**RECREATION
WITHOUT
HUMILIATION**

RECREATION WITHOUT HUMILIATION

BLACK LEISURE
IN THE TWENTIETH-CENTURY SOUTH

Mary Stanton

THE UNIVERSITY OF GEORGIA PRESS
ATHENS

Published by the University of Georgia Press
Athens, Georgia 30602
www.ugapress.org
© 2024 by Mary Stanton
All rights reserved
Designed by Melissa Buchanan
Set in Minion Pro

Most University of Georgia Press titles are
available from popular e-book vendors.

Printed digitally

Library of Congress Cataloging-in-Publication Data
Names: Stanton, Mary, author.
Title: Recreation without humiliation : black leisure in the
twentieth-century south / Mary Stanton.
Description: Athens, Georgia : University of Georgia Press, 2024. |
Includes bibliographical references and index.
Identifiers: LCCN 2024023491 (print) | LCCN 2024023492 (ebook) |
ISBN 9780820367668 (hardback) | ISBN 9780820367675 (paperback) |
ISBN 9780820367682 (epub) | ISBN 9780820367699 (pdf)
Subjects: LCSH: Leisure—Southern States—History—20th century. | African
Americans—Social life and customs—Southern States—History—20th century. |
Recreation—Southern States—History—20th century. | African Americans—
Social conditions—Southern States—History—20th century. | Amusement parks—
Social aspects—Southern States—History—20th century. | Southern
States—Race relations—History—20th century.
Classification: LCC GV54.A13 S75 2024 (print) | LCC GV54.A13 (ebook) |
DDC 306.4/8120975—dc23/eng/20240628
LC record available at https://lccn.loc.gov/2024023491
LC ebook record available at https://lccn.loc.gov/2024023492

For Mary Ann Oglesby Neeley (1932–2018),
a historian who loved to laugh.

Even modes of leisure could undergird opposition.... For members of a class whose long workdays were spent in backbreaking, low-paid wage work in settings pervaded by racism, the places where they played were more than relatively free places to articulate grievances and dreams. They were places that enabled African Americans to take back their bodies, to recuperate, to be together.... Knowing what happens in these spaces of pleasure can help us understand the solidarity black people have shown at political mass meetings [and] illuminate the bonds of fellowship one finds in churches and voluntary associations.
ROBIN D. G. KELLEY, 1993

CONTENTS

Acknowledgments ◆ ix
Preface: The Limitations of Memory ◆ xi
Introduction: *Whites Only* ◆ 1

WASHINGTON, D.C.

Suburban Gardens, Deanwood ◆ 9 | Black Minstrel and Vaudeville Shows ◆ 11 | The Theatrical Owners Booking Agency ◆ 15 "Black Broadway," Greater U Street ◆ 19

MARYLAND

Highland Beach, Anne Arundel County ◆ 23 | Washington Park, Prince George's County ◆ 29 | Brown's Grove, Rock Creek ◆ 36 | Edgewater Beach Park, Turner Station ◆ 39 | Carr's and Sparrow's Beaches, Annapolis ◆ 42 | Wilmer's Park, Prince George's County ◆ 46 | The Chitlin Circuit ◆ 48

VIRGINIA

Seaview Beach Resort and Amusement Park, Norfolk ◆ 53

NORTH CAROLINA

Shell Island Resort, Wilmington ◆ 59 | Sea Breeze and Bop City, New Hanover County ◆ 65 | Chowan Beach, Winton ◆ 69

SOUTH CAROLINA

Mosquito Beach, James Island ◆ 75 | Atlantic Beach, Horry County ◆ 78

TENNESSEE

Church's Park, Memphis ◆ 87 | Greenwood Park, Nashville ◆ 95

KENTUCKY

Frederick Douglass Park, Lexington ◆ 99

GEORGIA

The Atlanta Cotton States and the International Exposition ◆103 | King's Wigwam Country Club, Kennesaw ◆106 | Sweet Auburn/ Atlanta's Stroll ◆ 113

FLORIDA

Overtown, Miami-Dade County ◆119 | Manhattan Beach and Jacksonville's Movies ◆125 | Butler's Beach, St. Augustine ◆ 131 | American Beach, Anastasia Island ◆ 135 Paradise Park, Silver Springs ◆ 140

MISSISSIPPI

Gulfside Assembly, Hancock County ◆ 147 | Farish Street, Jackson ◆ 153

ALABAMA

Tuxedo Junction, Ensley ◆ 159 | Black Mardi Gras, Mobile ◆ 162 The Ben Moore Hotel and the Laicos Club, Montgomery ◆ 165

LOUISIANA

Congo Square and Storyville, New Orleans ◆171 | Crescent Stars Stadium, New Orleans ◆ 174 | Seabrook and Lincoln Beaches, East New Orleans ◆ 176

ARKANSAS

Wiley Jones Park and Race Track, Pine Bluff ◆181 | Bathhouses and Spring Training, Hot Springs ◆ 184

MISSOURI

Deep Morgan, St. Louis ◆ 191 | Fairground Park Pool, St. Louis ◆ 195

TEXAS

County Line/Upshaw, East Texas ◆ 199 | The Victory Grill, East Austin ◆ 201 | Black Rodeos and Trailblazers, West Texas ◆ 204

STATE AND COUNTY FAIRS AND NATIONAL PARKS

Colored State and County Fairs ◆ 211 | The National Park Service ◆ 216

Epilogue: Litigation, White Flight, and Theme Parks ◆ 221
Notes ◆ 225
Bibliography ◆ 243
Index ◆ 255

ACKNOWLEDGMENTS

In their memoir, *Deep Family*, Nicholas Cabell Read, Jean Craik Read, and Dallas Read argue that "some of the greatest story tellers are from the South, and this goes for many who did not write their stories down. They just told them within the circle of their friends."

I am grateful for everyone who took time to talk with me, to share memories, to point me in the right direction, or to walk along for a bit when I visited the South.

I am also indebted to my extraordinary editor, Nathaniel Francis Holly, who believed in this project from the get-go and never lost his enthusiasm.

PREFACE
The Limitations of Memory
❖❖❖
If Paris is France, Coney Island, between
June and September, is the world.
GEORGE C. TILYOU, 1886

Brooklyn's Coney Island was a thrilling if sometimes frightening place for a seven-year-old. Between wafts of fried clams and warm knishes and the pounding rhythms of calliopes and carousels, there was this *edginess*—an anticipation of something about to happen. Although I couldn't have named it, experts refer to it as the "exhilaration of controlled terror"—something akin to being suspended on a rope bridge over a canyon—with a safety net below.

After the long subway ride from Queens to Brooklyn's Stillwell Avenue terminal, my father and I would walk along Surf Avenue, passing fortune tellers, freak shows, Skee-Ball arcades, and saltwater taffy stands on the way to George C. Tilyou's Pavilion of Fun at Steeplechase Park, "the Funny Place." There the huge "Funny Face" painted across the windows just above the entrance smirked a welcome with his broad, mildly demonic grin. If he had a name, I never knew what it was.

Five years after visiting the 1893 Chicago World's Fair, Tilyou built Steeplechase Park, complete with a Ferris wheel, parachute jump, and the iconic "steeplechase" itself—a roller coaster–like mechanical horse race running on rails inside and outside the main building.

I have no recollection of the park's demise more than fifty years later. The 1964 World's Fair in Flushing Meadows Park used up all the oxygen that year. I stumbled onto the Steeplechase story much later, and it raised questions that I might never have otherwise asked—like how could such a beloved amusement park disappear virtually overnight? Steeplechase welcomed people who couldn't swim or hated rides—people-watching was a popular pastime—and the park became one of the city's most exciting tourist destinations.

In 1914, when founder George Tilyou died, his daughter Marie became president of the Steeplechase Amusement Company, and her brother Edward stepped up as CEO of Tilyou Realty, the parent company.[1] For almost forty years they operated successfully, but by the late 1950s the fabric of Coney Island began to fray. Admission prices increased, and, when popular Coney Island rides wore out, many weren't replaced. Jones Beach on Long Island, Rye Playland in Westchester County, and Palisades Park in New Jersey were the new competition, and as more families were able to afford cars their dependence on the subway ended.

White families were moving in droves to Nassau County just across the Queens border, and, as more African Americans visited Coney Island, they were less welcome. On July 2, 1964, *New York Times* correspondent Martin Tolchin reported, "[African Americans] now comprise half the weekend tourists [at Coney Island] and the concessionaires believe that their presence has discouraged white persons from visiting the area."[2]

Two weeks later, when a fifteen-year-old black teenager was shot and killed by an off-duty white police officer in Harlem, rioting spread to Bedford-Stuyvesant and eventually to Coney Island. That was the final blow for the Tilyous. Marie demanded that they sell the park immediately, but Edward refused, provoking some nasty infighting between the siblings. There were other problems, of course, including difficulty in renewing the lease and the need to invest in additional property for parking. There were also more muggings and gang "rumbles" and rumors of urban renewal projects, and seasonal help was harder to find. When demonstrators disrupted opening day at the World's Fair to protest job discrimination and police brutality, Marie was livid. Edward died later that year, and Steeplechase went on the market. Irving Rosenthal, owner of New Jersey's Palisades Park, was interested, but Marie refused to sell to him. When developer Fred Trump, Donald Trump's father, offered her $2.5 million in cash, she accepted. Marie explained to her nephew, "Naturally I feel very sad to even think of the park closing, but one night walking along Surf Avenue after dining at the Clam Bar and mixing with the horrible types one sees in the summer now, I decided that Steeplechase with all its splendor, drama and real beauty stood out like a gorgeous rosebush in a garbage can."[3]

Steeplechase closed for the season on September 20, 1964, and when the sale was announced on February 5, 1965, the Coney Island Chamber of Commerce, local residents, concessioners, and civic leaders were outraged. Fred Trump had just completed "Trump Village," a seven-building high-rise apartment complex in nearby Brighton Beach, and there were rumors that he planned to build more Miami Beach–type luxury apartments on the Steeplechase site. Charles Denson in his 2004 book, *Coney Island Lost and Found*, wrote, "Trump's racist tenant relocation tactics at Trump Village had destroyed the lives of many poor families in Brighton Beach who were relocated to the dilapidated bungalows of Coney's West End community."

Because the Steeplechase property was zoned "amusement-only," Trump sought a variance. After more than a year without success, he was angry. If *he* couldn't have the property, he vowed that nobody would have it. A wealthy and powerful man, Trump could afford to exact revenge, and that's exactly what he did.

On September 21, 1966, Fred Trump invited a group of friends to an evening "amusement park funeral," specifying formal attire. As bikini-clad hostesses in hard hats served hot dogs and champagne, he handed each guest a brick. For the night's entertainment they smashed the huge "Funny Face" that had grinned above the Steeplechase entrance since 1904. Trump had learned that the community board was attempting to turn the park into a historical landmark, and he told the press he "wasn't going to leave them anything."[4] No police arrived that night to investigate or limit or end the black-tie revelry, and demolition of the park began the following day. By January 1967 it was over. Trump never built any apartments on the site, high-rise or otherwise. Instead he sold the property to New York City for $4 million.

That event was the inspiration for this book. The mid-twentieth-century practice of rich and powerful developers destroying whatever got in their way was old news. Other people's good times had always been dispensable, and many white amusement parks preferred to close rather than integrate. By 1964, Coney Island was becoming too black, many whites thought, and many avoided it and drove to the newer and whiter parks upstate and in New Jersey.

It made me wonder if there had ever been any *African American* amusement parks, and I learned that, yes, there were, and at one time they were all over the United States. Like all amusement parks they suffered plagues of fire, insufficient capital, and high insurance rates and maintenance costs, with the added burden of white disdain up to and including a determination to destroy them.

Finding eyewitness accounts of these places, mining for oral histories and documentation about them, and searching for photographs and surviving ephemera were challenging, but visiting sites long ago abandoned or destroyed was well worth the effort. The story of African Americans pushing back against a culture that invested enormous amounts of time, energy, and money in keeping them out of public spaces, humiliating them, and forcing them to provide their own recreation or go without, is neither a well-known nor a proud chapter in our cultural history. I have set what I discovered against the backdrop of national events from the Reconstruction period through passage of the Voting Rights Act of 1965 to tell the story.

What follows sheds some light on the many and the brave who worked to provide the African American community with amusement, leisure activities, and fun. Their audiences and patrons—children and adults—admired, supported, and loved them for it. The survey is necessarily selective, and one can only imagine how much history has been lost.

Limiting the search to eleven states of the Old Confederacy, four border states, and the District of Columbia, I found some fifty-plus sites. Five are still in business as of this writing, five more are attempting comebacks, three have been designated as state parks, and the rest are gone. The book is arranged as a road trip, beginning in Washington, D.C., and ending in Texas.

This story of the struggle to establish recreation and amusement venues for black people and the efforts to keep them operating is a largely overlooked chapter of our national past. I am indebted to the foundational work of Dr. Andrew W. Kahrl, Dr. Nadine George-Graves, Dr. Kevin M. Kruse, and Dr. Robin D. G. Kelley for their scholarship and insight, which helped to guide my journey.

**RECREATION
WITHOUT
HUMILIATION**

INTRODUCTION
Whites Only

❖❖❖

All paradises, all utopias, are designed by who is not there,
by the people who are not allowed in.
TONI MORRISON

While access to public space, facilities, and services were major objectives of the American civil rights movement, there was also a strong focus on education, housing, transportation, and employment. Nevertheless, in 1954 Robert McKay, dean of the New York University Law School, asserted, "The actual fact is that the differences are more pronounced in [recreation] than in any other area in which distinctions based on race persist."[1]

In a 2015 study, *Landscapes of Exclusion*, William O'Brien, professor of environmental studies at Florida Atlantic University, argues, "White supremacy [in the South] was maintained in part by making inequality *visibly apparent*, as evidenced in the exclusion of African Americans from most state parks."[2]

Researchers who measure the effects of racial segregation on children argue that, because it fosters powerful perceptions of who belongs where, who are let in and who locked out, segregation damages children especially, during the years when their racial attitudes are forming.[3] Martin Luther King's 1963 *Letter from Birmingham City Jail* underscores this. He describes his six-year-old daughter Yolanda repeatedly asking him to take her to Atlanta's segregated Fun Town Amusement Park. "How could I explain that she could not go because she is colored?" he asks.

Ultimately, he told his daughter that Fun Town didn't allow colored children. But he assured Yolanda that even if she couldn't go inside, she should remember that she was as good as any child who could. How did Yolanda King process that information without feeling different and subsequently less?

O'Brien explains, "Violence and intimidation are significant means of enforcement, [but] deprivation and discrimination are the bedrock of racial subordination. Denial of amenities such as public parks that were on par with those available to whites was aimed at halting the development of greater confidence among African Americans." Traditional amusement parks and playgrounds, at their best, provided children (and adults) with safe fun. They delivered the experience of "good fear"—that adrenaline rush that kicks in during roller coaster rides. "Good fear" has been demonstrated to improve and enhance mood. People exiting a roller coaster are often flushed with pride at having conquered their terror.

By the 1920s, some municipal playgrounds were being designed to socialize white children by offering structured recreational activities, including group games and sports, that stressed fair play and encouraged self-control, responsibility to others, and opportunities for children to assert themselves appropriately to build positive self-concepts. These benefits were generally denied to African American children.

As early as the 1890s, municipal parks were promoted as alternatives to antisocial forms of amusement, consistent with turn-of-the-century progressivism, which held local government responsible for assimilating immigrants. That practical and humane policy was seldom extended to native-born African Americans, however.

So, what did black folks do? In 1928 Forrester Blanchard Washington, a black social work pioneer, published his findings from a survey of twelve amusement parks conducted in the South. In "Recreation Facilities for the Negro," Washington reported that "no amusement parks in the South admitted whites and blacks together and blacks were admitted only on selected days."[4] In the northern states, two-thirds of amusement parks also practiced segregation.

During World War I, Dr. Washington served as director of Detroit's Urban League, where he witnessed the city's rapid growth during the Great Migration of black people from the South. In 1923 he published "The Negro in Detroit," in which he reported that while "housing, health, crime, and family disorganization" had been studied in that city before, "very little thought" had been given to recreation, despite the fact that "Negro migrants [had] left the South on a quest for a better life."

AN AMERICAN DILEMMA

More than a decade later, in 1938, the Carnegie Commission tasked Swedish economist and sociologist Gunnar Myrdal with studying the "obstacles to full participation that Negroes experience[d] in American society." Myrdal's subsequent findings, published in 1944 as *An American Dilemma: The Negro Problem and*

American Democracy, would later be cited by the plaintiffs in the 1954 *Brown v. Board of Education* suit. Myrdal observed,

> America is probably more conscious than any other country of the great importance of recreation. The need for public measures to promote wholesome recreation has been shown to be particularly great for youth in cities and especially in such groups where housing conditions are crowded and unsanitary, where incomes are low and consequently opportunities for enjoying sound commercial entertainment restricted, where many mothers have to leave their homes for gainful work during the day, where the proportion of disorganized families is great, and where juvenile delinquency is high. This all means that, on the average, Negroes have greater need for public recreational facilities than have whites ... [but] not only beaches and playgrounds, but also public parks are often entirely closed to Negroes, except for Negro nurses watching white children....
>
> There is no doubt about the fact that provisions for Negroes are much inferior to those for whites.... The visitor finds Negroes everywhere aware of the great damage done to the youth by the lack of recreational outlets and of the urgency of providing playgrounds for the children. In almost every community visited during the course of this inquiry, these were among the first demands on the program of local Negro organizations.
>
> The Southern whites are unconcerned about how Negroes use their leisure time, as long as they are kept out of the whites' parks and beaches.[5]

IMMIGRANTS AND URBAN PARKS

Municipal streetcar companies operating in large cities during the late nineteenth century often established gardens, gazebos, cafés, and picnic groves at their terminals to boost weekend ridership. As the number of passengers increased, band concerts, carousels, and fireworks were added. Brooklyn's Coney Island was initially a trolley terminal park. White progressives in places like New York, Boston, and Chicago also championed "City Beautiful" programs to pave the streets, build playgrounds, and commission public art, including monuments. Sociologists who studied white European urban immigrant communities determined that many problems were based on environmental factors like poor sewage facilities and lack of access to health care. In African American communities, however, such unhealthy and often dangerous conditions were attributed to racial pathology.

Urban parks provided relief from overcrowded neighborhoods and a respite from dangerous working conditions, and while some African Americans surely benefited from New York's Central Park and Brooklyn's Prospect Park, most sociological studies focused on white working-class families and the assimilation of white European immigrants.

HOMER PLESSY

In 1883 the U.S. Supreme Court determined that the Civil Rights Act of 1875, which forbade racial discrimination in hotels, trains, and other public modes of transportation and in public spaces was unconstitutional. States (not limited to the South) subsequently passed Jim Crow statutes that historian C. Vann Woodward has described as the "most elaborate and formal expression of sovereign white opinion and constant reminders of the black man's inferior position."[6]

In Louisiana and Mississippi, Creoles had initially enjoyed excursions to the Gulf Coast casinos at Bay St. Louis and Pas Christian along with their white neighbors. That ended in 1890 when the Louisiana Assembly passed a railroad car accommodation ordinance relegating nonwhite passengers to the "last coach forward," a euphemism for the smoke-filled car behind the locomotive. In 1896, when Homer Plessy, a Creole from New Orleans, was denied admission to a first-class passenger car, he sued all the way to the Supreme Court, citing the Civil Rights Act of 1875, which guaranteed American citizens, regardless of race, color, or previous condition of servitude, "equal enjoyment of accommodations, advantages, facilities, and privileges of inns, public conveyances on land or water, theaters and other places of amusement."

Businesses and transit that required licenses (hotels, theaters railroads, and streetcars) were subject to penalties and fines for racial discrimination, and their victims could sue for damages. In its time the Civil Rights Act of 1875 was considered the most controversial federal legislation ever passed. Sponsors and supporters were charged with trying to blur the lines between "civil" and "social" rights.

On May 18, 1896, Plessy appeared to be vindicated when the Supreme Court in its *Plessy v. Ferguson* decision determined that every American citizen had a constitutional right to equal access to public accommodations. There was a catch, however. The court ruled that *separate but equal* arrangements met that requirement. Later court decisions would permit individual states to define what "separate but equal" meant. After *Plessy*, many theaters, restaurants, beaches, parks, and other public venues, while remaining segregated, welcomed African Americans on designated days when whites stayed away. African Americans could either fight these restrictions, cope with them, or provide their own education, transportation, employment, and recreation. It took nearly sixty years for the Supreme Court to overturn *Plessy* in the 1954 *Brown v. Board of Education* decision ("Separate is inherently unequal," the 1954 court unanimously ruled).

PLEASURE SPACES

Black Americans living in the South established spaces of their own, outside of white authority, where they could experience leisure and pleasure. They created an alternative culture based on mutuality and fellowship in an atmosphere of laughter, music, and dance.

Historian Robin D. G. Kelley in his study *Race Rebels* notes, "In the shadow of 'Whites Only' signs and police officers aggressively monitoring the color line, they found pleasure and fellowship, fun and games, in these segregated spaces."[7] Earl Lewis, another black historian, perhaps put it best when he observed that black people in the South turned segregation into "congregation," and congregation "symbolized an act of free will, whereas segregation represented the imposition of another's will."

In 1976 African American artist Ernie Barnes painted *The Sugar Shack*, a large acrylic-on-canvas work featuring a wild, splashily colorful rendition of black men and women dancing, with their arms waving above their heads, clearly enjoying themselves. Their elongated bodies seem boneless as they gyrate. Barnes maintained that *Sugar Shack* was inspired by a North Carolina childhood memory of sneaking into the Durham Armory in 1952. "I wasn't allowed to go to a dance," he explained, "and I wanted to go so much when I was eleven."

Sugar Shack was used as a backdrop to the credits of the television series "Good Times," which ran from 1974 to 1979, the story of a Black family living in a Chicago housing project. *Sugar Shack* was later selected as the cover illustration for Martin Gaye's award-winning album *I Want You*, released in 1976.

Ernie Barnes was born in North Carolina in 1938, attended North Carolina College at Durham (now North Carolina Central University) on a football scholarship, majoring in art, and after graduation played pro football for five years before focusing on an art career. Barnes died of leukemia in 2009, and thirteen years later Bill Perkins, an African American art collector, bought *The Sugar Shack* for $15.2 million at a Christie's auction. Today actor Eddie Murphy is the proud owner.

"We never remember days, only moments," Italian novelist Cesare Pavese observed. Ernie Barnes captured an important moment on canvas.

❖❖❖

What follows is a look at more than fifty African American beaches, resorts, amusement parks, green spaces, juke joints, theaters, country clubs, casinos, and music and sports venues that once prospered in the American South. While not exhaustive, it represents the ingenuity, energy, and raw courage required to provide and maintain recreation for black people and offer some good times in a segregated society. It introduces the founders, builders, and visionaries—men and women—farmers, fishers, cooks, vaudevillians, musicians, doctors, gamblers, politicians, entrepreneurs, lawyers, and preachers, and it demonstrates what could be accomplished in spite of extraordinarily difficult and dangerous circumstances, guided by the spirit of the African proverb that cautions against standing in a place of danger and trusting in miracles.

WASHINGTON, D.C.

SUBURBAN GARDENS, DEANWOOD
"The Negro Coney Island"
◆◆◆
Hard times require furious dancing.
ALICE WALKER

Suburban Gardens, the mid-Atlantic's most successful (and D.C.'s only) African American amusement park, was located in the northwest quadrant of the city. Designed by black architect Howard Woodson in 1921, it was developed by John H. Payner, a black realtor, and financed by the African American Universal Development and Loan Company.

The Gardens covered seven acres in Deanwood, a rural black community within the D.C. limits, and it would expand to twenty acres before closing in 1940. The land was leased from the Washington, Baltimore and Annapolis Electric Railway Company, whose tracks ran from 15th and H Streets, across the Benning Road Bridge to the Deanwood terminal. Transportation from downtown D.C. was convenient.

Deanwood had earlier been home to the Benning Race Track, a white society playground that attracted affluent whites like Alice Roosevelt Longworth, daughter of President Teddy Roosevelt and wife of Nicholas Longworth, Speaker of the House. Benning sponsored Fourth of July galas and political fund-raising events. Deanwood was a racially mixed working-class neighborhood, and African Americans were routinely employed as jockeys, trainers, and stable hands.

In 1908, when bookmaking was outlawed the track closed, but the site was used to board and train horses. Locals, black and white, kept their seasonal jobs working with horses, but after a 1915 fire the facility closed. As the community became an African American neighborhood of single-family homes, plans to build an amusement park raised hopes that some jobs might return, and some did.[1]

For a ten-cent admission fee, the Gardens offered a carousel, a scenic railway, a band shell, strolling gardens, picnic grounds, visiting carnivals, daredevil shows, and circuses. By the mid-1920's it was being called the "Black Glen Echo," a reference to the white amusement park in nearby Maryland. Popular jazz singers, orchestras, and vaudeville stars made regular appearances. Beach lovers could take a steamboat across the Chesapeake to a landing near Annapolis where two African American waterfront parks, Carr's and Sparrow's Beaches, were located.[2]

In 1929, as the Great Depression descended, Abe Lichtman, white owner of District Theaters, Inc., purchased Suburban Gardens and kept it going for another decade for Black clientele.[3] Lichtman added a swimming pool, a miniature golf course, a Ferris wheel, a roller coaster, and a fun house. He also owned Deanwood's six-hundred-seat Strand Theater, located just two blocks from the Gardens as well as the Lincoln and Howard Theaters on D.C.'s "Black Broadway" (U Street). They were popular stops on the "Chitlin Circuit," a booking agency network of black-owned nightclubs, dance halls, juke joints, amusement parks, and theaters.[4] "Chitlin" referred to "African Americans making something beautiful out of something ugly, like top notch cuisine out of hog intestines or world-class entertainment provided by those who were excluded from white clubs and theaters."[5]

Deanwood's Strand Theater had a pool hall and a dance hall on its second floor and an auditorium on the ground floor where artists like Fats Waller, Bessie Smith, Lena Horne, and the Mills Brothers performed. In 1940 Lichtman closed both Suburban Gardens and the Strand, and three years later the old Gardens were leveled in order to build temporary army barracks. After World War II the Suburban Gardens Apartments, a 203-unit federal housing project, was constructed for African American veterans and their families. Future D.C. mayor Sharon Pratt (1991–95) spent much of her childhood in the Suburban Garden Apartments. Lichtman retired in 1946 after managing forty-six black theaters in a chain that stretched across D.C., Maryland, Virginia, and North Carolina.

BLACK MINSTREL AND VAUDEVILLE SHOWS
❖❖❖
A dazzling display of heterogeneous splendor designed
to educate, edify, amaze and uplift.
EARLY VAUDEVILLE POSTER

Uniquely American, minstrel shows were white racist productions inspired by Thomas Dartmouth ("Daddy") Rice, a New York City stage actor who, while touring in Louisville, Kentucky, in 1828 watched a crippled black stable hand hop and shuffle as he sang to himself, "Weel about and turnabout/ And do jus so/ Eb'rytime I weel about/ I jump Jim Crow."

When Rice returned to New York he added a new stage character, Jim Crow, based on this unfortunate man. Jim Crow was portrayed by white men in blackface along with other minstrel show stock characters like the dandy Zip Coon who dressed and spoke "above his station," the obsequious Mammy, the soldier, Aunt Jemima, Uncle Tom, and the trickster slave—stereotypically happy, stupid, lazy, or sly and devious.[1]

During the 1830s and 1840s some black entertainers, like their white counterparts, also performed in burned-cork blackface, with their lips outlined in white face paint. Sunny Craver, partner of the black comedian Pigmeat Markham, explained that he chose blackface so white audiences couldn't tell whether he was black or white. "When a black comedian wore blackface," Craver explained, "he wasn't a black comedian any more! He was a comic."[2]

Minstrel shows followed the same circuits as many traveling opera companies and circuses and performed in major American cities. Minstrel shows generally opened with some banter between a master of ceremonies (or interlocutor) and some wisecracking character, often accompanied by music or tap dancing or both. A second act might include individual skits or a short farce, while the third usually featured a slapstick plantation skit.

The young composer W. C. Handy once served as bandmaster for the Mahara Minstrels, and wrote about it in his autobiography, *Father of the Blues*. "[Black] minstrels were a disreputable lot in the eyes of a large section of upper-crust Negroes," he explained. "But it was also true that all the best talent of that generation came down the same drain."[3] Handy was likely thinking about black vaudeville

FIG. 1. 1887 poster for Bert Williams and George Walker's *Enjoy Yourselves*, a comedy review promising "two real coons" as opposed to white entertainers in blackface. They became one of the most popular vaudeville teams on Broadway.

stars like Bert Williams and George Walker, who had toured with Martin and Selig's Mastodon Minstrels before becoming stars on the vaudeville stage.

ON THE ROAD

Vaudeville began replacing the minstrel show in the 1880s. In September 1896 veterans Williams and Walker were cast in Victor Herbert's operetta *The Gold Bug*, which opened at New York City's Casino Theater on West Thirty-Ninth Street. Billed as "Two Real Coons"—("the real thing," as opposed to white actors in blackface)—they performed as gangsters and cheap, flashy fools, in an effort to spoof "blacks playing whites playing blacks." Theater historian James Dormon explains that the joke was lost on white New York audiences who simply accepted what they saw on stage as "the reality of blackness"—"the reality of the coon." These same white audiences would howl with laughter at stereotypical Irish drunkards, Italian gangsters, and blustering Germans, all the while accepting those stage portrayals as entertainment.

Seven years later Williams, Walker, and Walker's wife, Aida Overton Walker—who had toured with the Black Patti Troubadours—made Broadway history when they starred in *In Dahomey*, the first full-length musical comedy written and performed by black entertainers. It opened at the New York Theater on West Thirty-Third Street on February 18, 1903, and ran for fifty-three performances before touring the United States and ultimately playing in London for another four years.

At that time New York City's Theater District ran from Twenty-Fourth Street to Forty-Second Street and from Fifth to Seventh Avenues, overlapping a red-light district and Hell's Kitchen, the white (primarily Irish) ghetto where young white men enjoyed beating up young black men who arrived during the Great Migration. In 1900 Hell's Kitchen exploded when Arthur Harris, a black man, arrived on the corner of Eighth Avenue and Forty-First Street to meet his wife and found her being accosted by a white man. In the ensuing struggle, Harris killed that man who turned out to be an undercover police officer who was attempting to arrest his innocent wife for soliciting. Angry whites went searching, not for Harris necessarily but for a black man to attack. The black vaudeville star George Walker was then performing at the Winter Garden in Times Square. They would teach *him* a public lesson. Walker and the cast locked themselves inside the theater, and fifty people were injured in the melee that took place outside.

Black entertainers often found respite at the Marshall Hotel on West Fifty-Third Street, ten blocks north of the Theater District. Owned by Jimmie Marshall, who was black, it offered a ballroom and a twenty-four-hour restaurant. The Marshall became a gathering place for black and white artists, entertainers, writers, and social justice activists.

The "New Negroes" of the Harlem Renaissance, advocates for black dignity who refused to submit quietly to Jim Crow, often gathered at the Marshall to socialize and collaborate. Vaudevillians Williams and Walker, songwriters Bob Cole and Billy Johnson, NAACP activists W. E. B. Du Bois and Walter White, boxer Jack Johnson, musician Eubie Blake, and poets Paul Laurence Dunbar and James Weldon Johnson were often joined by whites like Florenz Ziegfeld, Diamond Jim Brady, W. C. Fields, and Lillian Russell.

James Weldon Johnson wrote of the Marshall,

> On Sunday evenings the crowd became a crush; and to be sure of service one had to book a table in advance. This new centre also brought about a revolutionary change in Negro artistic life.
>
> A good many white actors and musicians frequented the Marshall, and it was no unusual thing for some among the biggest Broadway stars to run up there for an evening. So there were always present numbers of those who loved to be in the light reflected from celebrities... To be a visitor there, without at the same time being a rank outsider, was a distinction.[4]

After Williams and Walker's 1906 triumph in *Abyssinia* at the Majestic Theatre on Columbus Circle, they worked together for the last time in *Bandanna Land*. Three years later Williams joined the Ziegfeld Follies as the "Jonah Man" character, the "unluckiest man in the world." Although he shared billing with white stars like Fannie Brice, Eddie Cantor, and W. C. Fields, Williams was required to find separate lodgings while on tour. As he told his lawyer, "They keep me out of a hotel where loafers are admitted without question, so long as they're white. Then a professor or a lawyer or a doctor invites me up to his house. It's a great, sad little world."[5]

THE THEATRICAL OWNERS BOOKING AGENCY
Protecting Black Talent

❖❖❖

Vaudeville was the theatre of the people, its brassy assurance a
dig in the nation's ribs, its simplicity as naïve as a circus.
DOUGLAS GILBERT

Vaudeville, using the best of the minstrel, variety, and traveling show traditions, created a new magic beginning in the 1880s. Vaudeville theaters remained open six days a week, noon to midnight, and offered continually changing shows. You could enter or leave at any time, and if you didn't like a particular act or routine, a new one would begin every fifteen minutes. As in the minstrel shows, there were comedy skits, acrobats, dancers, musicians, and trained animals, but vaudeville also included short plays, musicals, and comic operas.

Just as white showmen B. F. Keith and Edward Albee established the United Booking Artists in 1900 to recruit and promote white talent, Sherman H. Dudley, a black man, would later partner with the Theatrical Owners Booking Agency (T.O.B.A) in 1921 to encourage and promote black actors and performers.

KING OF THE FUN MAKERS

Sherman Dudley, an actor, entertainer, and vaudeville empresario, was born in Jonesville, Louisiana, in 1872 and began his career performing with circuses and traveling medicine shows. At age twenty-five he organized the Georgia Minstrels and toured across Texas, playing everything from "concert saloons" to Houston's Grand Opera House.

In 1903 Dudley married fellow vaudevillian Alberta ("Bertie Mae") Ormes, and the following year their son and only child, Sherman H. Dudley Jr., was born. At the time, the Dudleys were touring and performing in Chicago with the Smart Set, billed as "the smartest set of colored people ever put together on one stage in America." Dudley not only managed and directed but also starred as "The King of Fun Makers." His stage banter with Shamus O'Brien, a live mule dressed in overalls, was the high point of the show. The Smart Set played Church's Auditorium in Memphis along with Ma Rainey and her Black Bottom Band, a troupe of "acrobats, clowns, dancing girls and operatic stars."[1]

Dudley, five foot eight, had boundless energy and a steely determination to succeed. On May 9, 1911, he costarred with Smart Set diva Aida Overton ("Queen of the Cake Walk") at New York City's Majestic Theater in the musical comedy *His Honor the Barber*. A *New York Times* critic noted that the show "had enough saving grace to make a visit to the Majestic worthwhile."

Dudley established the Colored Actors Union in Washington, D.C., in 1913, leaving the Smart Set in the capable hands of the Tutt Brothers—J. Homer Tutt and his brother Salem Tutt Whitney—who had performed with the Black Patti Troubadours. Dudley subsequently purchased D.C.'s Minnehaha Theater and recruited several black theater owners to create, "Dudley's Circuit," the first black vaudeville network. By 1914 the circuit was representing twenty-three theaters owned or managed by African Americans. Historian David Nasaw argued,

> In southern cities, the theater-building campaign proceeded with such alacrity that Salem Tutt Whitney, a black producer and performer commented in 1910 that, while Booker T. Washington could hardly have been thinking of show business when he "maintained that the South is the natural field of endeavor for the colored man . . . a trip through the south will convince one that there had been no more rapid progress along any line than in things theatrical. Every town of importance has its colored play-house, and for the most part they are well attended. From empty storerooms and lots in the walls there have grown many creditable theatres with all the modern equipment, capable of seating from 500 to 1,000 persons."[2]

In 1917 Dudley began producing musical comedies, and two years later he joined with white producers Sam Reevin of Chattanooga and Martin Klein of Nashville to organize the United Vaudeville Circuit. When E. L. Cummings, a white Florida booking agent, joined them, they became the Southern Consolidated Theater Circuit. In those days white promoters controlled all the major vaudeville venues and had virtually unlimited power to advance or destroy careers. They allowed only one "colored act" per show. Under Dudley's leadership the Southern Consolidated Theater Circuit marketed African American talent directly to African American audiences. He knew what they wanted—entertainment that spoke to them, and they did *not* want to be mocked.

In the 1980s William Dillard, an African American trumpeter who had worked with Louis Armstrong, explained just why black vaudeville was so important: "We only had church and ballrooms and the vaudeville theaters," he recalled. "You wouldn't be allowed in the opera house."[3]

In 1921 Milton Starr, a founder of Nashville's all-white Bijou Circuit, joined with Dudley, Reevin, and Klein. He had formerly managed an independent chain of African American theaters across the Deep South, Texas, and Oklahoma. This merger completed formation of the legendary Theatrical Owners Booking Association (T.O.B.A.) or "Toby," which did for African American entertainers what the Keith and Albee circuits did for white performers. After some initial struggling, Starr became president of T.O.B.A., Dudley vice president, and Sam Reevin treasurer. E. L. Cummings, unhappy with the arrangement, withdrew.

T.O.B.A. artists performed in Tennessee, Louisiana, Mississippi, Alabama, Georgia, Florida, and South Carolina. Southern tours were generally humiliating and often proved to be dangerous. Even very popular black stars were required to use service entrances, and when overnight accommodations couldn't be secured it meant sleeping in dark and deserted train stations. Actors, musicians, and stage hands worked seven days a week, sometimes contracting for four shows a day. Their dressing rooms, stage lighting, and simple creature comforts were all inferior to those provided for white performers.

Dudley negotiated contracts, wrote group agreements, arranged travel, secured lodging, and offered black and white audiences a wide range of entertainment. He was determined to get black entertainers as much security as possible. Unfortunately, that didn't translate to higher wages. Some complained that T.O.B.A. stood for "**T**ough **o**n **B**lack **A**sses." While popular acts like the Whitman Sisters and J. Leubrie Hill's *Darktown Follies* were well compensated, overall the pay scale was low. Still, despite internal conflict and inferior accommodations, the T.O.B.A. enjoyed a full decade of success. During the Jazz Age it represented more than forty theaters.[4]

Dudley, however, an astute businessman, knew that the future of entertainment was motion pictures. After the Great War, he watched vaudeville wind down its fifty-year run. Public tastes were changing. He subsequently contracted with REOL Productions, a New York City affiliate of Richard Norman's Film Studios in Jacksonville, Florida, and produced film versions of two musical comedies. He stared in *The Simp* and *Easy Money*, which were both released in 1921. Unfortunately, REOL filed for bankruptcy two years later.

In 1926 Dudley invested in the Philadelphia-based, white-owned Colored Players Film Corporation and contracted to work as a producer while continuing to direct musical comedies for the stage. As late as 1929 he complained to a *Baltimore Afro-American* reporter, "White booking agents and producers [won't] book black shows in first class white theaters[,] and [I] do not want to book first class entertainment in second class theaters."[5]

Unfortunately, the T.O.B.A. did not survive the Great Depression, and Dudley was forced to sell his theaters, including D.C.'s Minnehaha, in 1930. He shared his disappointment in the *Pittsburgh Courier* in an interview published on January 10, 1931. "Was it the mismanagement of the [T.O.B.A.] organization or was it the shows?" he asked.

> Salaries were small, but the actors worked all the time and could be working now if they had only made a study of the show business. This they did not do, so the audiences got tired of seeing the same thing week in and week out. Then the talking pictures with elaborate settings, beautiful women, [and] gorgeous costumes came along with something new[,] and the audiences of today fell for it. Now, as to the managers: they never encouraged the producers of these shows for the T.O.B.A. to put out shows of the better kind by classifying them and paying a decent salary to those who would and could produce better attractions, nor would they do things to build up their business. All they cared for was to count the receipts and live for today without looking into the future. I pleaded with them at each meeting to do these things[,] and now they see their mistakes. . . . Essentially, the curtain descended for the T.O.B.A. circuit.[6]

Dudley retired in 1935, and he and his wife Bertie bought a farm in Oxen Hill, Maryland, where they bred racehorses. He died in 1940, and their only son, Sherman Dudley Jr., enjoyed a successful career as a performer and producer.

"BLACK BROADWAY," GREATER U STREET

❖❖❖

We weren't pushing black is beautiful. We just showed it.
KATHERINE DUNHAM

During the Jazz Age, the Roaring Twenties, and throughout the 1940s and '50s, the Greater U Street district in Washington, D.C., was "Black Broadway"—ground zero for black café society. The district vibrated with jazz clubs, cabarets, and dance halls. White entrepreneur Abe Lichtman, owner of the Republic, Howard, Booker T., and Lincoln Theaters, staffed them with African Americans, including all his managers and supervisors. Popular entertainer Pearl Bailey maintained that "Black Broadway was Harlem before Harlem was Harlem," and she insisted that both the Lincoln and Howard Theaters predated Harlem's Apollo by at least five years.[1]

From the lobby of the Lincoln, patrons were able to access a brick tunnel that opened into the Lincoln Colonnade, an after-hours dance hall featuring Cab Calloway's Cotton Club orchestra. The Republic Gardens, the Jungle Inn, the Capitol Grill, and Murray's Palace Casino, where Calloway also performed, were just down the street.

In 1922 John W. Lewis, black founder and president of the Industrial Savings Bank, opened the Crystal Caverns nightclub in the basement of the Davis Pharmacy on Eleventh Street—directly across from his office. Lewis reimagined the former speakeasy with no windows as a subterranean jazz club, picturing a "rendezvous of the socially elite." Regulars referred to it simply as "the club." There musicians and "shake dancers" entertained in a cave-like setting complete with plaster stalactites and stalagmites. In 1959 the black manager Tony Taylor bought the club, renamed it the Bohemian Caverns, and in the years to follow booked Miles Davis, Herbie Hancock, Aretha Franklin, and Roberta Flack as well as an up-and-coming comic, Bill Cosby.[2] The day after Aretha Franklin's debut in 1966, John Seagraves noted in "After Hours," his column for the *Washington Evening Star*, "No one laughs when Aretha Franklin sits down to play, or for that matter when she stands up to sing. Instead, they yell, stomp their feet, whistle, and generally make a child's final days of school seem like a funeral procession in comparison."[3]

The Bohemian Caverns club was not unique. The Murray brothers, who printed the *Washington Tribune* by day, became the hosts of the Palace Casino after hours. Their closest competitor was Club Bengasi, established in 1943 and a favorite of Nat King Cole and Art Tatum. Twenty years later Benjamin Cardwell's Club Bali, the first to institute a cover charge, introduced the "jumpin' and jivin' Cats & The Fiddle," who performed two shows nightly and three on Sunday. Louis Armstrong, Errol Garner, Billie Holiday, Sarah Vaughn, and Dinah Washington all regularly performed there. Like most Black Broadway night spots, the Bali welcomed whites, and whites came.

The Greater U Street District was also called the "Black Man's Connecticut Avenue"—D.C.'s black business district as well as its political capital. In August 1927 Langston Hughes, "the voice of the New Negro Movement," commented in the NAACP journal *Opportunity*, "Never before, anywhere had I seen such persons of influence—men with some money, women with some beauty, teachers with some education—quite so sure of their own importance and their high places in the community."

In 1954, when the U.S. Supreme Court ruled that segregation was unconstitutional in *Brown v. Board of Education*, and African Americans were free to patronize formerly whites-only clubs, the Lincoln Theater and the Crystal Caverns (by then called the Bohemian Caverns) lost revenue, and both closed down in the late 1960s. More businesses folded in the wake of the 1968 riots that devastated the nation's capital following the murder of Dr. Martin Luther King Jr. But, while it lasted, U Street was Black Broadway.

MARYLAND

HIGHLAND BEACH, ANNE ARUNDEL COUNTY
"A Summer Colony"
❖❖❖
Smell the sea and feel the sky. Let your soul and spirit fly.
VAN MORRISON

In the winter of 1892, Major Charles Douglass and his wife Laura Haley Douglass were looking forward to celebrating their twelfth wedding anniversary with dinner at the Bay Ridge Hotel on the Chesapeake Bay. Charles, the youngest son of Frederick Douglass, the African American abolitionist, made reservations for December 30 at the Annapolis Dining Room, which he and Laura had previously enjoyed. That evening, however, the maître de refused to seat them. Initially stunned, Douglass quickly became angry. The Douglass family belonged to D.C.'s "Black Four Hundred"—a community of affluent, educated, and civic-minded people. A Harvard graduate, Charles had served in the Fifty-Fourth Massachusetts Infantry and fought to preserve the Union.[1]

After the Reconstruction Act of 1867, the District of Columbia banned racial discrimination in public places of amusement, including theaters and restaurants. For two decades the middle classes—white and black—engaged each other across political and economic lines. Now, a quarter-century after Appomattox, neither Douglass's social standing nor his education or family wealth shielded him from this humiliation. Like many of his friends, Douglass disagreed with Booker T. Washington's insistence on African American self-sufficiency because he was convinced that assimilation was imminent. Perhaps not for *all* African Americans but certainly for educated, respectable professionals like himself whose values were compatible with those of the white middle class. In 1893, one year after the insult, Douglass purchased forty acres on the Chesapeake Bay in Anne Arundel County, Maryland, and with financial assistance from his father he built Highland Beach, "a private colored summer colony."

HIGHLAND BEACH

Charles Douglass divided his property into 104 building lots, and by 1894 fifty-two summer cottages were standing. Former Reconstruction senator Blanche K. Bruce; P. B. S. Pinchback (who had served as interim governor of Louisiana),

James T. Wormley (owner of the Wormley Hotel who had served with Douglass in the Fifty-Fourth Massachusetts); and the capital's black grand dame Mary Church Terrell, daughter of black Memphis millionaire Robert Church, were just a few of the aristocrats of color who had invested.

They and their guests brought everything they needed with them during that first season since Highland Beach was initially a resort without services. Several seasons would pass before all the indoor plumbing, electricity, and paved roads were completed. An iceman delivered bread and milk, and a local farmer sold them chickens, corn, watermelons, and peaches. Those who enjoyed playing farmer grew tomatoes, onions, squash, and peas.[2] Situated thirty-five miles east of D.C., Highland Beach was surrounded by white communities whose residents proved less than welcoming.

In 1900 Douglass added riding stables, a guest house, and tennis courts, and for two decades the beach was a popular summer residence for retired black army officers, former congressmen, Howard University professors, lawyers, physicians, and businessmen and their families. The writers Paul Laurence Dunbar and Langston Hughes, activists Paul Robeson, Mary McLeod Bethune, and W. E. B. DuBois, and even Booker T. Washington himself visited. As owners, renters, or weekend guests they enjoyed boating, swimming, riding, croquet, crabbing, lectures and concerts in the guest house, and lively conversation. Shortly before World War I, Dunbar described Highland Beach as "such a gathering of this race that few outside of our own great family circle have ever seen."[3]

When Charles Douglass died in 1920, ownership of the beach passed to his twenty-eight-year-old son Haley, his only child with Laura Douglass. Haley was educated at Howard and Harvard and taught history and science at D.C.'s Dunbar High School. His first challenge as manager of Highland Beach came when residents of neighboring private communities began to encroach on his waterfront. The adjoining black summer community of Venice Beach, established in 1922, had limited waterfront access, and, despite warnings and threats, its residents continued to trespass onto Highland Beach. Haley Douglass's solution was to string barbed wire along the Venice-Highland border to remind everyone of who was paying taxes on the waterfront property. It was torn out almost immediately, however, and cooler heads prevailed.[4]

Douglass subsequently convinced the Highland Beach property owners to apply for a charter and incorporate as a town. In 1923 they elected him town supervisor, but four years later the trespassing resumed. The frustrated Haley Douglass complained to Ralph Matthews Sr., a columnist for the *Baltimore Afro-American*, "We are still confronted with the problem of unauthorized picnicking and bathing parties. The failure of large cities to provide adequate bathing and recreational facilities has placed upon us the burden of protecting our property from roving trespassers whose ignorance or lack of self-respect permits them uninvited to impose upon residents who bought their homes for the benefit of their own families and friends."[5]

Before he died, Charles Douglass prevailed on his friend Richard Ware, owner of the only black department store in D.C., to purchase four Highland Beach lots and build a hotel. He had been concerned that only 34 of the original 129 lots had been sold by 1920 and wanted to generate more interest in the colony. Douglass did not live to see the Ware Hotel open in 1925, however, with twenty guest rooms, a ballroom, and a dining room overlooking the Chesapeake Bay. Ware later added a lounge, pool room, and slot machines for the Jazz Age set, a group of writers, artists, and rebels who enjoyed gin and gambling. The more sedate cottage owners were soon grousing that Highland Beach was "becoming another open town." During the 1926 season, they complained to Haley Douglass that his guests were loud, crude, and rude. While Ware attracted attention, as Charles Douglass had hoped, none of these visitors became buyers. They were young, restless, weekend guests looking for a good time. Tempers grew short. Things got nasty.

On July 12, 1930, Ralph Matthews reported, "All is not well on this little sector of beachfront on the Chesapeake Bay. The feud that has been going on between residents of this fashionable colony of Washington, Baltimore and Philadelphia society folks and ordinary folks who would like bathing in the Bay at this point, flared up on the Fourth of July when the distinguished elocutionist Nathaniel Guy discovered three persons dressing under his cottage [deck]." Matthews defended the hotel guests—and especially Richard Ware as a "man of the people": "He caters to the public and cares for them without regard to their status in life. The residents [of Highland Beach] would have him close his hotel because they hold that his patrons are undesirable."

Unfortunately, the hotel was firebombed later that year. After Ware collected the insurance payment, he moved on to Arundel-on-the-Bay, a former white summer colony transitioning to a mixed-race Jazz Age playground.

Although Haley Douglass was a gifted educator, he had not been blessed with his father's tact or with any ability whatsoever to take the long view. He faced more headaches as the number of speculators who bought land and built vacation homes and summer colonies along the bay increased. Highland Beach's old guard was taken to task by a new (and vocal) public for its "pretentiousness." On June 30, 1932, the *Baltimore Afro*'s Ralph Matthews published a letter to the editor. "In order to be actually recognized [among the] Highland Beach upper crust," the writer complained, "you either have to possess a fadeout complexion or plenty of filthy lucre and the less you have of the former the more you have to have of the latter."[6]

A furious Haley Douglass tried to convince the owners to rescind the town charter and reorganize as a home owners' association, a move historian Andrew Kahrl calls "the last straw." But by then the community had grown tired of Douglass's officious manner, and several owners accused him of using his office to dispense favors to his friends, punish his enemies, and advance his business and real estate interests. To be fair, Douglass was not enriching himself, and he was actually right about creating a home owners' association.

In 1933 the owners established a hybrid town–home owners' association. In return for relinquishing their rights to use their property as they wished, they would be "relieved of the threat of rogue neighbors violating community standards with impunity, or the introduction of persons and land uses that threatened to alter the character of the community and depreciate property values."[7] Commercial development was prohibited.

By 1950 forty-five privately owned summer cottages and five year-round structures remained. The 2020 census recorded 118 residents in forty-four households and twenty-seven families. Despite some rocky times, Ray Langston, who had served as mayor of Highland Beach from 1995 to 2003, affirmed, "[It] was a wonderful place. We could get away from the segregation and the degradation of where you could and couldn't go. All our friends and parents knew each other. It was a very carefree life for youngsters."[8]

EAGLE HARBOR AND CEDAR HAVEN

It is difficult to overstate the effect that summer colonies like Highland Beach had on middle- and working-class African Americans. Washington, D.C., was an overcrowded city and unbearably hot in the summer. Many residents sought escape along the Chesapeake Bay or by a river or lake. Black professionals—lawyers, dentists, undertakers, and business owner—could afford summer residences, but working-class people could not. However, when a desire surfaced in D.C., someone inevitably arose to satisfy it.

In 1925, as Highland's Ware Hotel was still under construction, Walter L. Beams was busy buying up defunct tobacco farms on Truman's Point in southern Prince George's County on the Patuxent River. Beams was working as an agent for John Stewart Sr., owner of Stewart Funeral Homes, the largest black funeral businesses in D.C. In partnership with state senator Landsdale G. Sasscer Sr., a white man who had represented the Fifth District of Maryland in the state legislature for seven terms. The plan was to create a middle-class African American summer colony, Eagle Harbor, at Truman Point, thirty miles from downtown D.C.

For generations Truman Point served as a Weems Shipping Line landing used by African American tobacco farmers to deliver their crop to market. After World War I, when the price of tobacco fell, many farms failed, and the Weems Line went bankrupt. Beams was subsequently hired by Stewart and Sasscer to buy up these farms, create lots that were twenty-five feet wide and one hundred feet long, and market them for fifty dollars each in the new summer colony of Eagle Harbor. The target market was D.C.'s Shaw district, where more than three hundred black businesses flourished.[9] An ad in the *Washington Times* described them as "parcels of Paradise on The Patuxent For the Better People."[10]

The lots sold quickly, and Eagle Harbor eventually boasted a hotel, bathhouses, a tearoom, and a park. Activities included bathing, fishing, boating, and cruising on "a large excursion boat." The old two-lane roads to Truman Point were repaved and expanded to accommodate summer residents, weekend visitors, and their guests. A citizens' association was created in 1928, and when Eagle Harbor incorporated as a town the following year the partners discovered that two of the project's underwriters were white brothers married to black women.[11]

Eagle Harbor's success inspired the Maryland Development Corporation, an African American organization, to buy up the farmland north of Truman Point on the opposite side of the Patuxent River. There in 1927 the owners established Cedar Haven—an African American summer refuge for working-class families. Advertising it as "a wonderful place for children far from the dangers of city streets," they marketed to teachers, nurses, clerks, and civil servants. Many who bought lots subsequently ordered home-building kits from Sears, Roebuck, and Company.[12] The Cedar Haven Hotel and several guest houses were subsequently constructed as well as a public bathhouse with eighty dressing rooms and lockers. Cedar Haven was marketed as "a miniature Atlantic City."[13]

Just a year later, James H. Shreve, the Prince George's County tax assessor, reassessed land use and tax rates in the county, specifically along the Patuxent, including the new developments of Eagle Harbor and Cedar Haven. He recommended that the tax rate be increased from $20 to $300 per lot annually on lots that sold for between $25 and $100. The recommendation was accepted.[14] It did not seem to make a difference that a sitting state senator was a major investor in in Eagle Harbor, and there is no surviving record of Sasscer either opposing the decision or trying to delay it or limit the rate increase to assist his African American partner. Such was the power of white communities to end any and all invasions by "undesirables." By 1928, options like property covenants and overtaxing residents were still available. There was more than one way to deny, destroy, or poison the simple pleasures of undesirable people.

WASHINGTON PARK, PRINCE GEORGE'S COUNTY
"The Coney Island of Colored Americans"

❖❖❖

Not everyone who chased the zebra caught it,
but he who caught it chased it.
AFRICAN PROVERB

In 1889 John (J. W.) Patterson, a light-skinned nineteen-year-old African American, left Richmond, Virginia, for Washington, D.C., to pursue his dream of getting rich. He became a minister, preached the gospel of "enterprise and success," practiced law, and by 1894 managed to convince enough friends, colleagues, and members of his congregation to invest in the People's Transportation Company, his first business endeavor.

Patterson purchased a steamer, the *Lady of the Lake*, to transport both black passengers and freight from D.C. to Norfolk, Virginia. He scheduled passenger stops at the Glymont landing in Maryland and at Virginia's Colonial Beach, where black visitors were permitted. Black churches and fraternal organizations hired him for cruises, sightseeing tours, and family excursions, and Patterson was successful until February 15, 1895, when the *Lady of the Lake* caught fire and sank, after which he was arrested for arson and insurance fraud. Just two months later, in April 1895, several disgruntled shareholders reorganized without him as the National Steamboat Company, purchased a triple-decker steamer, the *George Leary*, and resumed passenger service to Norfolk. This new National Steamboat Company purchased eight acres on Cobb Island on Virginia's eastern shore and built an excursion landing there with a dance pavilion, bowling alley, and shuffleboard courts for day visitors; a sheltered stage for Sunday services and revival meetings; and a several rental cottages. On July 27, 1895 the black *Washington Bee* described it as a "Colored Saratoga."[1]

Saratoga Springs, New York, was home to the original Chautauqua movement that promoted cultural events, music and drama, lectures, and other highbrow entertainment. In the spring of 1896 construction began on Cobb Island's "colored Chautauqua" but was interrupted by severe storms. Unfortunately, in 1897 violent weather again intervened. Then the ten-year-old *George Leary*'s engines failed, and it was taken out of service. This was the beginning of the end of the

Cobb Island Chautauqua. Within a year the National Steamship Company was in receivership.

At this very opportune time, J. W. Patterson resurfaced, bankrolled by a new group of investors and holding title to the steamer *Jane Mosley*. He had leased Collingwood Beach, near Mount Vernon, from L. J. Woolen, a white steamboat captain who, recognizing the potential of the African American excursion market, had developed it in 1888 and added a roller coaster, dance pavilion, merry-go-round, swings, and a bathhouse. Patterson renamed it Douglass Beach, but he very quickly ended up bankruptcy court for a second time, and his plans for Douglass Beach were dashed.

MOUNT VERNON AND MARSHALL HALL

The Mount Vernon and Marshall Hall Steamboat Company, one of the largest white Potomac fleets, held title to Marshall Hall Park, a landing in Charles County, Maryland, across the Potomac from Mount Vernon. It included a casino, penny arcade, Ferris wheel, carousel, roller coaster, and miniature golf course. White tourists and day-trippers visited the park on the *Mary Washington* and the *Charles Macalester* steamers and toured George and Martha Washington's Mount Vernon estate.

After the National Steamboat Company's plans for the Black Chautauqua on Douglass Beach imploded, Mount Vernon and Marshall Hall purchased the *River Queen* (an old side-wheeler once used by General Ulysses Grant) and entered the black excursion business. The company offered trips to Marshall Hall on Mondays (when whites stayed away) and also included a tour of Mount Vernon.

LEWIS JEFFERSON

Some combination of inexperience, inadequate capital, refusal of white bankers to write loans to black entrepreneurs, and high maintenance costs kept the number of black amusement venues in the region low, but a desire for them in the black community and the challenge of providing them motivated entrepreneurs. One of them was Lewis Jefferson, an African American building contractor with a gift for attracting white capital.

Born in 1866 to Hugh Allan, a white Canadian financier, and a free South Carolina black woman who died shortly after his birth, Jefferson was raised in Orange,

Virginia, by his maternal grandmother. He left home at fifteen, stowed away on a steamer to New York City, lied about his age, and enlisted in the navy. Discharged in 1887 after two world cruises, the twenty-one-year-old seaman settled in the nation's capital. Smart, energetic, and resourceful, he worked for a grocer, then a blacksmith, and finally for a general contractor, increasing his skills with each opportunity and attracting the attention of helpful whites like William Wilson Corcoran, founder of the Riggs Bank, who taught him the real estate development business.[2] Corcoran helped Jefferson to establish the Freedman's Transportation Land and Improvement Company and acquire property. Jefferson initially built affordable housing for black migrants arriving from the South. His father may also have assisted him. In any event, by the time he was thirty years old Lewis Jefferson was recognized as a "colored capitalist."[3]

In 1901 he purchased a minority stake in Frank Hume and Samuel Bensinger's Independent Steamboat and Barge Company. Hume, a wealthy white liquor importer, was the silent partner, while Bensinger, an avid gambler and a specialist in both land acquisition and amusements, was senior partner.[4] In 1903 Bensinger and Jefferson purchased Notley Hall, a 240-acre plantation on the Potomac River in Prince George's County. Once owned by Thomas Notley, deputy governor of Maryland, it was just twenty miles south of Washington, D.C., near the black community of Oxon Hill. For decades its abandoned riverfront was used as a picnic beach until white speculators purchased the property in the late 1800s to build a resort that unfortunately failed after four seasons. Jefferson was determined to build a "Coney Island for Negroes" on the site.

In 1904 he purchased Captain James Woolen's *Jane Mosely*, which had once belonged to J. W. Patterson. It was a two-hundred-foot double-decker steamboat with a checkered history that included *two* collisions with the *George Leary* (of Cobb Island fame). This likely allowed him to negotiate a reasonable price.[5] Jefferson subsequently signed a long-term lease for Somerset Beach, a failed white resort in King George's County, which included a hotel with a large outdoor dance pavilion. He reopened it as an African American resort.[6] A philanthropic capitalist, Jefferson arranged for poor black woman and their children to enjoy free two-week summer vacations on Somerset Beach. He was partial to children—by that time he had fourteen of his own.

By 1906 Lewis Jefferson was simultaneously booking cruises on the *Jane Mo-*

sely, managing Somerset Beach, and designing a new landing beach at Notley Hall outfitted with a dance pavilion, bowling alley, carousel, shooting gallery, "aero swings," and a penny arcade. During the first season at Notley Hall he purchased the *River Queen* from Mount Vernon and Marshall Hall, who no longer required it for African American excursions to Mount Vernon since the white Mount Vernon Ladies' Association had stopped welcoming black visitors there. Since whites refused to ride on it, that likely helped Jefferson negotiate favorable terms. He would use the *River Queen* to ferry visitors between D.C. and Notley Hall three times a day to free up the *Jane Mosely* for the more lucrative cruising business.[7]

Jefferson permitted both alcohol and gambling on board his steamers and was roundly criticized for it by W. Calvin Chase, editor of the *Washington Bee*. Chase maintained that on the *River Queen* "liquor flowed freely, the gambling tables were crowded, and fights were frequent." Staterooms, he reported, could be rented by the hour. The editor allowed, however, that Jefferson's *Jane Moseley* (advertised as "the only first-class excursion boat owned and operated by an African American," was more respectable.[8] Despite the criticism, or perhaps because of it, Jefferson's businesses flourished, and he was able to purchase another steamer, the *Angler*, for private charters. That one cost him $20,000—a fortune at the turn of the century.

Unfortunately, Jefferson's vision for Notley Hall ran counter to the Edwardian sensibilities of D.C.'s African American middle class, a largely mulatto elite. Their women's clubs famously dictated the standards of decorum, and their husbands, generally businessmen, educators, and Prince Hall Masons, exemplified Booker T. Washington's uplift ideology. None shared Jefferson's enthusiasm for "a democratic resort, like Brooklyn's Coney Island," where people from all walks of life would be welcome. Heaven knew, Jefferson argued, that there were enough "public" places along the Potomac where black people—from the lowest to the highest of social classes—were denied entry. He therefore appreciated the endorsement of Mary Church Terrell, an affluent women's club official, who in 1908 praised Notley Hall as "well-equipped with everything to amuse the people." "The children enjoy the merry-go-rounds immensely, . . . and it has the finest pier I've ever seen anywhere," she said.[9] That summer Jefferson added a roller coaster, expanded the bathing facilities, lit up the entrance with seven thousand electric lights, and changed the name of Notley Hall to Washington Park.

WASHINGTON PARK

Washington Park welcomed a diverse crowd—young and old, working-class men and women, middle-class families, church and fraternal groups, and migrants from the Deep South—all arriving with the expectation of a good time and with very different ideas about what constituted respectable behavior. Irritations, provocations, and insults could, and did, provoke aggression. As a result, black ministers and Prince Hall Masonic Lodge masters encouraged their members to boycott the park if things didn't improve. Preachers advised their congregations to return to "the safer option" of visiting the white landing beaches on Mondays. Some did. Many didn't. It made no sense to Jefferson and made him wonder if creating a democratic pleasure park like Coney Island was going to be possible. Compromise was difficult—harder than he had anticipated, and most of his attempts at it failed. Every action he took seemed to offend someone. He wasn't alone in this. At about the same time, Coney Island was being disdained as "Sodom by the Sea" by Rev. A. C. Dixon of Brooklyn's Hanson Place Baptist Church.

Jefferson agreed to reschedule activities that made his affluent supporters nervous. He limited casino gambling and boxing matches to after sundown and prohibited the sale of alcohol during the day. That seemed more reasonable than cutting these popular entertainments and amusements entirely, and he continued to defend his customers when they were unjustly harassed by the D.C. police. He argued that white excursioners also drank, gambled, and became rowdy, yet few of them were arrested. Their behavior was written off as high jinks, while the same conduct exhibited by blacks was considered threatening. Jefferson's nemesis, Calvin Chase, editor of the *Washington Bee*, actually supported him in this.[10]

Unfortunately, in 1910 Jefferson's *River Queen* caught fire and sank, forcing him to use the *Angler* to ferry customers to and from Washington Park. As a result, the charter business suffered. The following year the *Jane Moseley* developed engine trouble, and was taken out of service. Then, in a classic case of bad timing, Jefferson bought out Samuel Bessinger to become sole owner of the Independent Steamboat and Barge Company. While it freed him to make unilateral (even unpopular) decisions, responsibility for keeping Washington Park afloat was his alone, and many "respectable" black families continued to avoid the park.

In 1912, when Riverview Park's white gambling casino on Colonial Beach began admitting black patrons, it negatively affected Jefferson's business. By the end of the year, he was forced to sell the *Jane Moseley*, and the *Angler* would soon follow.

Although there wasn't another facility like Washington Park anywhere in the mid-Atlantic region, historian Andrew Kahrl maintains that "rather than seeing [the park] as a rebuke to white exclusionism and a visible symbol of black initiative, many [black] community leaders believed that it and the crowds it attracted corroborated white stereotypes and served to collapse the class differences that groups like the Masons strove so hard to attenuate."[11] In February 1913 a fire destroyed $30,000 worth of Washington Park property, and Jefferson was uninsured. The cause, believed to be arson, was never conclusively determined. Three years later Jefferson lost the land when he failed to meet his mortgage payments. Still, he refused to accept defeat.

THE *E. MADISON HALL*

By 1918, Lewis Jefferson was working for J. O. Holmes, reputedly the richest black man in Washington, D.C. He owned the Holmes Hotel and a high-class restaurant on Virginia Avenue, and he had purchased Jefferson's *Angler* in 1913, renamed it the *E. Madison Hall*, and entered the cruising business. Later he acquired one of J. Pierpont Morgan's yachts and subsequently hired Jefferson to manage this growing fleet.

Deeply concerned about respectability, Holmes outfitted the *Hall* with an all-black crew: a captain, first mate, purser, chambermaid, two engineers, two firemen, a coal passer, two cooks, two waiters, four policemen, and six deck hands.[12] He offered first-class on-board dining and would occasionally operate as a floating casino for private outings. Initially Holmes was spared the equipment failures, foul weather, and lawsuits that had plagued other steamboat companies, but his luck ran out in 1919 when he was sued by the family of a passenger who fell off the Colonial Beach gangplank and drowned. Prohibition brought more trouble. Like many in the entertainment business, Holmes was not averse to sidestepping the anti-liquor laws, but in 1922 he got caught, was arrested, and the *E. Madison Hall* was seized. The July 7, 1922, *Baltimore Afro-American* reported that "a shower of bottles, many containing liquor[,] were thrown over by excursionists ridding themselves of evidence as they greeted officers making the raid." That ended Holmes's foray into the cruising business and cost his crew their jobs.

Lewis Jefferson never recouped after Washington Park and had to sue J. O. Holmes for his back wages, but perhaps he took some consolation from the fact that his Independent Steamboat and Barge Company had changed the calculus on the Potomac River. No longer would exclusively white-owned companies profit from transportation and entertainment on the water. Lewis demonstrated that African Americans, despite being denied many important business tools and opportunities, could still make river cruising and amusement parks profitable.

BROWN'S GROVE, ROCK CREEK
"Owned and Operated by Colored People"

❖❖❖

If winning isn't everything, why do they keep score?
VINCE LOMBARDI

In 1896 George Brown, a young black man barely out of his teens, left his Washington, North Carolina, home for Baltimore to train as a machinist. As an apprentice he proved so skilled that his white boss eventually promoted him to foreman. In later years Brown liked to tell the story of that boss sending him to Maryland's Eastern Shore, where a white train conductor insisted that he ride in the baggage car with a dog. Brown maintained that the incident fired his determination to provide first-class transportation for his people.[1] Whether or not the story is true, George Brown made his dream a reality.

Like Lewis Jefferson, Brown was a self-made man, but unlike Jefferson he was a fairly rough one. He worked hard to earn his pilot's license and became the first African American member of Maryland's Masters, Mates & Pilots union. In 1905 he leased a side-wheeler for $25 a day to offer Baltimore's black community safe transportation across the Chesapeake, and within the year he was providing pleasure cruises on the Bay. Brown subsequently leased a picnic grove on Bear Creek to provide an excursion destination.

In 1907 he bought a half-interest in the steamboat *Dr. J. W. Newell* with a friend, Walter Langley, who had a talent for passing as white. Together they refurbished the *Newell*, renamed it the *Starlight*, and offered moonlight cruising. They would eventually add shipboard dining and dancing. Business was so good that Brown and Langley leased forty-five acres on Rock Creek to establish Brown's Grove, a waterfront family amusement park. It's likely that the realtor who brokered the lease believed that Langley was white.[2]

By 1910 several African American–owned steamers were operating on the Chesapeake Bay, but in 1913 Brown's Grove was the region's only black amusement park when Jefferson's Washington Park (on the Potomac) closed. Brown's Grove offered picnic grounds, a bathhouse, a fishing pier, a merry-go-round, pony rides, and eventually a "Racer Dip" roller coaster. Brown and Langley opened a midway restaurant and leased space to concessionaires for shooting galleries and penny arcades.³ They welcomed church and fraternal groups as well as baptisms and revivals and advertised in the *Afro-American Ledger* as "the only park in Maryland run exclusively for Colored People by Colored People."⁴

All summer the *Starlight* made the forty-five-minute trip from Fells Point on the Baltimore waterfront to Brown's Grove on the Severn River. The partners subsequently purchased the *Granite City* and the *Avalon* to offer excursion packages for YMCA groups, fraternal lodges, women's clubs, and Sunday Schools. Brown's *Favorite* sailed to Havre de Grace, a popular gambling landing on the bay's north end, and moored at Round Bay on the Severn. Built in the 1880s, Round Bay was a white-owned facility that welcomed African Americans, mainly from Baltimore, who could afford vacation packages at the Round Bay Hotel.

In 1904, however, the *Baltimore Afro-American* began referring to Brown's Grove as "The Great Colored Excursion Resort."⁵ It boasted a boardwalk, dance pavilion, bathhouses and annual athletic carnival.⁶ In 1911, the property was purchased by white developers to build a summer colony. Nevertheless, some African Americans returned for day outings on the *Favorite* to enjoy the waterfront and stroll the boardwalk again.

Brown's cruises had included onboard music and dancing, but Captain Brown would not permit alcohol, nor would he tolerate disruptive behavior.⁷ If a man smuggled liquor aboard or became disorderly, Brown would allegedly knock him out with a single punch and lock him in a cabin below deck until the *Starlight* docked.⁸ His strictness insured a safe, family-friendly outing.

Both Brown's Grove and the Brown and Langley fleet operated profitably until the captain's death in 1935. Langley attempted to carry on, but on July 5, 1938, the park's wooden roller coaster caught fire. By the time the Riviera Beach Fire Company responded, the blaze was out of control. In the end, the carousel, all the refreshment stands, the bathhouses, and the picnic area were destroyed. Brown's Grove never reopened. On the fifty-seventh anniversary of the fire, journalist Gilbert Sandler recalled in his column for the *Baltimore Sun*, that "Brown's was the first, last and only seaside resort of any black community in the Baltimore area with its own to and from excursion boats."⁹

Fire was a factor in the demise of so many amusement parks, black and white, because rides were generally made of wood and no insurance company would write a fire-loss policy on them. The parks were expensive to build and maintain, and customers were always seeking new experiences. The life span of a thrill ride was incredibly short.

EDGEWATER BEACH PARK, TURNER STATION
"Home of the Baltimore Grays"

❖❖❖

I am what time, circumstance, history, have made of me, certainly, but I am, also, much more than that. So are we all.
JAMES BALDWIN

During the first half of the twentieth century, Edgewater Beach was one of three popular black beaches in Anne Arundel County, Maryland. Carr's and Sparrow's Beaches were the others. Edgewater, established in 1929 by Joseph and Flavia Thomas, offered bathing, boat rides, children's amusements, a restaurant, an outdoor stage, and camping groves.

Joseph Thomas and his five sisters were raised in Turner Station. Their father Anthony settled there in the late 1800s when it was known as Sparrows Point. Beginning as a shipyard welder, Anthony Thomas later partnered in a grocery business and by the mid-1920s was selling real estate.

BETHLEHEM STEEL

In 1916, as the United States prepared to enter World War I, the Bethlehem Steel Corporation annexed the Sparrows Point Shipyard, doubled its size, and added a massive blast furnace to establish itself as the biggest producer of steel on the East Coast. The corporation built worker housing and a company town that included ten paved streets arranged in districts according to company hierarchy. Managers lived on A Street, supervisors and professionals on B and C Streets, and plant workers on D through H.

Black employees lived in a separate enclave, the North Side, on the opposite side of Sparrows Point by Humphrey's Creek.[1] Although they eventually made up a quarter of the Sparrows Point workforce, African Americans were not permitted to use the same cafeterias or restrooms as the white employees, nor could they aspire to the same promotions, and there were no black supervisors. As the plant expanded and the white company town became overcrowded, additional white worker housing units were constructed in nearby Dundalk. Whites were permitted to buy them and to make mortgage payments through payroll deduction.[2] Newly hired white immigrants—Finns, Czechs, Poles, Lithuanians, and Italians—generally rented in Baltimore's Highlandtown, a forty-minute commute on the Red Rocket trolley. African Americans who chose not to live in the North Side rented in Baltimore's Old West district, where blocks were designated as either "all-white" or "all-Negro."[3]

In 1920 Anthony Thomas and three of his North Side neighbors organized the People's Company. They leased a North Side building and opened a restaurant, ice cream parlor, barbershop, and eventually a boardinghouse for single black employees, with a savings bank in the basement.[4] In 1938 the Adams Cocktail Lounge, formerly a liquor store owned by Irvin Adams, booked Pearl Bailey, Redd Foxx, and Fats Domino. Thomas and his partners eventually expanded the bank to create the Tuxedo Savings and Loan Association, which offered African American families personal loans and mortgages. As wages rose after the war, black workers were able to save for homes of their own.[5]

During World War II, Anthony's son Joseph graduated from Howard University Medical School and then completed an internship in Johnstown, Pennsylvania, and a residency in a New Orleans hospital. There in New Orleans he met and married Flavia Ridley. In 1919 he brought her home to Turner Station where he established a medical practice and Flavia worked in his father's real estate business. It wasn't long, however, before the newlyweds were building and selling row houses themselves.

Dr. and Mrs. Thomas later invested in a dream that became Edgewater Beach Park, where they offered modern bathhouses, motorboat and aquaplane rides, horseshoe pits, children's amusements, and tennis courts. Dr. Thomas booked popular Chitlin Circuit stars like Billie Holiday, Gene Krupa, Count Basie, and Chick Webb, and a Miss Edgewater Park was crowned at the end of each season.

Before Edgewater Beach, Turner Station's North Side residents were required to make a considerably longer trip across the bay to Brown's Grove or to Carr's or Sparrow's Beaches. The white residents of Sparrows Point, on the other hand, spent their summers at the Bay Shore Amusement Park, fifteen miles outside Baltimore. The Baltimore, Sparrows Point & Chesapeake Railway provided direct service to the front gate of that thirty-acre park, which boasted bathhouses, bowling alleys, restaurants, a dance pavilion, and a two-thousand-seat music pavilion.

In 1932 Dr. Thomas purchased an eighty-three-foot surplus naval air-sea rescue vessel that he converted into an excursion boat, the *Fla-Joe*, for moonlight cruising along the South River and into the Chesapeake Bay. An avid baseball fan, in 1936 he purchased the Sparrows Point Giants, a Negro Southern League semipro team and sponsored the local Turner Station Hawks and built the Water's Edge Field for them. When the Giants joined the Negro Major Leagues in 1942 (and took the name Baltimore Grays), the doctor took time from his practice to tour with them. Baseball was a popular pastime in most African American communities. Historian Gary Ashwill maintains, "Black baseball players sustained a level of craftsmanship (some might call it artistry) that links them with the creators of jazz or the writers of the Harlem Renaissance as makers of African American culture during a time of especially harsh oppression."

On July 4, 1942, the Water's Edge Field hosted an exhibition game between the Grays and the Cincinnati Clowns, baseball's equivalent of the Harlem Globetrotters. Despite Clowns star Peanuts Davis pitching from a wheelchair and Pepper Bassett catching from a rocking chair during the last inning, the Clowns won 7–4. It was the highlight of the season.

As a young man, Charles Douglass, who had established the Highland Beach summer colony in Annapolis, had played third base for the Washington, D.C. Alerts. African American novelist, poet, and NAACP director James Weldon Johnson later pitched for Jacksonville's Cuban Giants and is remembered as the first Negro League pitcher to master the curveball. Johnson believed that the Clowns brought something new to the professional diamond: baseball comedy. "Their coaches kept up continuous banter while players staged a comic pantomime for the spectators, generally after a good play," Johnson noted. "The whole team would cut up and make the grandstand and bleachers roar . . . white baseball was a dignified and rather grim performance by contrast."

During World War II, Dr. Thomas closed Edgewater Park after many of Turner Station's young men and most of the Grays enlisted. His son, Joseph Thomas Jr., was completing his training at the U.S. Naval Academy. When the war ended, however, the doctor did not reopen the park but instead built the Anthony Theater, a seven-hundred-seat, state-of-the-art, air-conditioned entertainment center that he and Flavia managed. The grand opening on March 22, 1946, featured John Wayne in *Dakota*, and the Anthony would often be favorably compared with Baltimore's Royal Theater. It operated, profitably, until 1956. When the doctor died, Flavia donated it to the Red Brick Baptist Church. Joseph Thomas Jr. subsequently pursued a successful career as an attorney.

CARR'S AND SPARROW'S BEACHES, ANNAPOLIS
"Black Feet in White Sand"

❖❖❖

Everything that happened to me as a child involved music.
It was part of everyday life, as automatic as breathing.
NINA SIMONE

During the 1950s and '60s, Carr's Beach—"The Beach," as it was called—attracted African Americans from Washington, D.C., Baltimore, and Philadelphia. It was the place to go on summer weekends. In 1927 siblings Elizabeth Carr Smith and Florence Carr Sparrow had established side-by-side "sister bathing beaches" on the Chesapeake Bay, directly across the from D.C.'s Suburban Gardens.

Sparrow's Beach, with its spacious picnic grounds, Ferris wheel, pony rides, basketball courts, and baseball diamonds, catered to families and welcomed day camps and church groups. Sunday afternoons on Sparrow's Beach were all about family fun and sports. Carr's, on the other hand, was all about music. Elizabeth Carr Smith brought Cab Calloway, Billy Eckstein, Ray Charles and Dinah Washington, Chick Webb, and James Brown to the bay.

The sisters inherited their properties from their father, Fred Carr, who had been a fugitive slave and served in the Union navy during the Civil War. He later worked as a Naval Academy cook. Over twenty years, Fred Carr accumulated 180 acres on the Annapolis neck, and in 1902 he and his wife Mary Wells Carr opened a picnic and bathing beach on the bay, including summer boarding accommodations. After Fred Carr died, his daughters established their own beaches.[1] Both were listed in *The Negro Motorist Green-Book*, a guide first published in 1936 and updated every year into the mid-sixties by the Victor H. Green Company to help black travelers avoid difficulties, danger, and embarrassing situations while traveling in their own country.

When Elizabeth Carr Smith died in 1948, her son Frederick and his wife Grace inherited the twenty-six acre Carr's Beach and subsequently partnered with Baltimore venture capitalist William L. "Little Willie" Adams to commercialize it. A former numbers runner, Adams had helped to fund many African American businesses, including Baltimore's members-only black Sphinx Club on Pennsylvania Avenue, where black politicians, judges, lawyers, and other professionals gathered.

The new Carr's Beach Amusement Company built a huge bandstand pavilion, and, when Anne Arundel became the first county in Maryland to legalize slot machines, it added the Bengasi Night Club.[2] Beginning in 1952, Charles "Hoppy" Adams, Little Willie's brother and a popular disc jockey on WANN-AM Baltimore, broadcast live from the bandstand on the beach, making Carr's one of the most popular stops on the Chitlin Circuit. When Fats Domino performed there in the early 1950s, traffic was reported to have been backed up for thirty miles. When Chuck Berry arrived in July 1956, only eight thousand of the seventy thousand who came to see him were able to get in.[3]

"We couldn't go anywhere else," explained Nevada Smith, who came to Sparrow's Beach on church-sponsored excursions in the 1950s. "You had Sandy Point

FIG. 2. Sparrow's Beach, 1927. A family picnic and bathing beach on the Chesapeake Bay near Annapolis, bordering on Carr's, its sister beach.

FIG. 3. Dancers enjoying a good time in the Carr's Beach Pavilion, 1956. It was the most popular African American Beach and music venue on the Chesapeake. WANN Radio Station Records, Archives Center, National Museum of American History.

(on Chesapeake Bay's north shore) but there were separate facilities there and Ocean City wasn't welcoming."[4]

In the 1960s, Carr's Beach welcomed young whites who had discovered black music. As music trends expanded, Little Willie and the Carrs sold the business to white events promoter Mike Schreiebman in 1972. The following season Schreibman renamed it the Great McGonicle Seaside Park and leased it for rock concerts. Frank Zappa's concert that year was its very last show. In 1974 the beach closed after forty seasons, and the property was eventually purchased by developers who built the Villages of Chesapeake Harbor condominiums. Sparrow's Beach had closed three years earlier after Anne Arundel County condemned the property to build the Back Creek Sewer Treatment Plant.

Vincent Leggett, who spent many weekends at Carr's Beach as a young man, recalls that "the beaches attracted thousands of visitors from Philadelphia, New

York, Baltimore, Wilmington and Washington, D.C. The slogan was 'Black Feet in White Sand,' and it was all so empowering—no one could tell you to sit down or to stand up. You could just come out and enjoy the Chesapeake Bay. Enjoy the music, the food, enjoy the fellowship. Just to see people of color in charge, running something was very empowering."[5]

FIG. 4. Young women ready for a day at Carr's Beach, ca. 1958. Note the likeness of Hoppy Adams to the right on the rear quarter panel of the car. Adams was a popular deejay who broadcast on WANN from Carr's Beach on weekends. WANN Radio Station Records, Archives Center, National Museum of American History.

WILMER'S PARK, PRINCE GEORGE'S COUNTY
"A Musicians' Showcase"

❖❖❖

Music is a verb.
ORNETTE COLEMAN

Wilmer's Park in rural Brandywine, Maryland, was one of very few African American–owned and -operated entertainment venues that continued to thrive after integration. Once an eighty-acre tobacco farm owned by the family of African American photographer and film maker Gordon Parks, it was purchased by Arthur Wilmer for $6,500 in 1947 to create a sports park and entertainment center. He constructed outdoor stages and booked musicians like Duke Ellington, Otis Redding, the Temptations, Patty LaBelle, and a young Stevie Wonder.

For twenty years before Wilmer moved to rural Maryland, he had owned and operated the Little Harlem Supper Club on D.C.'s Black Broadway, serving dinner and drinks to musicians like Cab Calloway and Ella Fitzgerald before and after their performances in the U Street nightclubs. He also supplied jukeboxes and cigarette machines to black clubs all over Black Broadway. As he approached his fiftieth birthday, however, Wilmer decided that it was time to pursue another dream: a sports park and entertainment center conveniently near both D.C. and Baltimore. So he sold his supper club, purchased the tobacco farm, and opened "Wilmer's Park" three years later.

Wilmer's Park featured picnic areas and two baseball diamonds to accommodate semiprofessional Negro League games, and Wilmer later added hot air balloon rides, a restaurant and lounge, and a six-thousand-square-foot dance hall. By the mid-1950s Wilmer was offering live concerts. He built a covered outdoor stage and added a fifteen-unit motel for weekend guests.[1] The park became a fixture on the Chitlin Circuit, filling the slot between Baltimore's Royal Theater and Carr's Beach.

Wilmer's early shows featured Ray Charles, James Brown, and Marvin Gaye, and later ones showcased Otis Redding, Gladys Knight & the Pips, and Count Basie. Although many African American amusement parks, beaches, and resorts closed after passage of the 1964 Civil Rights Act, Wilmer's Park survived because Arthur Wilmer adapted to newer and broader musical trends, including the music of white bands like Led Zeppelin and the Grateful Dead. During its nearly half-century run, Wilmer's Park featured rhythm and blues and hard rock. Natalie Hopkinson of the *Washington Post* maintained that Wilmer hosted everyone "from hippies to hip-hoppers." Wilmer also organized annual Woodstock anniversary celebrations, and he helped to launch several heavy metal bands. The park was transformed into a showcase for festivals, jams, and raves, and it was the venue for an annual Jerry Garcia Festival. Wilmer featured hard rock, folk rock, zydeco, and reggae bands. He promoted all kinds of musical talent, and his long run was ended only by his death in 1999.

Wilmer's Park operated for three decades longer than most of Black Broadway's movie palaces, theaters, and nightclubs. In 1999 when James Martin, a D.C. police officer who as a young man had played black sandlot baseball there, heard of its closing, he recalled, "All the country girls were out there, that's why all the fellas went."[2]

THE CHITLIN CIRCUIT

❖❖❖

Even chitlins smell good to a starving man.
GREG ILES

Black America's musical legacy celebrates jazz and the blues as well as ragtime, swing, and later rock and roll, rhythm and blues, and soul. By the 1920s, radios, jukeboxes, record players, and affordable records made this music part of the American experience. The Chitlin Circuit helped.

Until 1930, agents, promoters, and business managers controlled the careers of those black musicians who were barred from white venues. They were initially represented by T.O.B.A. and later played the Chitlin Circuit. Music historian Preston Lauterbach describes this circuit as

> a network of black-owned nightclubs, dance halls, juke joints and theaters in the South, on the East Coast and in parts of the Midwest, most located on or near "the Stroll" [the black main drag]—Memphis' Beale Street, Auburn Avenue in Atlanta, and the U Street District in D.C. During segregation these were safe venues for black performers. After the collapse of T.O.B.A in 1930, Sea and Denver Ferguson, black Indianapolis nightclub owners, established the Ferguson Brothers Booking Agency, and Denver Ferguson is remembered as "the man who invented the Chitlin Circuit."

The Chitlin Circuit's most popular stops were Baltimore's Royal Theater, the Royal Peacock in Atlanta, the Ritz in Jacksonville, the Apollo in New York City, Memphis's Hippodrome, Birmingham's Carver Theater, the Fox in Detroit, the Howard in D.C., and the Lyric Theatre in Lexington, Kentucky.

On September 14, 2014, Tyler Perry, a black actor, producer, and filmmaker, made a guest appearance on *The Arsenio Hall Show* and recalled the old network. "You had all these people who could not perform in white establishments," he explained, "so they went on the road and played in all these small juke joints with chicken fries and chitlins, and they traveled all over the country and became so famous among their own people that they were able to support themselves and live well."

Why "Chitlin"? Some believe that it was a reference to slave times when the master ate "high on the hog" (taking all the ham and bacon), leaving the less desirable parts for the slaves. Chitterlings (chitlins) are fried or steamed pig intestines, the cheapest meat on the market. Chitlins were a staple in the poorest sections of the South, and they were dinner for touring musicians.

"Beginning in the midsummer of 1947," Lauterbach writes, "the Chitlin Circuit hit its full, hectic stride, with important events and new artists breaking over the map, all at once. But by the end of the decade the Circuit was out of business as talented black musicians began to leave the South and were picked up by name orchestras in New York or Chicago."[1] Eventually record companies controlled these artists in the same way that movie studios controlled actors and actresses.

Lauterbach notes, "[By the mid-1950s] the tour business which had been the moneymaker for black musicians and promoters during the Circuit's first twenty years declined. When *Billboard* started publishing a *Rhythm and Blues Chart* in 1949, former Chitlin' Circuit stars could make a living without leaving the studio."[2] They didn't have to tour. Finally, he laments, "The Circuit as we came to know it on the road to rock n' roll was eliminated by degrees as urban renewal programs eviscerated once vital black neighborhoods nationwide. There would be no return to the old Circuit or to black Main Street's importance in American culture."[3]

Almost twenty years later, in 1964, Dr. Martin Luther King Jr. spoke at the first Berlin Jazz Festival. At that time Berlin was still divided by the infamous wall. He reminded the gathering,

> Jazz speaks for life. The Blues tell the story of life's difficulties, and if you think for a moment, you will realize that they take the hardest realities of life and put them into music, only to come out with some new hope or sense of triumph.
> This is triumphant music.
> Modern jazz has continued in this tradition, singing the songs of a more complicated urban existence. When life itself offers no order and meaning, the musician creates an order and meaning from the sounds of the earth which flow through his instrument. . . .
> Everybody has the Blues. Everybody longs for meaning. Everybody needs to love and be loved. Everybody needs to clap hands and be happy. Everybody longs for faith.
> In music, especially in this broad category called Jazz, there is a stepping stone towards all of these.[4]

VIRGINIA

SEAVIEW BEACH RESORT AND AMUSEMENT PARK, NORFOLK
"The Largest and Best Negro Beach Resort in America"

❖❖❖

We are made to persist, that's how we find out who we are.
TOBIAS WOLFF

In 1920 the African American community of Norfolk, Virginia, almost 50 percent of the population, petitioned the city council to create a black municipal park. For three years the council dragged its feet before finally offering up Lafayette Municipal Park, which was neither attractive nor maintained.[1] A 1923 Norfolk *Journal and Guide* editorial noted that:

> [Lafayette Park] could be had only under the most humiliating circumstances[,] neglected and unkept as it was, its condition ever presented a silent but sinister reminder that the Negroes were not welcome anywhere in the park. Few Negroes would compromise their self-respect and use that spot under conditions plainly meant to humiliate them.[2]

Nearly a decade later, in 1930, P. B. Young, publisher of the African American *Journal and Guide*, and Dr. R. J. Brown, a local dentist, organized an interracial committee and recruited one thousand residents to attend a city council meeting to publicly petition for a black municipal beach. The white council members predictably argued that a black beach would negatively affect white property values and "make for a shoreline spectacle." White businessmen complained that such public-sector competition was unfair to them.[3]

Eugene Diggs, the committee's African American attorney, informed the council that under the circumstances the only option left for the city's black residents was to sue to integrate white Buckroe Beach, since it was being maintained with tax dollars. They hadn't done this previously, he explained, because they wanted to keep the peace.

Attorney Diggs continued, "The Negro has waived his rights for so long that many of you have come to believe he has none. I am wondering if the time has not come when the colored man will have to stop waiving his basic citizenship rights."[4] Diggs made clear that gaining access to public space did not mean that the black community was anxious to socialize with whites. No. What they demanded was access to a first-rate public facility or otherwise a public beach of their own. Separate but equal was fine as long as it was truly equal. During this period the NAACP's demand for desegregation was gathering strength, but it would not come into its own for another decade. In any event, the city council passed a resolution to purchase property and to create an African American municipal waterfront park. It subsequently acquired ten acres from the Pennsylvania Railroad Company.

Construction began in 1934, partially funded by the federal Civil Works Administration. On June 16, 1935, Norfolk's City Beach celebrated its grand opening, showcasing a boardwalk, a bathhouse, an outdoor pavilion, and a ballroom. Over successive seasons it attracted an average of five thousand weekend visitors. Kathleen Edwards, a Norfolk historian, recalls, "The white residents around the Beach heckled us and had our cars towed, but we went in droves anyway because finally we had some place that was for us."[5]

During World War II, Norfolk's shipyard workers—black and white—were logging significant amounts of overtime, and in 1944 four African American entrepreneurs, who recognized a potential market when they saw one, organized the Seaview Beach and Hotel Corporation. William T. Mason (president of Metropolitan Realty and one of the first black millionaires in Virginia), attorney Wilbur Watts and his brother Irving Watts (a dentist), and William E. Waters, principal of Norcom High School, recruited eighteen African American business and professional leaders to study the feasibility of building an African American resort and amusement park.

They raised $75,000 to purchase a two-story building and six and a half acres on the Chesapeake Bay. Once owned by the white Knights Templar fraternity, the building had a large ballroom, forty guest rooms, and an outdoor dance pavilion, the Starlight Plaza.[6] From opening day, May 31, 1945, activities of "the Club" were chronicled in the *Journal and Guide*'s weekly "Social Whirl" column under the banner "See You at Seaview." Local chapters of the National Negro Business League, the Prince Hall Masons, Odd Fellows, and black Elks, and Kappa Alpha Psi and Omega Psi Phi fraternities would subsequently schedule all their formal affairs at "the Club."[7] By 1946 the trustees added a full-service restaurant with a dining balcony overlooking the dance floor. That year they contracted with Dudley Cooper, white owner of Norfolk's Ocean View Amusement Park, to design an amusement park for them. Cooper agreed to build it and to purchase, install, and maintain the equipment.

Seaview Amusement Park opened on July 11, 1947, with a Ferris wheel, a carousel, and bumper cars, and it soon attracted a weekly average of fifteen hundred visitors. Board member Irving Watts maintained that "it was not uncommon to see between thirty-five and fifty chartered busses in the parking lots on weekends."[8] *The Negro Motorist Green-Book* recommended five safe hotels in Norfolk where black tourists who visited Seaview could affordably stay. The annual guide listed restaurants, tourist homes, hotels, parks, taverns, and even beauty salons and barbershops across the nation that accepted African American customers.

The combined staff of the club and the amusement park ultimately swelled to nearly a hundred. The park was a family destination, while the club came alive after dark. In 1947 *Life* magazine noted it as "a gathering place for Norfolk's Negro elite."[9] The club featured entertainment by Ruth Brown, Count Basie, Mercer Ellington, and Ella Fitzgerald, and neither Norfolk's City Beach nor Bay Shore Beach in nearby Hampton, Virginia, could compete.

Hampton's Bay Shore was adjacent to the white Buckroe Beach, and both had been destroyed by the brutal hurricane of August 23, 1933. When they rebuilt, white Buckroe added rides, carnival games, bumper cars, a Ferris wheel, a fun house, a carousel, and a Dixie Flier roller coaster. Bay Shore replaced its roller coaster and bumper cars and added a dance pavilion. Live performances by the likes of Cab Calloway, Dizzy Gillespie, and James Brown became the major attraction. White locals and sailors stationed in nearby Norfolk were known to slip inside the Bay Shore Pavilion to dance, listen to, or watch the performers. Although no one asked them to leave, the penalty for blacks who slipped into the white Buckroe Beach was a night in jail. Buckroe's management eventually constructed a "boundary pier"—a series of wooden pylons running from the boardwalk into the Chesapeake Bay to separate "the black sands and waters of Bay Shore from the white sands and waters of Buckroe."[10]

Seaview's advantage over both Bay Shore and City Beach was its ability to add attractions every season. The board was never hesitant about spending money. In 1947 it replaced the bumper cars, offered fireworks all weekend, and expanded the parking lots. In 1948 a bigger and better Ferris wheel was installed, and the Moon Rocket ride made its debut. In 1957 the club's facilities were updated, and a golf course and tennis courts were added. The amusement park rides were overhauled, and a new bathhouse was built. Both the park and the club enjoyed almost two decades of success before club manager Ike Wells got fired for permitting illegal gambling on the premises.

The board was subsequently reorganized, and the four trustees who had been replaced sued the corporation. They charged "financial improprieties," and the litigation dragged on. The 1964 Civil Rights Act, however, delivered Seaview a mortal blow. Wilbur Watts told Obie McCollum of the *Journal and Guide*, "We couldn't compete with the [white] amusement parks at Ocean View and Virginia Beach once they let the Negroes in."[11]

Seaview Amusement Park closed in 1965, the property was sold, and the beloved club was demolished. Bay Shore closed a short time later, but Buckroe continued as an integrated park until 1985. Dudley Cooper's Ocean View Park also desegregated in 1965, and Cooper remained in business for another thirteen years until competition from the King's Dominion theme park made it impossible to continue.

NORTH CAROLINA

SHELL ISLAND RESORT, WILMINGTON
"The National Negro Playground"

❖❖❖

It appears that my worst fears have been realized: We have made
progress in everything, yet nothing has changed.
"GENEVA CRENSHAW," IN DERRICK BELL'S *WE ARE NOT SAVED*

In 1898 Wilmington, North Carolina, municipal elections, white southern Democrats did not win control of the city government, though they controlled the state legislature. Republican mayor Silas P. Wright, who was white, won reelection on the Fusion Party ticket (of Populists and Democrats), as did a black city treasurer, customs collector, jailer, and three black aldermen. The white Democrats had run a nasty campaign that summer, pledging to protect white women from sexual assaults by black men (such claims were unsubstantiated). At that time Wilmington's population was 55 percent black.

On August 11, 1897, Mrs. Rebecca Felton, one of the more prominent white women in Progressive Era Georgia, a socialite and former slave owner, addressed the Georgia State Agricultural Society with a recommendation to increase the number of lynchings of black men in order to protect rural white women from being raped. "When there is not enough religion in the pulpit to organize a crusade against sin; or justice in the court house to promptly punish crime, nor manhood enough in the nation to put a sheltering arm about innocence and virtue ... then I say lynch, a thousand times a week." The *Raleigh News and Observer*'s white editor Josephus Daniels not only published her speech in its entirety but also supported Rebecca Felton's campaign to remove "the incubus of black rapists."[1] The editor had expressed on more than one occasion that the greatest crime in the history of the United States had been granting Negroes the vote.

Furious over Felton's inciting words, on August 18 Alex Manly, black editor of the *Wilmington Daily Record*, confronted both Felton and Daniels in his editorial entitled "Mrs. Felton's Speech": "Our experiences among poor white people in the country teach us that the women of that race are not any more particular in the matter of clandestine meetings with colored men than the white men are with the colored women." Then Manly articulated the unmentionable: "You set yourselves down as a lot of carping hypocrites, in fact you cry aloud for the virtue of your women while you seek to destroy the morality of ours. Don't think ever that your women will remain pure while you are debouching ours. You sow the seed—the harvest will come in due time."[2] White Wilmington was enraged.

The son of former Delaware governor Charles Manly and his "house slave" Corrine, Alex Manly owned and operated the *Wilmington Daily Record* in partnership with his brother Frank. The following day both were evicted from their offices. Manley's editorial was reprinted on the front pages of all the white papers until election day in order to raise the ire of white voters.

The day before the election, former Confederate officer Alfred Moore Waddell, chair of Wilmington's White Government League, encouraged Wilmington's white voters: "Go to the polls and if you find the Negro voting, tell him to leave the polls. If he doesn't, kill him."[3] After all the ballots were counted and it became clear that the biracial Fusion candidates had won again, Waddell's militia torched Manly's *Daily Record* offices and threw his printing presses into the Cape Fear River. Fourteen African American men were randomly murdered, but Manly escaped North Carolina before the militia could find him. He likely got away because he was light-skinned enough to pass for white.

Another hundred black men would die before it was over. A white mob of almost two thousand roamed the city destroying black businesses and properties. At gunpoint Waddell forced Mayor Wright, the black aldermen, and the chief of police to resign and subsequently declared himself mayor. The following day Josephus Daniel's banner headline screamed: "Negro Rule Is at End in North Carolina Forever."

No action was taken to stop or to subdue the violent mob. Even Governor Daniel Russell remained silent, and not one member of President William McKinley's administration stepped up to condemn the violence, despite intervention by Ida B. Wells, the black Memphis journalist and activist who begged the president to act. Not only did he not act, during its 1899 and 1900 sessions the North Carolina legislature passed a series of Jim Crow statutes limiting the voting rights of African Americans. Two thousand blacks had fled the city by then, and in 1902 only sixty-one hundred black people remained on the state's voter registration rolls.[4]

A decade later, in 1913 President Woodrow Wilson appointed Josephus Daniels secretary of the navy. By that time Daniels had expressed regret over the role he had played in the 1898 Wilmington Insurrection. Still, he insisted that he had been a victim of circumstances.

Thomas Cripps, a Morgan State University professor, later explained, "The Wilmington Massacre effectively announced that white violence against blacks for the next quarter of a century would be organized, collective in strength, in daylight, and against concentrations of blacks in their ghettos."[5] And so it was. For seventeen years the white Redeemer Democrats held on to North Carolina's state legislature.

THE SHELL ISLAND RESORT

Two years after the 1898 insurrection and massacre, Wilmington was one of the busiest deepwater harbors on the Atlantic Coast. Opportunities in shipping, shipbuilding, fishing, and the tourist industry seemed limitless for white people. Hotels, resorts, and spas sprang up along the inlets and there was little unemployment in any quarter. In 1905 the Oceanic Resort Hotel at Wrightsville Beach advertised itself as the "Playground of the South"—the *white* South, of course.

In 1917, on the eve of America's entry into World War I (and almost twenty years after the Wilmington insurrection), a group of prominent African Americans—clergymen, lawyers, doctors, federal employees, and businessmen—whose livelihoods did not depend on white men, met with Hugh MacRea, president of the Tidewater Power Company and controller of Wilmington's trolley lines, to petition for the use of some property on the southern tip of white Wrightsville Beach (sufficiently removed from the white resort area), to build an African American public bathing beach that they were prepared to fund. The Tidewater Power Company had constructed Wrightsville Beach's Lumina Entertainment Pier in 1905, a three-level, twenty-five-thousand-square-foot wonder illuminated by six thousand electric lights.

Wrightsville's mayor Thomas H. Wright (a descendent of former mayor Silas Wright) supported their request and took it to the community board, where the white Wrightsville summer community petitioned against it. They maintained that a black beach would lower white property values. The African American petitioners subsequently withdrew.[6]

Mayor Wright, a vice president of the Wilmington Home Realty Company, was one of three partners. Charles Parmalee and Robert Northrup were the other two. When an uninhabited island across the Queen's Inlet from Wrightsville Beach became available in 1922, the mayor contacted Dr. Frank Avant, leader of the 1917 petitioners, and offered to buy it and create a Negro beach and resort community if Avant could raise $75,000.[7] Avant raised it—some indication of the amount of capital that was available in the black community twenty-four years after the insurrection.

Announcement of the impending Negro resort on Shell Island was made on February 16, 1923. Back in 1917 the original black petitioners had requested a simple public bathing beach, but by 1923 it was the Jazz Age, a war had been fought and won, and Wilmington's affluent African American community wanted its own Atlantic City.[8]

That was fine with Mayor Wright, who planned to make his money selling real estate (a total of 270 building lots) and financing summer bungalow construction. He hired white contractor Luther Rogers to design and build a community with fourteen streets, bathhouses, a restaurant, a music pavilion, a pier, and public beach.

Avant predicted that Shell Island would become the premier Negro resort of America, "the national Negro playground." He described it in the *Wilmington Journal* as "two miles of ocean front spreading itself out like some fairyland along the mighty water."[9] By April 16, 1923, the *Journal* reported that the Shell Island pavilion was nearing completion.[10] Opening day was scheduled for May 30, 1923.

The Tidewater Power Company operated an electric trolley line between Wilmington and Wrightsville, and president Hugh MacRae agreed to construct a spur from downtown Wilmington to Harbor Island, where the white-owned R. R. Stone Towing Company would provide ferry service to Shell Island for black people. Four daily round trips were scheduled.

Wrightsville Beach's wealthy white summer residents (some of whom lived in Wilmington) were concerned about the number of black people that would be traveling to and from Shell Island. The thought of having to swim with them, even from opposite ends of the inlet, was apparently offensive. These were affluent, influential white people whose experiences with black people were limited to interactions with their domestic servants. Many had live-in cooks, maids, and nannies who traveled with them between their permanent residences and summer homes. They believed that it was not only unseemly but *unnatural* for servants and yard help to aspire to resorts and summer residences.

On Shell Island the three-story pavilion that would serve as a recreation and entertainment center was quickly completed, as were boardwalks, a bathhouse, and several piers. The pavilion became a wildly popular music attraction—especially jazz nights. Duke Ellington, Ella Fitzgerald, and the Southern All Star Orchestra all performed there and drew large weekend crowds, with many coming from out of state.

Norfolk's *New Journal and Guide* maintained, "[Shell Island] promises to be not only a convention and excursion center, but to be the summer home for some of the best citizens of the race." The white *Charlotte Observer* congratulated Wilmington itself. "Perhaps no city in the South has done quite so big a thing for its negro population as Wilmington has," it proclaimed.

A MYSTERY

A little over a year later, on October 7, 1924, Mayor Wright abruptly resigned in the middle of his term. Failure to sell more than a dozen Shell Island building lots had sent him into a financial spiral. Nine months later he and his partners, Parmalee and Northrup, dissolved the Home Realty Company. In the meantime, while Wrightsville Beach summer residents continued to complain about the Shell Islanders, there were no major problems until almost two years later when, on June 2, 1926, a suspicious fire destroyed the great pavilion.

This would not be an isolated incident. As the number of black beaches, amusement parks, and resorts increased, reports of sabotage, fraud, onerous tax assessments, eminent domain filings, arson, and violence escalated. In the spring of 1926, for example, a firebomb destroyed the Pine Crest Inn, an abandoned white waterside resort in Salem, Virginia, near Roanoke. African Americans had purchased it, refurbished it, and opened it for business that year. While some whites were only too happy to unload failing businesses on black entrepreneurs, others feared that African American ownership would cheapen surrounding property values. The Pine Crest Inn disaster occurred just a few months after black bathers were run off a beach at Kessler's Mill near Roanoke's white Lake Pleasure resort.[11]

More suspicious fires continued to plague Shell Island. After several cottages were destroyed, others were abandoned. By the end of June 1926 everything was gone. Who was responsible? Whites blamed affluent blacks who they maintained were turned off by the ferry boatloads of lower-class black people who streamed onto the beach every day. But more than that was at work.

The black community no doubt suspected members of the white Wrightsville community for starting the fires, and white people in turn likely suspected members of the black community. It was not until 2021 that Wilmington historian Marc Farinella, while reviewing land transaction documents in the New Hanover County Register of Deeds Office, learned what had gone on. After reading years of minutes of the Wrightsville City Council, he discovered that the Shell Island Beach Resort and Development Company (the African American group organized by Avant in October 1923), had disbanded in 1925, leaving former mayor Thomas Wright's Home Realty Company holding a very bad investment indeed.[12] Home Realty had purchased Shell Island and financed cottage construction because Wright was confident that he would make money selling the 270 building lots. As noted, that didn't happen. The project was a marketing disaster. Historian Andrew Kahrl, who studied the Shell Island situation, explains, "Black families with the means to buy a lot would want to avoid coming into contact with the black working poor who thronged to the Shell Island beach on weekends." This was a cultural issue that had been overlooked, undervalued, or simply ignored.

Dr. Avant's black Shell Island Development Company agreed to staff the hotels, restaurants, nightclubs, and recreation facilities, but those were never built, and the Shell Island Resort lasted less than three years. Investors who had counted on the remoteness of the island for protection found that it had instead isolated them, and, once ferry service became available, Shell Island was unable to limit the expansion of the public beach. So, who burned it down? White investors? Black investors? Members of the white Wrightsville Beach community? An angry day visitor? No one knew, but everyone had an opinion.

In 1933 the white Wrightsville Beach community passed a series of ordinances to prevent black people from walking on their beachfront, on their boardwalk, or in front of their cottages that lined the ocean. One year later a raging fire destroyed over a hundred buildings on the white north end of the beach, including the majestic Oceanic Hotel. Hurricane Hazel arrived two decades later to level two hundred homes and damage another five hundred. In an effort to prevent such damage in the future, the Army Corps of Engineers filled in Moore's Inlet in 1965—permanently (and ironically) connecting Shell Island with Wrightsville Beach. New homes were built on the site in 1968, and serious development began in 1985 when Wrightsville Beach annexed Shell Island and extended public roads and utilities.

SEA BREEZE AND BOP CITY, NEW HANOVER COUNTY
"Something for Everyone"

❖❖❖

Those who cannot dance say the music is no good.
NIGERIAN PROVERB

In 1923, as Shell Island Beach was opening to great fanfare in Wilmington, North Carolina, Rowland Freeman was constructing "Freeman's Beach" twelve miles south in the coastal village of Sea Breeze. In 1788 his great-grandfather Alexander Freeman, a fisherman and free person of color (Black and Native American), had acquired hundreds of acres along the Myrtle Grove Sound between the Cape Fear River and the Atlantic Ocean. In 1876 Alexander's son (and Rowland's grandfather) Robert Bruce Freeman purchased an additional twenty-five hundred acres in New Hanover County for one dollar per acre. Robert Freeman's sons Rowland and Nathan Freeman used it to develop Freeman's Beach.

At the beginning of the twentieth century, Ellis Freeman, their uncle, permitted Captain John Harper, of the New Hanover Transit Company, to build railroad tracks through the Freeman property to Carolina Beach in exchange for free transportation. Ellis Freeman subsequently sold William L. Smith of the Southern Realty and Development Company seventy-two acres on which Smith and Harper built Carolina Beach, a white resort with thirty-four summer bungalows, and the Oceanic Hotel and Seaside Club.[1]

The New Hanover Transit Company ran a rail line from Wilmington directly to Carolina Beach to accommodate white vacationers and day-trippers. Harper added a Carolina Beach landing to the Wilmington to Southport Steamship Line's schedule and built the "Shoo Fly" shuttle to transport hotel guests the two miles to and from the landing. This was a small steam engine capable of pulling five open passenger cars, and tourists loved it.

In 1902, when their father died, Rowland Freeman and his ten siblings inherited the twenty-five hundred acres of New Hanover County. Rowland would live to regret that his uncle had ever dealt with Harper and Smith since Carolina Beach would eventually not only bar African Americans but also deny them access to Freeman's Beach.[2]

When World War I ended, a booming economy enabled Wilmington's African

American shipyard workers to increase their earning power, and Rowland Freeman was anxious to have them spend their money at his beach. During the Jazz Age, Uncle Ellis marketed building lots to Wilmington's affluent black community and managed to attract a few former Shell Island investors. Victoria and Tom Lofton, who had earlier planned to build the Shell Island Hotel, instead built the twenty-five-room, three-story Russell Hotel and Dance Hall at Freeman Beach.

The Loftons were willing to invest in Sea Breeze because, unlike Shell Island, it was all black-owned and -operated. There were no white investors, backers, or advisers. Freeman's Beach would become one of the most popular exclusively black waterfront resorts on the East Coast. The Loftons' success encouraged another former Shell Island supporter, Peter Simpson, to build the Sea Breeze Simpson Hotel in 1925.

In 1930 *Pittsburgh Courier* columnist Geraldyne Dismond described the Sea Breeze cottages as "resembling transplanted Seventh Avenue [Harlem] tea rooms" and remarked that "the sporting crowd dressed in linen suits and driving roadsters" was "not to be missed." In 1931 the *Wilmington News* noted that the Negro Insurance Association planned to hold its annual convention at the Sea Breeze Resort. In the 1950s , after Fats Domino, James Brown, and Ike and Tina Turner played to white Wilmington audiences, they came to entertain and to spend the night at the Lofton Hotel.

When the Wilmington Bus Company added a Sea Breeze line, Rowland Freeman built a bingo hall and a music pavilion for day-trippers. Restaurants like Daley's Breezy Point, the Edgewater and Anchor Inns, Barbeque Sam's, and Mom's Kitchen quickly followed. Freeman Beach's legendary juke joints were also revived. Cottages, hotels and affordable inns, restaurants, casinos, and pool halls offered something for everyone.

In 1942, when the U.S. Marine Corps began accepting African Americans, black servicemen training at Montford Point, North Carolina, often spent their furloughs at Sea Breeze. While considered heroes in their own communities, they were denied access to white recreation facilities in Jacksonville, North Carolina, near Montford Point, and routinely ignored by the Camp Lejeune USO. The federal Works Project Administration funded, and the Civilian Conservation Corps (CCC) built, a bathhouse for them at Sea Breeze. Their trip from Jacksonville to Wilmington and on to Sea Breeze was seventy miles one way.

After World War II, Freeman's Beach added boardwalks, an entertainment pier, and a children's carnival run by a Native American known as Snake Man, who offered (in addition to his snake show) a Ferris wheel, a carousel, and a sideshow featuring "The Woman with No Body." He also had a candy store and at least one after-hours casino. Concessionaires rented space on a midway lined with refreshment stands and games of skill and chance. Although Freeman's Beach couldn't compete with Carolina Beach's state-of-the-art amusement park rides, outdoor bowling alleys, and high-end casinos, its forte was music.[3] Carolina Beach's young white summer residents, many of whom lived in Wilmington and visited for the summer, slipped into the Freeman Beach strip known as Bop City to dance to "race music." For them it was exotic, exciting. Some historians maintain that Bop City was the birthplace of the partner dance called the Carolina shag.[4] Located just north of Carolina Beach facing the Myrtle Grove Sound, Bop City's juke joints—the Ponco, the Big Apple, Daley's Breezy Pier, and Bruce's Tavern—booked swing, jazz, and rhythm and blues artists. Jump blues entertainer Joe Liggins as well as Louis Jordan, Lionel Hampton, Wy Harris, and Ike Turner regularly performed there.

Getting to Bop City required a short wade across the sound to a barrier island at Federal Point. It was detached from the mainland in 1930 when the Army Corps of Engineers created the Snow's Cut canal to provide direct access from the Cape Fear River to the Intracoastal Waterway. The crossing became increasingly difficult to negotiate, and fifteen years later the only access to Bop City was overland through Carolina Beach, a route that African Americans were denied. This threatened Lulu Hill and her husband Frank's investment in Monte Carlo by the Sea, a Bop City hotel, restaurant, and dance hall complex on Federal Point. Lulu Hill was Roland Freeman's daughter.

Monte Carlo featured Fats Domino, James Brown, and the Ike and Tina Turner Revue. As the sound continued to rise and patrons found it increasingly difficult to wade across it, Lulu Hill hired Margaret Green, a Freeman Fishing Company boat captain, to operate a passenger ferry across the narrow inlet, past Carolina Beach.[5] With improved access, the business was saved. Upwards of three thousand visitors attended annual Fourth of July and Labor Day music fests in Bop City. They swam, danced, played or listened to music, ate, drank, and soaked up the sun, and, to the everlasting frustration of Carolina Beach club owners, not all of them were black.[6]

White rhythm and blues aficionados made their way to Bop City, and, as in

Hampton Bay, Bay Shore Beach, Carr's Beach, and Wilmer's Park, none were asked to leave. They enjoyed themselves without fear of harassment. In the early 1950s Malcolm Ray "Chicken" Hicks, a white music fan from Durham brought R&B music to the beach and would later be inducted into the Beach Shaggers Hall of Fame. Chicken Hicks was also able to persuade a jukebox supplier to install some Bop City selections in the Carolina Beach jukeboxes.[7]

William Freeman, Roland Freeman's grandson, grew up in Sea Breeze and recalled, "It was fun. Black people came and danced and had a good time the whole weekend. That had to be a great thing for us psychologically. All those places—blacks owned them all. It was far more valuable than we knew it was."

When Hurricane Hazel struck the Carolina coast on October 15, 1954, many Sea Breeze and Bop City restaurants and hotels, including Monte Carlo by the Sea, were destroyed, as were most of the summer cottages. The oceanfront was also badly eroded, and the will to rebuild was dampened by the tremendous cost of replacement and the lack of insurance. Much Freeman family land had been sold off by that time. Daley's Pier, Barbecue Sam's, and Bruce's Tavern (a two-story restaurant and dance hall with a fishing pier) all closed in the 1980s, and Hurricane Fran demolished what was left of the summer bungalows in 1996.

Assata Shakur, Roland Freeman's great-granddaughter, a militant black civil rights activist who published her autobiography in the 1980s, included a 1950s memory of Freeman Beach:

> One of the moving things for me was when someone saw the ocean for the first time. It was amazing to watch. They would stand there, in awe, overpowered and overwhelmed, as if they had come face to face with God or with the vastness of the universe. I remember one time a preacher brought an old lady to the beach. She was the oldest-looking person I had ever seen. She said that she just wanted to see the ocean before she died. She stood there in one spot for so long, she looked like she was in a trance. Then, with the help of the preacher, she hobbled around, picked up the mundane shells and put them into her handkerchief as if they were the most precious things in the world.[8]

CHOWAN BEACH, WINTON
"The Fountain of Youth"
♦♦♦
The heart is the real fountain of youth.
MARK TWAIN

Untangling the history of North Carolina's Chowan (pronounced "CHOW-On") Beach requires determination. Some researchers (this one included) have assumed that it was a resort for African Americans built and run by a white man. That was not the case. Frank Stephenson's *Chowan Beach: Remembering an African American Resort*, a critical resource, does not specify founder J. Eli Reid's racial identity, and the photos accompanying the text reflect a visibly white Reid family. A history of the Chowan Beach community, posted on the town's Recreation Association website, does not include information about *any* African American contributions to the founding of Chowan Beach or the surrounding communities.[1]

Eli Reid, founder of Chowan Beach, was in fact an African American raised in Winton, North Carolina, one of three towns (the others being Cofield and Ahoskie), in Hertford County's mixed-race "Winton Triangle," a community founded by free land-owning people of color. Their descendants were of mixed African American, Native American, and white European ancestry, and most were famously nonblack in appearance.[2]

Early settlers migrated from North Carolina's Outer Banks in the 1740s and established the three settlements that produced nearly all the goods and services they required. Black freemen and white European settlers subsequently intermarried with Chowanoke Indians, other white and black women, and some immigrants from India. By the coming of the Civil War these three settlements had been prospering for over a hundred years. Later they were known as the Tri-Racial People of the Triangle. They farmed, built schools, were impressed into service during the Civil War, established businesses, founded churches, and created local government.[3] Unlike the Freeman family in Sea Breeze who lost their property, these farmers deeded land to succeeding generations and kept it within families.

Eli Reid, who looked white, served in World War I and was a trustee of Winton's First Baptist Church, an African American congregation. He and his family lived north of Main Street in Winton's majority white district. Ben Watford, a life-long member of First Baptist, believed when he was a child that "Mr. Reid," tall and light-skinned with sandy brown hair, was a white man passing for black. Eli's brother Charles Ray Reid, a successful Winton businessman, after all, was visibly black.[4]

Eli Reid owned a summer home on Chowan Beach three miles north of Winton where he managed a successful herring fishing business. He also owned a Winton gas station and worked as a regional jukebox distributer for Wurlitzer and Rockola equipment. Reid's sales calls often took him to Virginia, primarily to Norfolk. In 1926, as Shell Island was burning down, Reid purchased four hundred acres along the Chowan River, initially to expand his fishing business, but he later built a family beach that became another family business. In the mid-1930s he purchased a German carousel and swings, commissioned a "Laff Land" fun house, rented canoes, and offered boat rides. While it is impossible to determine if the incidents on Shell Island played any part in inspiring the commercialization of his family beach, it remains a possibility.

Chowan Beach became a popular resort for African American professionals— doctors, lawyers, professors, engineers, pharmacists, and bank and insurance executives and their families, many of whom lived and worked in Washington, D.C. In the 1940s Reid added rental cottages, a pavilion, and a dance hall and provided a clubhouse for the bridge players who returned every season. After World War II he built a restaurant for public and private dining and a dormitory to accommodate family reunions and church and fraternal outings, and he offered weekend fishing excursions. Reid advertised his beach in the Norfolk *Journal and Guide* as "the fountain of youth," "a gathering place," and "a vacation destination."[5] The *Journal and Guide* was the widest-circulating African American newspaper in Virginia. While he targeted the black middle class, he also invited local farmers, manual laborers, and domestic workers and their families to come and picnic for the day or buy tickets for the weekend entertainment—which was exceptional—or both. Reid wanted to make Chowan Beach a high-class stop on the Chitlin Circuit, and he succeeded. He welcomed recording artists B. B. King, Ruth Brown, James Brown, Sam Cooke, Earl Grant, and the Drifters, who performed on both indoor and outdoor stages. On Sundays he offered gospel music. Reid also established a 4-H camp in a separate beach area and welcomed school outings.

His daughter Caroline later described Chowan as being a beautiful place. "It was much more than a beach," she said. "[It was] a place of quiet dignity where people could come and enjoy themselves. . . . It was the result of my father's dream of providing a setting, and a clean and well-kept one, for not only what we called the picnic crowd, but also for the cottage guests."[6] For two generations Eli Reid offered his customers quality recreation and amusements, and when he retired in 1967 he sold the beach to Sam Pillmon, an African American entrepreneur from Ahoskie, North Carolina. Pillmon kept the beach going another twenty years—well beyond passage of the 1964 Civil Rights Act. Nevertheless, generational preferences, desegregation, and access to and competition from King's Dominion theme park in Hanover County all chipped away at the revenues. Attendance dwindled in the 1980s, and Pillmon closed the operation in 1990. Hurricane Floyd hit hard in 1999, washing out much of the riverfront. He sold the property in 2004, and today it is the site of the Chowan Beach Subdivision in Edenton, a private gated community.

SOUTH CAROLINA

MOSQUITO BEACH, JAMES ISLAND
"A Buzzing Oasis"

❖❖❖

Don't be afraid to bite on a giant, learn from the mosquito.
BANGAMBIKI HABYARIMANA

Mosquito Beach, at the south end of James Island, South Carolina, is a swampy stretch of shoreline on the Kings Flat Creek, four miles from the formerly whites-only Folly Beach, located on the ocean side. The land was owned through the late nineteenth century by Solomon Legaré, as part of his Savannah cotton plantation, and there had been two Civil War skirmishes on James Island involving the African American Fifty-Fourth and Fifty-Fifth Regiments of the Massachusetts Voluntary Infantry. Major Charles Douglass, youngest son of Frederick Douglass, had commanded the Fifty-Fourth.

In 1874 Legaré sold James Island to Charles Seele, who subdivided it and offered former slaves an opportunity to buy fifteen-acre lots. The Green, Left, Lafayette, and Wilder families bought them and raised okra, beans, onions, figs, watermelon, cantaloupe, and corn, which they sold in the Charleston markets. Residents of this low country marshland were known as the "Sol Legarians."

In an August 1880 issue of the *People's Advocate*, an African American weekly published in D.C., the editor noted, "Day labor on the Sea Islands is becoming scarce, owing to improvement in the condition of the laborers. Colored men, who ten years ago worked as field hands for fifty cents a day, now own their own lands and earn a comfortable support from them.... On James Island the colored people own 1,600 acres."

THE FACTORY

In the 1920s George Varn, a white Beaufort oyster merchant, signed a ten-year lease with Nelson Left for two acres on John's Island facing the Kings Flat Creek to establish his Unity Oyster Company of Charleston. Varn subsequently harvested and packaged oysters and crabs and hired Sol Legarian residents to work in his factory. After his death in 1934 the factory remained a gathering place for former employees and island residents. Joe Chavis opened the first convenance store nearby, and soon Machi & Nucca's Dance Hall Pavilion was raised, followed by the

Harborview Club and Jack Walker's Club. A shoreline entertainment district with the disconcerting name Mosquito Beach evolved. Swamp, sweat, and mosquito infestations made for an interesting ambiance. Chavis's son Joe Jr. later opened the Seaside Grill, which had a jukebox and a pool table. Mosquito Beach's nearest competitor was black Atlantic Beach in Horry County—two hours away.[1]

In 1953 Andrew "Apple" Wilder and his wife, Laura, built a boardwalk, and they later added a pavilion with bumper cars. Mosquito Beach soon attracted black visitors from other James Island communities and the nearby Charleston area. Word spread quickly, and by 1963 Apple Wilder owned and operated the fourteen-room Pine Tree Hotel. Managed by his wife and large family, it permitted vacationers from out of state to stay awhile and enjoy the music and seafood specialties. The beach developed a reputation as both a great "dating scene" and a mecca for local musicians. While the beach was never part of the Chitlin Circuit network and not listed in the *Green Book* travel guide (as Atlantic Beach was), Labor Day and the Fourth of July were always busy weekends.

Edward Wilder, who was Apple and Laura's son, recalled enjoying the rhythm and blues bands and dancing the shag in Machi & Nucca's. In April 2019 Richard Brown, then sixty-six years old, remembered that as a child he and his siblings would "go to bed listening to music and [wake] up to it."[2] Most clubs had jukeboxes and later live bands, some broadcast over WPAL, Charleston's black radio station hosted by deejay Big Bob Nichols, who opened and closed every session with "I see you out there . . . awww . . . you're lookin' good!"

The local black TV station (Channel 5, CBS), sponsored *Jump Time* an *American Bandstand*-like dance show hosted by Nichols. He also served as master of ceremonies for special live shows featuring Margo Mayes and her "Shake a Plenty" review—a semi-striptease act with a nine-foot boa constrictor, and the Lady Chablis, a popular drag queen from Savannah (featured in John Berendt's *Midnight in the Garden of Good and Evil*), a very popular attraction. They were strictly Saturday-night adult fare, however. Sundays were family days. Bill (Cubby) Wilder, Apple's grandson, recalls, "People enjoyed their culture and each other. The girls were always looking over the guys, and of course we were looking back at them."

White Folly Beach, on the ocean side of James Island, was culturally and economically a universe away. Many Sol Legarians worked there during the summer as housekeepers, maids, waitresses, and handymen. Russell Roper, Apple Wilder's nephew, recalled that if they missed the last bus from Folly Beach, which was at 7:00 p.m., they had to walk the four miles back, and it could be dangerous.

On July 2, 1964, the Civil Rights Act became law, and one week later Roper, who was working in Folly Beach that summer, and a few of his friends drove there intending to walk along the oceanfront now that it was legal to do so. On their way back to the parking lot they were surrounded by a group of white men, one of whom told them "you need to leave." Others, according to Roper, "spewed abusive language and became aggressive." One hit his friend and broke his nose. As he fell, the men began to kick him. Police escorted the young men to their cars where they discovered that sand had been put in their gas tanks.

Susan Chavis, a Sol Legarian, explained," [Mosquito Beach] was intended to give African Americans a place to enjoy visiting with friends, listening to music, and dancing, to enjoy seafood and to flirt. People could put aside the pressures and negativity associated with racial inequality and simply enjoy life." It was one of five small beaches built by and accessible to African Americans in the Charleston area. The others included Seaside Beach on Edisto Island, Frasier Beach on Johns Island, Peter Miller's Pavilion on Wallace Creek, and Riverside Beach in Mount Pleasant. Over time most succumbed to hurricane damage, neglect, the effects of the owners' children and grandchildren moving away, and to integration. Historian Andrew Kahrl explains that a few "fell prey to developers and skyrocketing property taxes that accompanied the rise of vacationing and tourism along the coast."[3]

In 1959 Hurricane Gracie destroyed Apple and Laura Wilder's pavilion as well as the Harborview Club and Manchi & Nucca's, leaving only Jack Walker's Club, the Pine Tree Hotel, Uncle Jimmy's Place, and Joe Chavis's original store. In September 2019 the Mosquito Beach Historic District was established, and it was listed as part of the National Park Service's African American Civil Rights Network in June 2021. That year the Park Service announced a grant of almost half a million dollars to stabilize the historic Pine Tree Hotel, which the owner planned to reopen as the Mosquito Beach Hotel.

Folly Beach was finally integrated in the 1970s.

ATLANTIC BEACH, HORRY COUNTY
"Black Pearl on the White Strand"

Telling us to stay in our place didn't mean we were going to get a place to stay in.
MAMIE GARVIN FIELDS

In 1899 Franklin Burroughs and Benjamin Collins, partners in a South Carolina real estate, mercantile, and transportation conglomerate, won the bid from the South Carolina Assembly to complete the final installment of the Conway Seashore Railroad from Conway, the county seat, to the coast. Burroughs died before the project got under way, and his three sons joined with Collins to complete the job and establish New Town on the oceanfront.

The Seaside Inn & Bath House opened in New Town in 1901, and the resort was renamed Myrtle Beach, for the myrtle trees that grew near the shore. This was at the suggestion of Frank Burroughs's widow.

A boardwalk, rental cottages, and a dance pavilion were added, and a spur from the Coast and Western Railroad, brought visitors, vacationers, and weekend guests. The Strand Hotel, a theater, several cafés, and many service businesses soon dotted the streets of Myrtle Beach.

In 1911 Collins retired, and the Burroughs brothers worked with financer Simeon Chapin to organize Myrtle Beach Farms, which sold building lots, developed land, and constructed summer cottages. Three years later the state completed a twenty-mile paved road from Conway to the coast, and oceanfront property was considered gold.[1]

ARCADY

In 1917 John T. Woodson, owner of six Greenville, South Carolina, textile mills, purchased 65,000 acres from Myrtle Beach Farms to build Arcady, a resort complex. He began with the Ocean Forest Hotel, a ten-story white tower with fifth-floor wings jutting out. Some said it looked like a wedding cake.[2] The project included engineering and constructing roads and bridges. Woodson increased his workforce using day laborers, including tobacco sharecroppers and tenant farmers he hired from the nearby Georgia Sea Islands for the backbreaking work.

When the Ocean Forest Hotel was near completion, Woodson began construction of the Pine Lakes International Country Club—a member-owned resort with four miles of beachfront.[3] While this project was completed on February 21, 1930, Woodson was subsequently ruined by the 1929 stock market crash, and Myrtle Beach Farms Company repossessed the hotel.

Designed by the architects who created New York City's Rockefeller Center, the Ocean Forest was a 202-room marvel—fireproof and storm-resistant, with European chandeliers and Italian marble floors, and including a ballroom, dining room, convention room, theater in the round, and shopping arcade. There were elevators, tennis courts, gardens, indoor and outdoor pools, stables, and a patio for dancing under the stars. It would eventually employ a huge staff of African American porters, cooks, bellhops, dishwashers, groundskeepers, maintenance men, and housekeepers, who, unlike their white counterparts, were not permitted use of the beaches.

Myrtle Beach gets brutally hot from May through September, and it was particularly oppressive for the manual laborers, most of whom were black. George and Roxie Dyson, black owners of a laundromat and a dry cleaning business in Conway, came to the rescue. George Dyson, who dabbled in real estate, had purchased forty-seven oceanfront acres on Myrtle Beach in 1934 from two of his white customers, Ernest and Robert Ward, now facing financial ruin. Dyson subsequently opened a beach and bathhouse there for the black community—including the Ocean Forest construction crews and hotel staff.[4]

Dyson later established the Black Hawk Nightclub, and he encouraged his friends and neighbors to invest in a black Atlantic Beach. He continued to buy oceanfront property and to sell it to African American developers for $300 per lot. Dr. A. J. Henderson built the first private vacation cottage there in 1934, Dr. Robert Gordon established the Hotel Gordon, and W. K. Smith built both the Smith and Marshall Hotels. All served African American tourists in addition to the black entertainers who performed at white Myrtle Beach resorts but who, as in Miami Beach and Wilmington, were denied overnight accommodations.

In 1941 Tyson purchased Pearl Beach, a forty-nine-acre tract, increasing his Atlantic Beach holdings to almost one hundred acres. Pearl Beach connected Atlantic Beach to the white "Grand Strand"—sixty unbroken miles of white beachfront hotels, nightclubs, and amusements.[5] Whites whose property bordered on Atlantic Beach built barricades to separate themselves from black bathers, just as whites in Hampton's Buckroe Beach had constructed their "boundary pier" to separate themselves from the adjoining African American Bayshore Beach.

Whites floated orange ropes, as if attempting to keep the very waves separate. Years later, Alice Graham, a frequent visitor to Atlantic Beach, recalled, "I cannot understand how they thought if we were in the water confined to one spot that they wouldn't be contaminated by our blackness just because they put up a rope. It was water and it flowed, and it made no sense."[6]

During World War II, motels grew up beside old family businesses on Atlantic Beach's Twenty-Ninth Avenue. The Bluebird Inn, the Rainbow Inn, the Cotton Club, a movie theatre, grocery and liquor stores, and beauty salons and barbershops flourished. The black residents of Carteret County, from physicians to day laborers, invested in Atlantic Beach. The Cotton Club's open-air pavilion became the place where black musicians, who performed for white audiences in Myrtle Beach, shared their music with the black community. Every Thursday was "maid's day."

In 1942 George Dyson retired and sold his last ninety-six acres to the Atlantic Beach Corporation, a consortium of black entrepreneurs led by Dr. James W. Seabrook, president of Fayette College; Robert K. Gordon, M.D., owner of the Hotel Gordon; and Peter C. Kelly, M.D., founder of the Kelly Clinic. They were determined to keep oceanfront property in black hands.[7] A year later the Atlantic Beach Corporation built an amusement park with bumper cars, a merry-go-round, and a Ferris wheel. During World War II the beach also provided housing for African American soldiers who were building an air force base near the white North Myrtle Beach community. Some of these men would later return with their families and build summer cottages. Historian P. Nicole King notes, "A thriving recreational beach for all African Americans completely controlled by wealthy black people was quite an accomplishment along the Grand Strand of 1940s South Carolina."[8]

During the fifties and early sixties, Atlantic Beach was a popular black resort town. It boasted the Black Magic Club and the Hawk's Rest, Patio, Baby Grand, and Big Apple Clubs offering rhythm and blues, beach music, and rock and roll, with artists like Count Basie, Ray Charles, James Brown, the Drifters, Chubby Checker, Martha and the Vandellas, and Bo Diddley. The Holiday Motel and Hotel Marshall were comfortable tourist accommodations. For the affluent, there was the upscale Hotel Gordon.

The "Black Pearl on the White Strand" was the only slice of oceanfront where black visitors to the South Carolina coast could book overnight accommodations.[9] It would remain a public beach, never making admission contingent on membership or property ownership.[10] Atlantic Beach hotels, motels, and guest houses held a virtual monopoly on African American entertainment and the oceanside resort trade for almost three decades.[11]

THE KLAN

The Ku Klux Klan visited Atlantic Beach in the summer of 1950. The large number of seasonal jobs in the Myrtle Beach area sometimes resulted in strong if temporary interracial friendships, attractions, and even love affairs. One club owner who could be counted on to look the other way when interracial couples danced the shag in his establishment was Charlie Fitzgerald, proprietor of Whispering Pines on Carver Street in Conway's "Nigger Hill" district. The Pines was a half-hour ride from white Myrtle Beach. A successful businessman, Fitzgerald also owned a hotel, a taxi company, and several beauty salons and barbershops, and his prosperity rankled many Conway whites. Rumors circulated for years that his light-skinned wife, Sarah, was white and that they were running a prostitution ring out of their motel.[12] The truth is that Fitzgerald had gotten rich by providing accommodations for entertainers like Dizzy Gillespie, Little Richard, Duke Ellington, Billie Holiday, and Lena Horne after they performed at nearby white hotels where they were unable to book rooms. They also entertained at his club and attracted appreciative local audiences.

On August 25, 1950, Thomas Hamilton, the newly appointed Grand Dragon of the South Carolina Realm of the KKK, brought a contingent of Knights to Conway. After parading up and down Main Street they went to Atlantic Beach to amuse themselves by terrifying black tourists. Several merchants on Twenty-Ninth Street South called the police to report that their customers were being driven away, and when the sheriff came to disperse the Knights the frustrated Grand Dragon brought them back to Conway and up Carver Street, where they called on Charlie Fitzgerald. Fitzgerald also called the police, and again the Klansmen were dispersed.

Infuriated, they left Whispering Pines without incident but returned the following night to smash Charlie's furniture and shatter his jukebox. His customers fled through every available door and window, while the Klansmen kidnapped Charlie, stuffed him into the trunk of a car, and took him into the woods, where they beat him. The only fatality that night was Conway police officer James Daniel Johnston, who was wearing a Klan robe over his uniform. Apparently a stray bullet hit him in the back, and his brother Knights left him to bleed out on Charlie's floor. He was pronounced dead on arrival at the Conway hospital.

Myrtle Beach's white resort, hotel, and restaurant owners roundly condemned the attack and were not at all interested in Sheriff C. E. Sasser's explanation that the Klansmen had been "misled into violence" by a new Grand Dragon. Neither did the sheriff's assurance that he had warned Fitzgerald about race mixing interest them. The white moguls were only interested in protecting their investments and in keeping reports of local violence quiet. Racial violence was guaranteed to turn away white customers.

Fitzgerald was subsequently taken to Columbia where he was held in custody "for his own safety."[13] Ten Klansmen, including the Grand Dragon, were charged with conspiracy to incite mob violence, but in October 1950 a Horry County grand jury refused to indict them. The Grand Dragon was removed from his position, and the mystery of who killed Officer Johnson was never solved.

About sixteen years later, in 1966, Atlantic Beach incorporated. When the white beach towns of Windy Hill, Crescent, Ocean Drive, and Cherry Grove merged to create the municipality of North Myrtle Beach two years later, Atlantic Beach chose not to join them. The decision to remain autonomous, questioned at the time, was discussed periodically, and issues about future development and direction sometimes became contentious. Atlantic Beach had flourished when it fought a common enemy, but internal dissension was more difficult to manage.

Today Atlantic Beach's eight hundred year-round residents, who are not affluent, repeatedly refuse to support construction of a hotel and convention center, a project proposed by descendants of the founders who owned land in Atlantic Beach but live elsewhere.[14] Gertha Gibson, a resident of Fayetteville, North Carolina, who held title to seven building lots, explained in 1989, "The people who own property are proud that it is a black town and want to see it developed in a way that blacks will continue to have access to it, but the year-round residents want money and jobs by whatever means they can get them."¹⁵ The stalemate has resulted in Atlantic Beach becoming the only municipality on the Atlantic Coast that has failed have a thriving tourist industry.

BIKEFEST

In 1980 the Atlantic Beach City Council approved a proposal to host an annual Bikefest on Memorial Day weekend. This was not a new idea. Twenty years earlier the white North Myrtle Beach communities of Windy Hill, Crescent, and Ocean Drive had established a Harley Davidson Festival—an annual ten-day mid-May event. Like the Harley Davidson Festival, Bikefest became a financial success. Black bikers patronized Atlantic Beach's remaining hotels, motels, restaurants, and nightclubs, and the town raised $40 million, enabling it to pay down some debt. Unfortunately, when biker participation spiked to 250,000 participants, the four-block town was overwhelmed, and North Myrtle Beach petitioned to shut the black festival down. Residents complained that black bikers were "wilder and louder" than the white bikers and that they "partied in a different way."¹⁶ During the 1998 Bikefest police presence was increased, and Ocean Boulevard, the main drag, was closed to traffic. This made access to Atlantic Beach difficult.

A complication arose in 2002 when the national NAACP called for a boycott of South Carolina businesses and services due to the state's insistence on flying the Confederate Battle Flag over the state capitol. NAACP staff and volunteers gathered at rest stops along highways to encourage tourists to drive through the state without stopping. A furious Atlantic Beach mayor Irene Armstrong attacked the NAACP brass for throwing a wrench into the efforts to save Atlantic Beach.

The following year the NAACP supported twenty-five Atlantic Beach residents in filing a discrimination suit against North Myrtle Beach for making access to Atlantic Beach difficult during Bikefest weekend. Endless rounds of mediation resulted in a court-imposed remedy compelling both Myrtle Beach communities to follow the same traffic pattern—whatever it was—on Ocean Boulevard during the festivals. Both agreed to one-way traffic on Ocean Boulevard.

Six years later, despite the annual infusion of Bikefest funds, Associated Press journalist Jeffrey Collins reported, "Atlantic Beach is dying. . . . Taxes are high and the town contracts out all its major services except the police force. Its single biggest taxpayer, the Crazy Horse Strip Club, paid its 2009 [tax bill] early to keep from laying off its handful of employees as it struggles under hundreds of thousands of dollars in unpaid court judgements. The six-seat zoning board has one member left."[17] Bikefest has not rescued the historic beach.

Historian P. Nicole King maintains, "Atlantic Beach has floundered because the vast array of stakeholders—residents, business owners, preservationists, outside developers, and surrounding communities—cannot agree on a vision for the town's future. Yet this difficulty has arisen from attempts to integrate the perspectives of all of these stakeholders—insiders and outsiders alike—into a refashioned landscape. Preserving the past and developing the future of Atlantic Beach is important for future generations, but it is not easy work."[18]

# TENNESSEE

CHURCH'S PARK, MEMPHIS
"A Resort for the Colored People"

❖❖❖

In the beginning, people all over the country came to Memphis, came down the river and docked somewhere along there and came to Beale Street.... Beale Street was the black man's haven.

RUFUS THOMAS

In 1899 Robert R. Church built Church's Park and Auditorium on Beale Avenue in Memphis, Tennessee. To Black Memphis it would always be Beale *Street*, as it is named today. In the 1920s, journalist Gilmore Millen described its character: "A street of business and love and murder and theft, an aisle where merchants and pawn brokers, country Negroes from plantations, Creole prostitutes and painted fag men, sleepy gamblers and slick young chauffeurs, crooks and bootleggers and dope peddlers and rich property owners and powdered women meet and stand on corners and slip upstairs to gambling joints and rooming hotels and barber shops and bawdy houses."[1] As in the Deep Morgan district of St. Louis, Storyville in New Orleans, and Sweet Auburn in Atlanta, music blared on Beale Street, and drunken nightlife teemed in and around Pee Wee's Saloon, the Gray Mule, the Hole in the Wall, the Daisy Theatre, and Hammitt Ashford's Place.

Church's Park, however, was a high-class operation and the only facility of its kind in the state, the South, and likely the nation. The park was built, owned, and managed by a black man, for the exclusive use of black people. In 1889 Memphis built the East End Amusement Park for whites, offering a lake, a Ferris wheel, thrill rides, a merry-go-round, a roller skating rink, beer gardens, a dance hall, and the finest popular vaudeville acts. Ten years later, in 1899, Robert Church built Church's Park with a playground, slides and swings, gazebos, and strolling paths with footbridges that crossed over lush gardens. Tame peacocks wandered the grounds. A 1933 *Memphis World* retrospective noted, "Mr. Church ... [had] built a picnic ground and auditorium for the race [that] proved to be the pleasure spot of the city. He prided himself on keeping order, and no officers [white policemen] were allowed to come in the enclosure of the Park."[2]

Church's twenty-two-hundred-seat auditorium was said to be "the finest theater of its kind in America. The best and only place for amusement in the city for Colored People."[3] Church booked African American vaudeville stars like Black Patti and Her Troubadours, an African American musical troupe featuring the classically trained coloratura Matilda Sissieretta Joyner Jones, who had performed for four U.S. presidents and sung on the stages of many of Europe's finest opera houses. She was the first black diva to perform at Carnegie Hall and subsequently dubbed the "Black Patti," a name she despised, to invite comparison with the white Italian prima donna Adelina Patti.

Church also booked the Whitman Sisters—four daughters of African Methodist Bishop Albrey Whitman, a light-skinned black man whose wife, Cassie, was believed to white. Mabel wrote their music; Alberta, a male impersonator, performed as "Bert"; Essie was the featured soloist; and Alice, the youngest, tap-danced and performed ballroom dancing routines with "Bert." Managed by Mabel, the Whitman troupe included comedians, midgets, acrobats, and a band.

Church sponsored cakewalk dances in an outdoor pavilion every evening during the summer except Sundays. W. C. Handy, "Father of the Blues," conducted the orchestra. In 1916 Handy wrote "Beale Street Blues."[4] Cakewalks, which had been a staple of minstrel shows, were traditionally performed by slaves for the entertainment of their masters, and the prize for the best dancers was a cake—memorialized in the phrase "that takes the cake." Church's Auditorium was a showcase for black musicians like Handy and entertainers like Gertrude "Ma" Rainey, "Mother of the Blues." A heavy-set woman, Rainey performed in sequined black satin gowns with long strings of pearls, waving ostrich plumes, wrapped in furs, and flashing her gold teeth. "Georgia Tom," her accompanist and the arranger for her all-male Black Bottom Band was composer Thomas A. Dorsey, who wrote "Precious Lord, Take My Hand" and "In the Sweet By and By."

Distinguished visitors to Church's Park included President Theodore Roosevelt in 1902, President Woodrow Wilson in 1907, Booker T. Washington two years later, and James Weldon Johnson, national executive secretary of the NAACP. Robert Church's gift to black Memphis was a safe and comfortable place to enjoy popular entertainment. Memphis historian Preston Lauterbach maintains, "Church's Park and Auditorium outshone any place in the city where white people prohibited Negroes from entering."[5]

SOLID CITIZEN

Robert Church, born a slave in 1829 in Holly Springs, Mississippi, learned gentlemen's manners from his father, Captain Charles Beckwith Church, who also made him promise: "never . . . let anyone call you a nigger."[6] His mother Emmeline was a seamstress who died when he was twelve years old. At fourteen he began working as a dishwasher and cook on his father's side-wheeler fleet. By twenty-three he had risen to the rank of steward, the highest position an African American crew member could aspire to. During a Civil War battle on the Mississippi River in 1862, Union troops captured Captain Church's *Victoria*, and Robert became separated from his father. The young man made his way to Memphis, which was then occupied by Union troops. There he met and married Louise Ayers, a mixed-race former slave who owned a hair salon catering to "elite white women."[7] In the early years of their marriage, she was the breadwinner. Their daughter Mary was born in 1863, and they later had a son, Thomas.

Working at a series of jobs, Church was eventually able to buy property. His first investment was an old building in Beale Street's red-light district that he converted into a saloon. He had the audacity to open several brothels in that quarter and to employ white women in the trade. That made him infamous and eventually rich. In 1870 his marriage to Louise ended, and she took the children to New York City. Robert kept the Memphis property since no woman, black or white, could own real estate. That year the Memphis City Council voted to license brothels, and Church, suddenly legitimate, opened a saloon and pool parlor on South Second Street and Gayoso Avenue outside the red-light district.

In 1885, at the age of fifty-six, he married Anna Wright, who was so fair-skinned that she was hardly recognizable as black. The following year they had a son, Robert Reed Church Jr., and three years later a daughter, Annette, was born. Church joined the Emmanuel Episcopal Church and built the city's first "colored lodging house," advertising it in the *Memphis Watchman* as "the only first-class colored hotel in the city."[8] He counted several African American politicians among his friends, including P. B. S. Pinchback, Louisiana's first black governor, and Senator Blanche Bruce of Mississippi, a friend of Frederick Douglass and the only black Reconstruction legislator to complete a full term. Like Church, Pinchback was the son of a white man and had worked as a steward on a Mississippi Riverboat where he learned the fine art of gambling. In 1882 Church made a brief foray into politics by running for a seat on the city's Board of Public Works. He campaigned to increase recreation facilities for the city's African American residents but unfortunately was defeated.

BLUFF CITY ROYALTY

By the first decade of the new century, Church was counted among the Memphis African American aristocracy. He built a family mansion on South Lauderdale Street just blocks from the home of Tennessee's white senator Kenneth McKellar, and Anna Wright Church had adapted brilliantly to her role as granddame. Church's biographer, Lauterbach, attributes his embrace of respectability in part to the influence of Ida B. Wells, then a young black journalist who would later become a national anti-lynching crusader.[9]

Like Robert Church, Wells was raised in Holly Springs, Mississippi. She moved to Memphis in 1884 at the age of twenty-two to teach school in order to support her younger orphaned siblings. Wells submitted columns to several African American newspapers and within a decade was editing the *Memphis Free Speech*. Smart, tough, and determined, she perhaps reminded Church of his first wife, Louise. Her editorials infuriated white Memphis, especially one she wrote in 1892 after her friend Thomas Moss was lynched.

Moss had owned the People's Grocery Company, a food cooperative that competed with a grocery owned by William Barrett, a white man. Both businesses were located in the "Curve," a mixed-race neighborhood outside the Memphis city limits. On the afternoon of March 2, 1892, two young boys, one black, the other white, were arguing over a game of marbles in front of the People's Grocery. The argument became a fistfight that the black youth won, causing the white youth's father to jump in. Before long several black and white men were involved. When Moss's employees Will Stewart and Calvin McDowell tried to pull them apart, all were arrested for disorderly conduct. After sundown Moss, Stewart, and McDowell were taken from their jail cells, brought to a railroad yard, and shot. A white mob that had gathered for the spectacle returned to the People's Grocery and emptied it before burning it down.[10]

African American civic leaders and clergymen subsequently counseled Memphis's black citizens to remain calm and not to consider taking revenge. Ida Wells was so infuriated by their timidity that in a blistering editorial she urged every black resident to leave Memphis and never return. In her next *Free Speech* editorial, she wrote, "Eight Negroes were lynched since the last issue. Three were charged with killing white men and five with raping white women. Nobody in this section believes the old thread-bare lie that Negro men rape white women.... If Southern men are not careful, they will overreach themselves and public sentiment will have a reaction; a conclusion will be reached which will be very damaging to the moral reputation of their women."[11] Wells was in Chicago when it was published, and the following day an angry white mob destroyed her office, seized her equipment, and threatened to lynch her if she ever returned. She never did. T. Thomas Fortune, editor of the *New York Age*, offered her a job in Chicago.

During her years in Memphis, Wells wrote editorials criticizing the Prince Hall Masons for failing to open their "swollen treasuries" for the public good and had taken issue with wealthy light-skinned blacks for ignoring the plight of their darker-skinned brothers and sisters. What likely caught Robert Church's attention was her provocative question, "What benefit is a leader if he does not devote his time, talent, and wealth to the alleviation of the poverty and misery and elevation of his people?"[12]

Church apparently took her challenge to heart when he built Church's Park and Auditorium in 1899. Seven years later, he and his friends—attorney Josiah Settle, merchant Milton Clay, and mortician Thomas Hayes—established the Solvent Savings Bank, the first African American bank to operate in Memphis after the collapse of the Freedman's Savings and Trust Company in 1874. During the financial panic of 1907 many larger and more established banks failed, but Church and his colleagues stacked bags of money in the Solvent Savings Bank's plate glass window under the sign: "THIS BANK IS PAYING OFF TO ALL DEPOSITORS."[13] Solvent Savings continued to provide home mortgages and loans for the next twenty years. When the Beale Street Baptist Church faced foreclosure in 1909, the bank paid off its creditors and offered the trustees a liberal repayment schedule. That year Ida B. Wells and Church's elder daughter Mary Church Terrell became founding members of the National Association for the Advancement of Colored People.

In 1911, twelve years after the grand opening of Church's Park, the Memphis City Council earmarked funds for an African American municipal park. By that time there were five tax-supported whites-only parks. The proposal was attacked almost immediately, however. Every location that the Parks Commission proposed was opposed by white residents. The most telling concern was that "a black park would become a haven for whites in search of sinful pleasures."[14] Memphis Judge Jacob S. Galloway actually recommended that it be constructed on a virtually inaccessible island in the Mississippi River. No sane developer would have considered it, yet the judge maintained that African Americans would "be in their glory among all that tropical growth."[15]

After a series of meetings and ongoing debate, Frederick Douglass Park opened in 1913 on Ash Street on the city's north side. That was one year after Robert Church Sr. died.

THE BOSS OF BEALE STREET

During the last year of his life Church worked closely with his very capable son, Robert Jr., to prepare him to take over the family businesses. In 1912 Bob Church inherited Church's Park, the presidency of the Solvent Savings Bank, and responsibility for managing the family's real estate holdings. Unlike his father, Bob was a political activist who believed that political struggle and a secure ballot were the keys to change.[16] A member of the Republican Party ("the Party of Lincoln"), young Church in 1916 founded the Memphis Lincoln League, which offered voter education classes and organized voter registration rallies in Church's Auditorium. Bob Church made funds available to settle overdue poll taxes that prevented African Americans from registering to vote. In 1917 he helped to organize the Memphis chapter of the NAACP and two years later became its first national board member from the South.

Church became the most prominent African American Republican in the Jim Crow South. He was black Memphis's interface with the white Boss Crump. Elected mayor in 1909, Edward H. Crump resigned eight years later to run the city's Democratic Party machine. He would hold sway over Memphis politics until 1948. Bob Church proved a match for him, and his Lincoln League became the Black Republican machine. Church was the "Boss of Beale Street." He negotiated with Crump and on occasion provided the votes that the Boss needed to ensure victory. Crump was willing to work with Church on a biracial, bipartisan basis—a mutually beneficial arrangement until the advent of the New Deal. As African Americans left the Republican Party to join the new Democrats, Church's influence waned until Crump no longer needed him. In 1938, when Church refused to support Crump's mayoral candidate, Walter "Clift" Chandler, Crump exacted swift revenge. He had exempted Church from property taxes years before, but after this act of insubordination Crump retroactively revoked the privilege, plunging Church into debt. Ten family properties were seized for back taxes, and Church fled to Washington, D.C., to escape prosecution for tax evasion. Crump subsequently told Lewis O. Swingler, editor of the black *Memphis World*, "You have a bunch of niggers [in the Lincoln League] teaching social equality and stirring up racial hatred. I am not going to stand for it. I've dealt with niggers all my life and I know how to treat them.... *This is Memphis*."[17]

In 1941 Mayor Clift Chandler removed Robert Church Sr.'s name from Church's Auditorium and rededicated it as the Beale Street Auditorium. The Church family had sold it to the City of Memphis twenty years earlier with the stipulation that the name never be changed. Anna Wright Church, Bob's mother, would never have considered selling it otherwise.[18] In 1956 a new municipal administration restored the Church name, and the editor of the white Memphis *Commercial Appeal* explained, "The Park was built before the turn of the Century and named for the late Bob Church, Sr. A falling out between Church's son, a Republican Negro leader now dead [Bob Church Jr. died in 1952], and city politicians caused the Park to be given its present name in 1941."[19]

The auditorium was demolished in the 1960s in the wake of an urban renewal frenzy. Church's Park, however, was reclaimed, rehabilitated, and placed on the National Register of Historic Places. In 1993 it became part of the Beale Street Historic District. Boss Crump's political career ended in 1948 with the election of Senator Estes Kefauver. The *Memphis Press-Scimitar* noted, "Crump received notification that he no longer holds undisputed control in Memphis." Reporter Richard Wallace explained that "the Shelby County (Memphis) Citizens Committee which had supported Kefauver's candidacy, announced that instead of disbanding after the campaign as it had originally planned, it voted to become a permanent citizens organization dedicated to good government."[20]

But the Crump machine wasn't finished with the Church family. On February 26, 1953, the Victorian mansion Robert Church Sr. built on South Lauderdale Street burned to the ground. Several disgruntled Crump supporters who still held municipal offices had granted permission to a National Firefighter Convention held in Memphis that year, to use it to demonstrate a new model fog-nozzle fire hose. The African American *Tri Star Defender* described it as "an act of infamy." Two years later the lot was paved over.

GREENWOOD PARK, NASHVILLE
"Owned by Colored People,
Operated by Colored People, for Colored People"

❖❖❖

What then is freedom? The power to live as one wishes.
CICERO

Greenwood Park in Nashville, Tennessee, was the gift in 1905 of Rev. Preston Taylor, an ordained Disciples of Christ minister and a black entrepreneur. It consisted of forty acres and included elaborate fountains, gardens, a baseball park, rides, and bandstands and hosted special attractions like the annual State Colored Fair.

Born into slavery on November 7, 1849, in Shreveport, Louisiana, Preston joined the Union's 116th Colored Infantry Regiment as a drummer boy at age fifteen during the Civil War and earned his freedom. After Appomattox he moved to Louisville, Kentucky, worked as a porter on the Louisville and Nashville Railroad, and studied for the ministry. He was assigned to a congregation at age twenty-one in Mt. Sterling, Kentucky.

During Reconstruction, Taylor became concerned about the exclusion of African Americans from the construction industry and subsequently applied for and won a labor contract with the Big Sandy Railway to lay track between Mt. Sterling and Richmond, Virginia. He was the only contractor who employed black workmen, and his crews proved so efficient that his contract was repeatedly renewed. Taylor was a good businessman, and he eventually became rich.

In 1884 Preston Taylor moved to Nashville to pastor the Gay Street Christian Church, and four years later he married Georgia Gordon, one of the original Fisk Jubilee Singers. They had a son, Preston Jr., who died in infancy, and Georgia Taylor died in 1813. After her death Preston trained as a mortician and established the Taylor Funeral Company to provide dignified burials for Nashville's black community. In 1887 he purchased thirty-seven acres of dairy farmland to create Greenwood Cemetery for black residents. Three years later he purchased the land on which he would build Greenwood Park.

In 1904 Taylor joined forces with two black Nashville entrepreneurs, Richard Henry (R. H.) Boyd, founder of the National Baptist Publication Board, and attorney J. C. Napier, a member of the Nashville City Council and president of the National Negro Business League. The three founded the One-Cent Citizens Savings and Trust Company, the first minority-owned bank in Tennessee.

On March 30, 1905, the Tennessee Legislature passed a bill to segregate public transportation effective July 5, 1905. White conductors were granted authority to remove passengers from any seat and to arrest anyone who refused to move. African Americans in Memphis, Chattanooga, and Knoxville subsequently organized boycotts of their municipal transit systems, and the editor of the black-owned *Nashville Clarion* urged his community: "Trim your corns, darn your socks, wear solid shoes and walk."[1]

Reverend Taylor and his partners Napier and Boyd, fresh from organizing the bank, subsequently created an independent transit system. On August 29, 1905, they issued shares of stock in the Nashville Union Transportation Company for ten dollars each. With the help of other black businessmen, they raised $25,000 to purchase five steam-driven motor coaches that could accommodate from ten to eighteen passengers. On October 6 these buses began operating along four routes that fanned out from the black business district. Demand was so great that the Union Transportation Company contracted for an additional fourteen buses.[2]

In September Taylor opened Greenwood Recreational Park, the first park for African Americans in the city. It offered gardens, fountains, strolling paths, children's rides, a roller coaster, a carousel, a bandstand, a swimming pool, a skating rink, baseball diamonds, and a zoo.[3] He made sure that the Nashville Union's buses on the Fairview Route terminated at the park's entrance, and it soon became the busiest line in the system. In November 1905 the city council levied a tax on the buses, and whites began to vandalize them and to attack black passengers. Union Transportation managed to hold on for eight months before it was forced to shut down in June 1906. The general boycott ended in 1907 with segregated transportation having won the day.

The following September, Greenwood Park hosted the first Tennessee Colored State Fair. While Reverend Taylor died in 1931, the park operated until 1949—thus for a period of more than forty years. As a businessman, mortician, contractor, activist minister, and philanthropist, Taylor reflected the value that he placed on dignity. He understood that recreation was a human need on par with education and right up there with transportation and employment. Preston Taylor was a renaissance man who learned to operate successfully in a backward society.

KENTUCKY

FREDERICK DOUGLASS PARK, LEXINGTON
"A Segregated Landscape"

❖❖❖

Racial segregation in the South not only separated the races, but it
separated the South from the rest of the country.

ROBERT DALLEK

On July 5, 1916, the white *Lexington Herald* reported:

> Frederick Douglass Park, the first public park for colored people ever opened in Lexington, was dedicated yesterday afternoon with elaborate exercises, preceded by a parade fully a mile in length and managed entirely by the committee of colored citizens appointed to arrange for the celebration. A crowd estimated at 5,000 filled the park and heard the program of addresses and music which had been arranged. . . . All the addresses expressed the spirit of appreciation of what the officials of Lexington are trying to do for its citizens and were expressive of the good will and public spirit felt by the colored citizens of the city.

Frederick Douglass Park's twenty-five acres had been sold to the city of Lexington by a prominent black grocer. State law required:

> All public parks established and maintained for the recreation, pleasure, and welfare of the white population . . . shall be held, managed, and controlled by a Board of Park Commissioners (white) of the city wherein the parks are located, *and* all public parks established and maintained for the recreation, pleasure and welfare of the colored population . . . shall be held managed and controlled by a Board of Park Commissioners (Colored) of the city wherein the parks are located.

Eventually the two boards merged in 1956, and all city parks were subsequently maintained by a unified and integrated board.

Douglass Park boasted a swimming pool, basketball and tennis courts, a gymnasium, playgrounds, walking trails, a community center, and a bandshell. It hosted county fairs, concerts, beauty pageants, talent shows, summer carnivals, church and family reunions, and music festivals. Its most popular development occurred in 1967, however, when it sponsored a Dirt Bowl Basketball League Tournament, so named because the courts were built on pounded dirt. In 1983 *Sports*

Illustrated covered these games since by then the league had become one of the premier summer basketball associations in the country.

Douglass Park was a community treasure for the balance of the twentieth century, but it was not spared the endemic violence of the twenty-first. On January 21, 2015, during a basketball game five people were shot, and a young man died.

Stop the Violence rallies were subsequently organized in the park and all over the city as citizens vowed to take their neighborhoods back. Unfortunately, the violence escalated. As in many major American cities, violent crime had steadily increased during the first six months of 2015. One was apparently just as likely to be murdered while pursuing an amusement or engaging in sports as by taking part in more dangerous and/or illegal activities. By December 2015 the Brennan Center for Justice in Washington projected that among twenty-five of the thirty most populous U.S. cities, the murder rate in 2016 would likely increase by an average of 14.6 percent. Anger, resentment, and the availability of guns was a deadly combination.

The park's centennial was celebrated in 2016. The Centennial Commission, whose members represented neighborhoods, schools, churches, and businesses, worked with Habitat for Humanity to clean up the park, plant one hundred new trees, and design a new playground.

Lexington's mayor, Jim Gray, noted,

> Douglass Park is a special place where tens of thousands of the city's residents have grown up running and playing and enjoying each other's company.... We know that the history of Douglass Park also includes some troubling chapters, and in those times, we work together, as a community to ... ensure that Douglass Park can continue to serve neighbors, now and in the future.

Douglass Park, one of the few public places where African Americans could go for recreation and entertainment in the city of Lexington, has survived.

GEORGIA

THE COTTON STATES AND INTERNATIONAL EXPOSITION
"A World's Fair"

❖❖❖

The Paris Exposition had its Eiffel Tower, the Chicago World's Fair had its Ferris Wheel, but Atlanta had its Negro Building.
H. R. BUTLER, *ATLANTA CONSTITUTION*

During the second half of the nineteenth century, expositions, centennials, and world's fairs became the rage on both sides of the Atlantic. The events began in London in 1851 with the Crystal Palace's tribute to the Industrial Revolution. Two years later New York City celebrated an "Exhibition of the Industries of All Nations," and in 1876 Americans flocked to Philadelphia for the nation's centennial. By far the largest, most electrifying of these events, however, was Chicago's 1893 "Grand Columbian Exposition," marking the four hundredth anniversary of Christopher Columbus's "discovery" of America. This was the first exposition to offer a midway with games, rides, and the then-new Ferris wheel ride.

Brooklyn, then an independent city, got into the act in 1895 with Black America, an outdoor extravaganza, held in Ambrose Park in South Brooklyn. Black America tried to re-create the southern plantation experience with scenes of rustic simplicity, focusing on the lovable "true southern Negro." There was no Simon Legree in this paradise, nor were there any references to slavey. The cast included five hundred black men, women, and children (no whites in blackface), all appropriately costumed. They remained in character, working, singing, and smiling for the benefit of the strolling white audience. Demonstrations of ginning, baling, and pressing cotton were continuous.

On June 11, 1895, the *Brooklyn Eagle* described Black America as "a show for intelligent people rather than for the crowds who usually frequent open air and popular seaside resorts." Researcher Dorothy Berry compared it to Buffalo Bill's Wild West Show. "*Black America* presented . . . plantations without White antagonists," she wrote, " racial uplift without a whisper of who was keeping the race down to begin with."[1]

That year white Atlanta hosted its Cotton States and International Exposition, hoping to attract northern investment for southern manufacturing. Georgia's rich natural resources required processing, and that required financial help.[2] Already a regional railroad hub, Atlanta wanted to become more cosmopolitan. If Birmingham was the "Pittsburgh of the South," Atlanta could be its New York City. Movers and shakers understood, however, that this meant facing up to the "race issue." Solving the "Negro problem" required defining the social status of African Americans in a society committed to white supremacy.[3]

An African American delegation attended the expo's first planning session in March 1894, and a "Negro Building" was proposed in addition to the Fine Arts, Transportation, Government, and Women's Buildings. Designed by black architects J. T. King and J. W. Smith, and built exclusively with black labor, Atlanta's Negro Building would be a showcase for African American achievement and a center for conferences, lectures, and demonstrations during the expo's hundred-day run.[4] Exhibits focused on African American agricultural and industrial achievements as well as artistic and scholarly accomplishments. Students and faculty from Spellman College, Morehouse, Tuskegee Institute, and Howard University assisted with the planning. Atlanta bishop Henry McNeal Turner's collection of Liberian swords, spears, wood carvings, and leather work (ironically titled "Uncivilized Africa") became a popular attraction. African Americans, the bishop maintained, had always been "a skilled and industrious people."[5]

On opening day, September 18, 1895, President Grover Cleveland threw an electric light switch from his home in Massachusetts to symbolically open the exposition. He would visit Atlanta before the end of the year. Black and white veterans marched with their regiments in a grand inaugural parade, and in October the Liberty Bell arrived on loan from Philadelphia. As in Chicago and Philadelphia, Atlanta offered a carnival midway with games, live circus acts, and displays of exotic foods and native peoples. A replica Dahomey village displaying "forty cannibals and fifteen Amazon warriors" was very popular, and easy access was provided to Buffalo Bill's Wild West Show performing on an adjacent site.

Booker T. Washington delivered one of the many opening day speeches at the expo. Addressing a racially mixed audience, he endorsed segregation as the most pragmatic solution to the New South's "race problem," and he assured potential investors that they would find a loyal, committed black workforce in Georgia—men and women who would not organize unions.

"In all things social," Washington explained, "we can be as separate as the fingers, yet one as the hand in all things essential to mutual progress." He counseled

African Americans to accommodate to white supremacy, at least for the present, and to accept "industrial progress in lieu of political rights and industrial training instead of classical education."[6] Whites were ecstatic over what would be remembered as his "Atlanta Compromise" speech. Even his nemesis, W. E. B. DuBois, congratulated him that day on "a fine job." Washington encouraged African Americans to work within the system, to focus on acquiring land and investing in businesses of their own to demonstrate their competence.

This infuriated Bishop Turner, however, who had represented Georgia in the 1868 Reconstruction legislature. He raged, "The colored man who will stand up and in one breath say that the Negroid race does not want social equality and in the next predict a great future in the face of all the proscriptions of which the colored man is the victim, is either an ignoramus or an advocate of the perpetual servility and degradation of his race." He assured his colleagues, "Booker will have to live a long time to undo the harm he has done to our race."[7]

On Negro Day, December 26, 1895, five thousand African Americans and five hundred whites visited the Negro Building, but while the Atlanta Expo included African Americans, it hardly welcomed them. Black people were required to use a separate entrance and were not permitted to eat anywhere outside the Negro Building. The black *Atlanta Daily World* railed: "The Fair is a big fake . . . for Negroes have not even a dog's show inside the Exposition gate unless it is in the Negro Building. Many people have written asking whether the Exposition is worth coming to see. . . . If they wish to feel that they are inferior to other American citizens, if they want to pay double fare on the surface cars and be insulted, if they want to see on all sides 'For Whites Only' signs . . . then come."[8] In the end, the Negro Building attracted the second-highest number of Expo visitors, bested only by the number of people who visited the other curiosity: the Women's Building.[9]

KING'S WIGWAM COUNTRY CLUB, KENNESAW
"An African American Country Club"

❖❖❖

No one can say, who has any respect for the truth, that
the United States is a civilized nation.
HENRY MCNEAL TURNER

In addition to African American amusement parks, bathing beaches, theaters, and dance halls there was at least one black country club operating in rural Georgia in 1916. This was King's Wigwam, located in Cobb County, fifteen miles northwest of Atlanta. A few years earlier Cornelius King, a successful African American realtor and contractor (and son-in-law of Henry McNeal Turner), built a family summer residence on several of the forty-seven acres owned by his wife. There they entertained friends and colleagues, most of whom belonged to the city's black elite.

King considered several commercial uses for the balance of the property and discussed them with his friend David Howard, who owned an Atlanta mortuary. In 1923 he would donate land for the David T. Howard Junior High School, whose prominent alums would eventually include Martin Luther King Jr., Atlanta mayor Maynard Jackson, basketball legend Walt Frazier, and civil rights activist Vernon Jordan.

David Howard and Cornelius King decided to partner in a country club venture. They chose a site, created an artificial lake, and built rental cabins, a central dining room and lounge, tennis courts, and an outdoor dance pavilion. King's Wigwam opened in September 1916 for weekend guests, vacationers, wedding parties, and family reunions. It was a spacious, safe, and comfortable retreat that businessmen, politicians, and members of the clergy regularly booked for conferences.

King hired his staff from nearby Kennesaw, a white community with a large Native American Cherokee population. His wife and children remained in Cobb County all summer, shopped in Kennesaw's stores, and were well known in the area. A manager ran the resort during the week, while King and Howard worked in Atlanta. They were members of the black professional circle that included Benjamin Davis, editor of the *Independent*; Alonzo Herndon, founder of the Citizens

Trust Bank; Alex Hamilton, a building contractor; Dr. John Hope of the Atlanta Baptist College; and Bishop Turner. The Wigwam enjoyed success from the spring of 1916 through September 1920.

❖❖❖

Born in Tennessee in 1861, Cornelius King was the son of George King, a free black carpenter, and Phyllis King, of Cherokee descent, who had been kidnapped and sold into slavery as a child. George King purchased her freedom, and so their children were considered freeborn.[1] When she died in 1876, he took them to McKee in the Indian Territory (later Oklahoma), where Cornelius completed his education and was apprenticed to a machine shop.

Ten years later twenty-five-year-old Cornelius met Bishop Turner and his daughter Lincolnia while they were touring the Indian Territory. The bishop had many questions about the complicated history of the Cherokee Nation, and he enlisted King as a guide.

In 1830 Congress passed the Indian Removal Act to uproot fifteen thousand members of the Cherokee, Chickasaw, Choctaw, Creek, and Seminole Nations, the "Five Civilized Tribes" living east of the Mississippi River. All would be relocated to the Oklahoma Territory, and their land would be reclaimed for white settlers. By that time, however, many Cherokees had adopted European customs and were economically integrated into white society. Many wore western dress, were literate, attended school, and worked at trades and businesses. Some farmed, while others owned plantations and even black slaves—the ultimate status symbol. Cherokee chief John Ross was a slaveholder, as was James Vann, the wealthiest Cherokee in Northeast Georgia.

By 1809 the Cherokee Nation included six hundred African American slaves. By 1835 that number had grown to sixteen hundred.[2] Despite high levels of education, wealth, and social status, all Cherokees along with their slaves were evicted and forced to travel west. From 1832 to 1837 forty-six thousand people were forcibly exiled to the Indian Territory, which eventually became Oklahoma. The poor walked along what would be recalled as the Trail of Tears.

During the Civil War the Oklahoma Cherokees supported the Confederacy in order to protect the institution of slavery since by 1860 the Indian Territory included 2,349 African American bondsmen.[3] Chief Stand Watie served as a brigadier general in the Confederate Army. After the war the federal government insisted that the Cherokees recognize their former slaves as members of their nation, an issue that was still being litigated in federal court in 2017.

Bishop Turner spent hours discussing this history with young King. Their conversations tended to reinforce the clergyman's low regard for the white race. King for his part, was delighted to make the acquaintance of Lincolnia Turner—and he followed the Turners back to Atlanta, where he found work first with the Western & Atlantic Railroad Company and later as a messenger with the white law firm of Hoke & Burton Smith. The firm defended railroads against claims brought by workers and their families for personal injury and death. King's family described his position as a "detective," and he may have worked undercover as a claims investigator for the Smith firm. At any rate, Hoke Smith, a future Georgia governor and U.S. senator, seems to have taken a special interest in him.[4]

Cornelius King married Lincolnia Turner on December 14, 1887, and they had two sons, George and Henry McNeal King, who died within weeks of their births. Lincolnia and their last son, Cornelius Victor King, died in May 1892, when she was twenty-eight years old. The following year, when President Grover Cleveland appointed Hoke Smith secretary of the interior, King went to Washington and Smith arranged a job for him.

In 1893 King was appointed a "Special Indian Agent," and the following year he married Nina Culver, a light-skinned mulatto woman who had grown up in an affluent Georgia family. King was subsequently assigned to the Dawes Commission, chaired by Republican senator Henry L. Dawes, who had sponsored the 1887 General Allotment Act (known also as the Dawes Act). His commission was charged with disbanding western tribal governments to prepare the Indian Territory for statehood.[5]

In 1894 Dawes arranged for a general assembly of tribal chiefs in Muscogee, and since King knew both the territory and the language he was assigned as an aide to the commissioners.

The subsequent move required Mr. and Mrs. King to travel in the "colored car" of the Missouri, Kansas, & Texas Railroad, where, King maintained, chief porter Dave McCurtain, an African American, treated them disrespectfully. When they arrived in Muscogee, King saw McCurtain in the colored dining room of the Hotel Adams, and according to the *Muscogee Phoenix* of April 5, 1894, he "threw pulverized Cayenne pepper in [McCurtain's] face and while the man was rubbing his eyes, . . . lashed him with a cowhide." King was arrested and charged with assault and battery but released on $150 bond provided by his employer. His fury spent, King settled down to support the commissioners in their deliberations with the representatives of the Cherokee Nation. Twelve years later Oklahoma became the forty-sixth state. By then Hoke Smith was governor of Georgia, and the Dawes Commission had enabled the sale of more than ninety million acres of formerly Native American land to white Americans.

In 1898 Bishop Turner convinced his former son-in-law to return to Atlanta with his new family to take advantage of the many opportunities the city offered to smart and ambitious black men. That year King, Nina, and their two-year-old daughter Bertha moved from Muscogee to Atlanta. In 1899 they welcomed a son, Turner; in 1902 another daughter, Nina, was born; and in 1911 Cornelius Jr. arrived.

Within a year of his return King had established Atlanta's first black real estate and construction firm. Three years after that Hoke Smith, then editor of the *Atlanta Evening Journal*, made a run for governor. During his 1906 campaign Smith won the support of populist leader Tom Watson by promising to remove black candidates from the Democrat/Populist fusion ticket. Not to be outdone, Clark Howell, editor of the *Atlanta Constitution* and Smith's competitor for the nomination, campaigned on a promise to "end the epidemic of Negro crime." They wore themselves out in a race-baiting contest.

On September 22, 1906, when both newspapers published unconfirmed reports of four white women being attacked by black men in a single day, a mob of armed and angry whites gathered in Atlanta's Five Points downtown district and vowed "to do something about it."[6] For the next two days white mobs randomly attacked, beat, stabbed, and shot African Americans. Black homes, churches, schools, and businesses were destroyed. When the smoke cleared, twenty-five black and two white men were dead. Five thousand African Americans left Atlanta that year, but King and his family remained. The Atlanta City Council subsequently passed Jim Crow ordinances, and whites abandoned formerly mixed-race neighborhoods. Some black families remained, while others relocated to undeveloped areas. Cornelius King stayed where he was, just east of downtown. His construction business was perfectly poised in a city badly in need of rebuilding.

As time passed, King sensed that many of the dark forces that fueled the riot remained. Their influence was unmistakable in both the 1913 lynching of Leo Frank and the Atlanta premiere of the silent film *Birth of a Nation* two years later. On April 26, 1913, Mary Phagan, a white thirteen-year-old employee of the Atlanta National Pencil Company, was raped and murdered, and her body was found in the factory basement. The company was owned by the Frank family, who were Jewish, and the girl's supervisor, Leo Frank, was charged with the crime on May 24. Tried and found guilty, Frank appealed all the way to the Supreme Court without success. After the governor commuted his sentence to life in prison, a mob kidnapped him from his cell and took him to Marietta, Mary Phagan's hometown, where they lynched him on August 17, 1915.

A few months later, on December 6, 1915, the epic D. W. Griffiths film *Birth of a Nation*, premiered in Atlanta. Griffiths had rewritten Reconstruction history, making lynching heroic, and casting every African American character (white actors in blackface) as a villain, an idiot, or a degenerate. Within a week of the Atlanta opening, William Joseph Simmons, a former minister, organized the Mary Phagan Klavern of the Georgia Ku Klux Klan. The wildly popular movie reinforced white perceptions (both locally and nationwide), that black men were sexual predators. Historian Wyn Craig Wade notes, "In an astonishing few months Griffiths had united white Americans in a vast national drama, convincing them of a past that had never been."[7]

THE WIGWAM

Less than six months after the riot, in the spring of 1916, King and Howard celebrated the opening of the Wigwam Country Club. The following year fire destroyed more than fifty blocks of Atlanta's black Fourth Ward. Two years after that, African American soldiers who had fought in France were returning home to find few jobs, virtually no affordable housing, and pervasive racial tension. "After fighting to make the world safe for democracy," historian Pete Daniels notes, "blacks returned to find it unsafe for themselves."[8] Unwilling to resume their place at the bottom of society, their resistance coupled with white pushback resulted in more than three dozen riots in major American cities, including Chicago, Tulsa, Omaha, Knoxville, and Washington, D.C. The summer of 1919 is remembered as Red Summer due to the blood that flowed in the streets.

Educator Ursula Wolfe-Rocca explains, "Throughout 1919 the exercise of black agency—black veterans wearing their military uniforms in public, black children swimming in the white section of Lake Michigan, black sharecroppers in Arkansas organizing for better wages and working conditions—was met with mob terror."[9]

Despite this, Atlanta's black middle class pushed back to establish a claim to the businesses and institutions they had built on Auburn Avenue. Many were able to escape on weekends to King's Wigwam for a respite, and so the black country club flourished.

❖❖❖

In September 1920 Bertram Hamilton, a student at Atlanta University and a friend of the King family, enjoyed a tennis weekend at the Wigwam. On Sunday evening he was arrested at the Kennesaw railroad station as he waited for a train back to Atlanta. Charged with raping a Cobb County white woman, Hamilton was taken to the Marietta jail. The white sheriff, accompanied by several Klansmen, interrogated all King's guests that evening. Edgar Webster, a white Atlanta University physics professor who was also a guest that weekend, recalled that the sheriff had warned King Sr. that there were "more angry people in Marietta that night than there had been at the lynching of Leo Frank."[10]

Bertram Hamilton was abruptly released, however, when the woman who had made the accusation against him said she'd been mistaken—he was *not* the young man who'd attacked her. But the Klan's visit to the Wigwam achieved its purpose. Cornelius King Sr., his family, and his guests would never feel safe there again. He and Howard sold the club and all its furnishings, and King disposed of the family compound at a substantial financial loss. Friends and family members were convinced that the rape allegation had been a plan to acquire his land cheaply. King's daughter Nina later explained, "I know that it's hard for people who have led hard lives to see another person, particularly a colored person, have a little success. Perhaps that was it. [Kennesaw] was a poor sharecropping town. It may have been difficult for them to see us there having such a good time."[11] Still, the Kings remained in Atlanta.

In 1941 the firm of Cornelius King & Son constructed an eight-unit cooperative apartment complex at 589 Auburn Avenue, one block east of the birthplace of

Martin Luther King Jr. (no relation). On opening day Cornelius King's grown children attached a steel cutout of an Indian warrior drawing his bow in the building's entranceway. The silhouette had once welcomed guests to King's Wigwam.

The "Wigwam Building," restored in 2004, is part of Atlanta's Old Fourth Ward historic district, rescued from a likely fate as a crack house. Most people pass by unaware that the African American man who built it once owned a country club in Cobb County that offered people who looked like him quality recreation and relaxation during very difficult times. Some whites, however, maintaining that black people didn't deserve a place like that, ran them out—just because they could.

SWEET AUBURN / "ATLANTA'S STROLL"

❖❖❖

You could get anything you wanted on Auburn Avenue.
C. C. HART

On May 21, 1917, a fire engulfed Atlanta's Fourth Ward, leveling most of the city's northeast quadrant. Nineteen hundred structures were destroyed, and ten thousand people were left homeless.[1] The Darktown and Buttermilk Bottom districts, overcrowded neighborhoods consisting of wooden boardinghouses, shacks, shanties, warehouses, and factories, burned quickly. Urban historian Kit Southerland maintains that the fire moved as fast as a person could walk.

John Bowen, editor of *Voice of the Negro*, a monthly magazine with a national circulation, described Decatur Street, the Fourth Ward's main drag, as "a hotbed of staggering men and swaggering, brazen women . . . people divested of all shame and remorse." It teemed with dance halls, nickelodeons, saloons, brothels, and dives all pulsating with ragtime music, and it featured the Crystal and the 81, two vaudeville theaters where Bessie Smith, Ma Rainey, Ethel Waters, and the Whitman Sisters performed.

Sweet Auburn, the city's black business and entertainment district, located south and east of downtown, was spared. Alonzo Herndon's Atlanta Mutual Life Insurance headquarters was located there, as was Heman Perry's Citizens Trust Bank and Henry Rucker's Georgia Real Estate and Trust Company. By 1917 Sweet Auburn counted seventy-two African American–owned and –operated businesses and twenty professional offices.[2] In 1928 the *Atlanta Daily World*, the nation's first black-owned daily newspaper, established its offices on Auburn.

Entertainment in Sweet Auburn was held to a higher standard than anything produced on Decatur Street. Author Herman Mason Jr. writes that "what Decatur offered in crass, Auburn provided in class."[3] While the loss of Decatur Street left a vacuum, it also created opportunity. The Sweet Auburn entertainment district would expand to accommodate the victims of the fire as well as promote new Jazz Age entertainment. After the armistice in 1919, Sweet Auburn's James and McKay Hotels added lounges and grills. In 1924 Benjamin Beamon and his partner Herman Nash established the Savoy Hotel on the top two floors of the Herndon Building and brought in new musicians, performers, and vaudeville stars.

A decade later, in 1933, the owners of the Royal Theater, who had initially rented space in the Oddfellows Building, constructed a five-hundred-seat auditorium for vaudeville performances and later for silent films. In 1937 the Top Hat Club, Atlanta's first nightclub, opened. Advertised as "The South's Smartest Ballroom," it boasted crystal chandeliers and entertainment by Cab Calloway, Louis Armstrong, Muddy Waters, Etta James, and Sam Cooke. One night a week the Top Hat Club opened exclusively for white clientele who paid a cover charge two and a half times the standard fee. Atlanta historian Cliff Kuhn explained that segregation prevailed in the city's clubs and dance halls because dancing suggested social equality and physical intimacy, and, while nobody wanted trouble, everybody wanted to make some money.

In 1947 Atlanta entrepreneur Benjamin Burdell (B.B.) Beamon bought the Sunset Casino & Amusement Park from music teacher J. Neal Montgomery and reopened as the Magnolia Ballroom. This large pavilion, once a boxing arena, sponsored up-and-coming jazz musicians as well as jitterbug and Lindy Hop contests for a twenty-five-cent admission fee. The Lindy Hop got its name at Harlem's Savoy Ballroom in 1927 in honor of aviator Charles Lindbergh.

In 1949 Jesse B. Blayton Sr., former chief auditor for Standard Life, purchased WERD-AM, an Atlanta radio station, and reprogrammed it for an African American audience. "Jockey Jack" Gibson became one of Atlanta's most popular radio personalities. WERD broadcast from the Prince Hall Masonic Lodge, which also served as the headquarters of Martin Luther King Jr.'s Southern Christian Leadership Conference.

In 1961 Benjamin Beamon opened the B. B. Beamon Café, a twenty-four-hour restaurant on the corner of Butler Street and Auburn Avenue, advertising it as "the place where Black Atlanta meets and eats." It became a popular postshow stop for many entertainers. Beamon provided a private dining room where Martin Luther King and Andrew Young met with other activists. By that time *Jet* magazine had celebrated Beamon as the South's number one music producer. He used his wealth and talent to make life easier for black entertainers and to make entertainment more accessible to working-class blacks. During a 1979 interview for *Living Atlanta*, Beamon was asked why he worked so hard. He replied that his restaurant and his shows were an opportunity to give back to segregated Black Atlanta. "The black community was fenced in and needed busting out," he replied. "I took pride in it because [I was] making people happy, they didn't have anywhere else to go. ... You felt like you were doing a service for people."

Civil rights leaders often held breakfast meetings at Beamon's. Andrew Young recalls, "Those breakfasts were part strategy sessions, and part church without the congregation. It was where the ministers gathered to plan the full employment drives and the economic activism that led to Atlanta's becoming a completely desegregated city."

THE ROYAL PEACOCK

In 1949 Carrie Cunningham, owner of the Royal Hotel in the Citizen's Trust Company Building, bought Atlanta's old Top Hat Club, renovated it, and reopened it as the Royal Peacock, "Atlanta's Club Beautiful." Here was a woman who understood show business. As a teenager she had run away with a tent show—Silas Green from New Orleans—that included a sixteen-piece band. She performed with them as a bareback rider appearing with legendary comic duo Butterbeans and Susie. Other Silas Green stars who went on to achieve wider fame were Bessie Smith and Muddy Waters.

In 1950, an older and wiser Cunningham became determined to rescue her son Big Red McAllister, a touring saxophone player and bandleader, from a life of illicit activity. Tired of bailing him and his friends out of jail, she offered Red the manager's job at the Peacock. Big Red accepted and not only reformed but also made the club one of Atlanta's most successful nightspots. He booked Ray Charles, Little Richard, Marvin Gaye, Nina Simone, Sam Cooke, and Nat King Cole and advertised the Peacock as "swanky" and "the South's version of Harlem's Apollo." It was a *very* popular stop on the Chitlin Circuit. Aretha Franklin recalled it as "hot as it could get."[4]

Steve Daugherty, popular author of *Experiments in Honesty*, described the Peacock as "an incubator for black music, keeping it hot and alive until it was allowed to be born, full-grown and screaming, into the midst of mainstream American pop. It's taken over now. American music is black music."[5]

FLORIDA

OVERTOWN, MIAMI-DADE COUNTY
"The Harlem of the South"

❖❖❖

Hark to the song of the smiling troubadours / Hark to the
throbbing guitars / Hear how the waves offer thunderous applause /
After each song to the stars.

RAY CHARLES

In 1878 Henry Flagler, a partner of John D. Rockefeller in the Standard Oil Company of Ohio, brought his wife Mary to Jacksonville, Florida, to spend the winter. They hoped that the mild climate would restore her declining health, but she died in the spring of 1881. Flagler remarried and two years later traveled to St. Augustine with his second wife, Ida Alice. St. Augustine was little more than a village at that time, and Flagler had nothing good to say about his accommodations. He described the landscape, however, as "a lush paradise" and considered building his own resort—perhaps the beginning of an American Riviera. He was serious enough to arrange a leave from Standard Oil and subsequently purchased the narrow-gauge Jacksonville, St. Augustine, and Halifax River Railway in 1893. Ultimately Flagler owned nearly every railroad in the state. He standardized a track size, extended routes, and provided through-service from Jacksonville to Daytona.[1]

In 1894 he reached what would become West Palm Beach, where he built the Royal Poinciana Hotel. It was the largest wooden structure (hotel or otherwise) in the world. The Palm Beach Inn (later renamed The Breakers) followed in 1901. By 1912 Flagler's Florida Coast Railway Company owned millions of acres. The state had awarded him land grants in exchange for building and extending the railroads. With easy access to property and capital, all he required was a dependable labor force, and he recruited African Americans as well as German and Italian immigrants. The black men were routinely assigned to the hardest, dirtiest, and most-dangerous details. Neither he nor his foremen believed that they were competent to handle the same tasks as white workers.

In 1896 Miami incorporated as a segregated city, and since African Americans were not permitted to live within the city limits, Flagler built worker housing in "Colored Town," a new area of the city that became the "Central Negro District."

Residents of Colored Town lacked basic municipal services like electricity, running water, and sanitation, and, because they lived in cramped quarters, they were subject to yellow fever, influenza, smallpox, and tuberculosis. Despite this, the district developed a strong economy since the majority of its residents were employed by the railroad, the construction industry, or as hotel and restaurant workers. Colored Town's economy was stable.

On Northwest Second Avenue, black-owned grocery stores, a barbershop and beauty salon, a pharmacy, an ice cream parlor, a furniture store, insurance agencies, medical and legal offices, and the Colored Town Bargain Store were conducting business. Eventually small manufacturing operations were established, including Osbourne Jenkins and William Sampson's Cola Nip Bottling Company, to provide additional jobs. The black residents of Coconut Grove, seven miles away, patronized Colored Town's shops and sought its services.

Like a lot of the residents of Colored Town, blacks who settled in West Coconut Grove were mostly Bahamians who had come to Florida to work on the railroad, pick and pack fruit, or staff the Bay View House, built in 1882 and later known as the Peacock Inn, a haven for artists, writers, and creative types from the North. The 1940 edition of the *Green Book* recommended that black vacationers make a stop in Coconut Grove. "Here we find a modern tourist camp, amusement pavilion and the beautiful home of Mrs. Mamie Cox, maid of the late Miss Marie Dressler, famous in the movies. All of this was provided through funds left to Mrs. Cox by Miss Dressler, with the stipulation that she would build a suitable place for the comfort of Negro travelers."

By 1905 Colored Town had a Colored Board of Trade and could boast Miami's first black millionaire, Dana Albert Dorsey. He had established the Miami Industrial Mutual Benefit and Savings Association and built the Dorsey Hotel just a decade after working as a carpenter on the railroad. Dorsey had saved his money, invested in real estate, and eventually built affordable housing.

In 1913 Geder Walker celebrated the grand opening of his four-hundred-seat Lyric Theater. A Georgia native, Walker offered vaudeville shows and later silent films. The Northwest Second Avenue corridor was eventually known as Little Broadway and was home to the Rockland Palace, the Ritz Theatre, The Harlem Square Club, and the Mary Elizabeth Hotel.

In 1915 Colored Town changed its name to Overtown, derived from "going over town," which was the expression of an intent to spend time on Little Broadway. Three years later, black physician William B. Sawyer founded the Christian Hospital to address the community's health needs and to treat victims of industrial accidents. Black mortician Kelsey LeRoy Pharr subsequently established the Lincoln Memorial Burial Park.

In 1918 D. A. Dorsey, by then called "the Black Flagler," purchased eighteen acres of an uninhabited island off the Florida coast to establish a black beach. He encountered three stumbling blocks, however: an exorbitant tax rate, no easy access to the island, and an inability to convince any black businessman to enter the ferry business. Discouraged, he sold the island to the Alton Beach Realty Company owned by Carl Fisher, a white real estate developer and chief promoter of Miami Beach. Sixty years later Fisher's Island was a private residential community with one of the wealthiest zip codes in the nation.

In 1922 several Overtown community leaders leased eighty-two acres on Virginia Key, a barrier island near Key Biscayne. They negotiated with Dade County, cleared the land, built cabanas, added picnic tables, a snack bar, and barbeque pits, and established Bear's Cut Beach. Dorsey's access problem had been solved when a young entrepreneur leased a steamer to offer scheduled runs from Overtown to Bear's Cut. Visitors often spent the night in Overtown and enjoyed Little Broadway before or after visiting the beach. The arrangement worked well for nearly a decade—until the stock market crashed in 1929 and Bear's Cut Beach closed.

During World War II the U.S. Navy leased a hundred acres on Virginia Key to train African American amphibious troops. This was necessary because the Dade County Code did not permit blacks to swim in whites-only areas. After the war Judge Lawson E. Thomas, who was black, petitioned Dade County to reopen and maintain Bear's Cut Beach as a county park. After the petition was denied, the judge and seven activists—five veterans and two women—staged a wade-in at North Miami's whites-only Haulover Beach to protest the dearth of black beaches. Two decades later, civil rights activists would employ the wade-in strategy in St. Augustine and famously in 1960 at Biloxi Beach on Mississippi's Gulf Coast.

VIRGINIA KEY BEACH

In 1946 Judge Thomas and his cohorts prepared to get arrested. Overtown's NAACP chapter alerted the press, and the judge arrived holding bail money. The police, however, were instructed not to make any arrests. White owners of nearby resorts were averse to any publicity that might put tourist dollars at risk, and Dade County was not anxious to broadcast its failure to provide even a "separate but equal" public beach. When it was clear that Judge Thomas, the NAACP, and the demonstrators were not going to go quietly, the Miami City Council took Carl Fisher's advice: "The best way to keep them off our beach is to give them a place of their own."[2] The council subsequently worked with state officials to make Bear's Cut Beach "a colored county park," entitled to the same amenities—a carousel and miniature train ride—offered by other state parks. This victory, though significant, was bittersweet. A peaceful accommodation had been reached, but Fisher's words stung.

On August 1, 1945, Virginia Key Beach opened with a "For Colored Only" sign at to the entrance. Florida historian Gregory Bush notes that while most older black Miami residents express nostalgia for this black-only beach, others harbor "mixed feelings and lingering resentment."[3]

NIGHTLIFE

Overtown was the only black district in Florida with its own police precinct and courthouse. As the Harlem Renaissance had taken off up north, so Overtown's reputation was enhanced by the African American entertainers who performed in Miami's nightclubs, hotels, and theaters and spent their nights in Overtown because they were not permitted to drink in the white bars or sleep in the white hotels. They were more than welcome at Overtown's Carver Hotel, the Josephine, the Dorsey, the Mary Elizabeth, the Sir John, the Dunn, and Ward Rooming House, built in 1925 by Victoria and Shaddrack Ward.

The biggest African American stars from the Roaring Twenties to the late 1950s performed in Overtown's Flamingo Room, the Zebra Lounge at the Mary Elizabeth Hotel, the Sir John Hotel's Knight Beat Club, and the Harlem Square Club. As the nightlife flourished, whites increasingly crossed the district border to enjoy the restaurants, cabarets, and late-night lounges that pulsated with music. Performers in Overtown, the epicenter of Miami's black wealth, included Bessie Smith, Cab Calloway, Lena Horne, Duke Ellington, Louis Armstrong, Billie Holiday, Count Basie, Nat King Cole, Aretha Franklin and Ella Fitzgerald.[4]

When distinguished black visitors like W. E. B. Du Bois, Mary McLeod Bethune,

A. Philip Randolph, Walter White, Langston Hughes, and Thurgood Marshall visited Miami they stayed at the Dorsey or the Mary Elizabeth, which were recommended by *The Negro Motorist Green-Book*.

Overtown's residential areas, however, were crowded and unhealthy. New arrivals grabbed any available living space they could find, including wooden shotgun shacks outside the district, cheaply built by white landlords. The front doors of these hovels faced each other along narrow rows of muddy unpaved streets. Most did not have electricity or indoor plumbing. Rents were high, and after-dark curfews were strictly enforced.[5] During the 1920s Rev. J. R. Evans, pastor of the Mt. Zion Baptist Church, reported that one hundred families lived on a single block with four or five individuals to a room. Children were often locked inside small quarters while their fathers were building the hotels where their mothers worked as maids and cleaning ladies. As living conditions in the urban ghettos of the North fueled resentment, Overtown's ghetto did likewise. None of this, however, deterred a steady stream of white men from coming, not for the music but rather to Railroad Front, the red-light district. Professor Ira Reid, a black sociologist who interviewed Overtown residents for his 1938 study *The Negro Immigrant*, referred to this crowded district as "a filthy backyard to the Magic City."[6]

❖❖❖

After the First World War, Miami Beach property that had once sold for $50 a lot suddenly shot up to an incredible $10,000, as rich Jazz Age speculators like Carl Fisher commercialized the promise of paradise. Thousands of affluent whites took the Dixie Highway to South Florida to buy and sell real estate. The idea was to turn a tract of land over several times in a single day and make a fortune. What many didn't realize was that most of these fortunes were made and lost on paper.

On September 17, 1926, a violent hurricane barreled across South Florida and struck Miami. Seventeen thousand homes were destroyed, and nearly four hundred people lost their lives. The town of Moore Haven on Lake Okeechobee was completely flattened, and both the tourist and construction industries tanked. Earlier, when construction was unable to keep up with demand, prices had risen, but storm damage, coupled with a saturated real estate market, brought panic selling, massive unemployment, and increased poverty—culminating there and elsewhere in the Great Depression.

Throughout the 1950s and into the new decade, Overtown was a Miami nightlife hot spot. On January 12, 1963, rhythm and blues artist Sam Cooke recorded his performance at Overtown's Harlem Square Club for release on RCA records as "One Night Stand." RCA execs, however, subsequently decided that they weren't comfortable with what they called his "down home, down to earth gut bucket live performance," and they buried it. Cooke was murdered in California on December 11, 1964, and the recording might never have been heard if Gregg Geller, a young RCA executive, hadn't discovered the tape in 1985 and released it as *Live at the Harlem Square Club, 1963*. This album is still judged as among the best live LPs ever recorded. *Rolling Stone*'s special issue "The 500 Greatest Albums of All Time" declared, "Cooke was elegance personified, but [on this album] he works this Florida club until it's hotter than hell, while sounding like he never breaks a sweat . . . when the crowd sings along with him, it's magic."[7] Overtown itself was magic.

LIBERTY CITY AND DISLOCATION

In 1956 President Dwight Eisenhower signed the National Interstate and Defense Highways Act, which established an interstate highway system that would alter patterns of community development across the nation. This $25 billion project, Florida Atlantic University professor Raymond Mohl explains, "dislocated blacks from Overtown and stimulated growth of a second ghetto in Miami, the infamous Liberty City."[8]

The Miami City Council routed an overpass to connect the I-95 and I-395 interchanges right through Overtown. Hundreds of homes and commercial properties were destroyed, and nearly forty-thousand people were displaced. Most relocated to Liberty City, the community that had grown up around the Liberty Square Housing Project. Overcrowding was inevitable, and the 1980s brought a crack epidemic and a sharp rise in crime.[9]

Miami historian Marvin Dunn maintains that Overtown's legacy can't be replicated. "What we know is gone," he says. "We cannot re-create that. No matter how many millions of dollars you spend on this or that project to bring it back to life, Overtown as it was will never happen [again]. All of the things that came together at just the right time, the right people, the right place—you can't recapture that."[10]

MANHATTAN BEACH AND JACKSONVILLE'S MOVIES

❖❖❖

We want to see our lives dramatized on the screen as we are living them, the same as other people the world over.

OSCAR MICHEAUX

In 1900 Henry Flagler moved his operations to Atlantic Beach, thirty miles east of Jacksonville, where he built the majestic Continental Hotel that boasted 250 guest rooms and a dining room that could seat 300. He subsequently hired a full staff of African American cooks, cleaners, maintenance workers, dishwashers, porters, maids, and gardeners and, as he had in Colored Town, and provided worker housing. This housing was in a district called "The Hill," which included oceanfront property. Residents renamed it Manhattan Beach, and it became Florida's first African American beach resort, a popular destination for black Jacksonville church groups, school outings, and family picnics.

In 1907 Flagler added a railroad spur from the Jacksonville terminal to Manhattan Beach, providing African Americans from LaVilla direct access. Enterprising Hill residents built a boardwalk, cafés, and a dance hall. By 1914 "The Hill" was "a colored playground" with swimsuit rental concessions, a merry-go-round, and Mack Wilson's pavilion, which offered a restaurant, a dance rotunda, and outdoor stages. Entrepreneur William Middleton built two smaller pavilions that included both lodging and entertainment. That year Lucy Bunch, a successful LaVilla businesswoman, also built a "first class respectable Negro resort" in the dunes to "provide accommodation and amusement for the better class."[1]

Manhattan Beach flourished until 1932 when the Florida East Coast Railway ended the link between Jacksonville and Mayport and it became more difficult for residents of LaVilla to get to the beach. By then LaVilla had become Overtown's competitor for the title "Harlem of the South," and it would ultimately share Overtown's fate when the eighteen-mile Jacksonville Expressway was engineered to avoid the city's prime real estate district and LaVilla was leveled. The expressway tore through the heart of the city's historic district.

LAVILLA

Bay Street, LaVilla's main thoroughfare, was once home to the black employees of Jacksonville's hotels, cigar factories, and breweries. It was also lined with hotels, small businesses, and warehouses. The Richmond Hotel opened in 1909, followed by the Ambassador and the magnificent Prince Hall Masonic Temple. Saloons and gambling houses sprang up in the city's southeast quadrant, and significant wealth was generated on a section of Ward Street known as "The Line." It was rumored to be home to sixty bordellos, among them the New York Inn, the Turkish Harem, the Spanish Marie, and the Court.[2]

Like Miami's Overtown, Tampa's Central Avenue, and The Deuces in St. Petersburg, LaVilla called itself "Little Harlem." Patrick Henry ("Pat") Chappelle, owner of the black Excelsior Hall offered minstrel and variety shows there and promised "hours of comedy skits, musicians, singers, dancers, acrobatic acts, and pretty girls cakewalking across the stage." Chappelle and his "Rabbit Foot Minstrels" had been touring since 1903, and Ma Rainey, Louis Jordan, and Rufus Thomas all performed at one time or other with them. Chappelle advertised "the Foots" as "The Greatest Colored Show on Earth." They played Alabama, Mississippi, Georgia, and Florida, entering each town with a parade, complete with a marching band. Chappelle boasted that he'd created a Negro show without the help of a single white man, and he referred to himself as "the Black P. T. Barnum." At the height of the troupe's popularity, they played Washington, D.C., Baltimore, and Brooklyn's Coney Island.

When Chappelle died in 1911, Frederick Swift Wolcott, white owner of a minstrel show company in Michigan, purchased the Foots and relocated to Port Gibson, Mississippi, from where they performed an annual thirty-stop Delta tour. A number of Mississippi blues singers and musicians, including Big Joe Williams, Sid Hemphill, Willie Nix, Jim Jackson, Bogus Ben Covington, and Dwight "Gatemouth" Moore, were members of the troupe. Ma Rainey later brought Bessie Smith into the company, and Daddy "Stovepipe" Watson performed with the Foots into the 1940s. Their last performance is believed to have been in 1959.

MOVIN' PICTURES

In 1907 J. P. Chalmers, white editor of *Moving Picture World*, opined, "Moving pictures do not appeal to the masses of negroes." "The average negro wants to see a show with an abundance of noise, something like a plantation minstrel [show] with lots of singing and dancing and horseplay."[3] He could not have been more mistaken.

Thomas Cripps in his study of the Negro in American films, *Slow Fade to Black*, maintains that it was only "white movies that never really touched the Negro world. The 'Negro market' was supplied by directors and producers who created movies by blacks for black audiences."[4]

"Black movies," Cripps wrote, "provided a reinforcement to growing postwar race consciousness by providing the newspapers with a visible example of the race's enterprise, talent, and demiurge for success."[5]

In 1916, Noble Johnson, a popular African American stage actor, established the Lincoln Motion Picture Company in Jacksonville and produced *The Realizing of a Negro's Ambition*, a silent film with an all-black cast. Widely distributed in black vaudeville theaters, it was very successful. Two years later Johnson attempted to purchase the rights to black novelist Oscar Micheaux's *The Homesteader*, but Micheaux wouldn't sell them unless he could direct the film. When they could not reach an agreement, Micheaux returned to Chicago, where he produced and directed the film and released it in 1918. Its success launched his film career, as well as the era of "race films."

While in Jacksonville negotiating with Johnson, Micheaux met Richard Norman, white owner of the Norman Studios, who was experimenting with race films. He had produced six feature-length movies with black actors portraying pilots, cowboys, and soldiers instead of the buffoons, criminals, and servants they played in most white productions. Micheaux briefly worked with Norman on his first film, *The Green Eyed Monster*, before launching his own Capital City Studios in Chicago.

Thanks to its mild winters, sunshine, cheap labor, and easy access to railroads, Jacksonville became an early center of the American film industry. In 1908 New York's Kalem Studios opened a facility there, and Thanhouser Films of New Rochelle followed in 1909. By 1914 both Fox and Metro Pictures each established a presence.

But Jacksonville would lose out to Hollywood due in part to the bad behavior of the filmmakers. Several directors pulled fire alarms downtown in order to film speeding fire trucks, and in 1910 they provoked a riot during the filming of a massive chase scene. Miami tried to steal the film business, but a violent hurricane in 1926 followed by a real estate bust three years later made that virtually impossible.

Richard Norman remained in Jacksonville, however, and achieved some commercial success with *The Flying Ace*. African American leading man Laurence Criner portrayed Captain Billy Stokes, and black actress Kathryn Bond played fe-

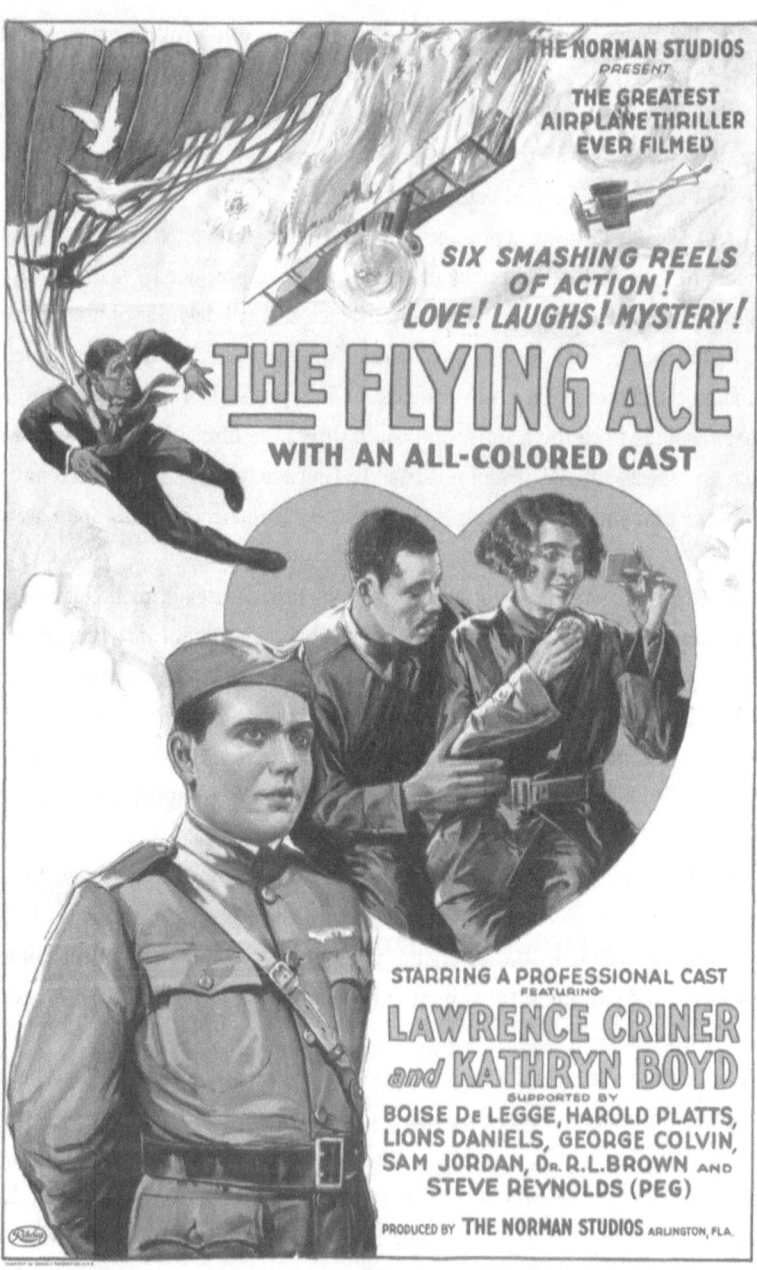

FIG. 5. 1926 poster for *The Flying Ace*, featuring an all-black cast and produced by Norman Studios. Richard Norman was the first white producer of race films to place African American characters in non-stereotypical roles.

FIG. 6. Poster for Oscar Micheaux's 1921 *The Gunsaulus Mystery*, a silent race film inspired by the 1913–15 trial of Leo Frank for the murder of Mary Phagan. It was filmed in Estee Studios in New York City.

male pilot Ruth Sawtelle, a character loosely based on Bessie Coleman, the African American aviator who would earn her pilot's license in France in 1921. In 1939 Norman cast Herb Jeffries, a former singer with Duke Ellington's band, as a singing cowboy in *Bronze Buckeroo*.

While Norman's films were popular with black audiences, they were nowhere near as commercially successful as the less polished work of Micheaux who wrote, directed, marketed, and distributed his own films. Like Micheaux, Norman pushed against white stereotypes, but Micheaux's scripts were edgier, grappling as they did with issues like job discrimination, lynching, rape, mob violence, and even interracial romance.

In 2016 *New Yorker* film historian Richard Brody criticized Micheaux as having been "overtly political" in his treatment of "the impossible dream of interracial marriage; the hostility of light-skinned blacks to darker-skinned ones; the great moral cost of trying to pass for white . . . [and] the ills of bootlegging, gambling, and prostitution that afflicted black communities deprived of education and opportunities."[6] Brody either undervalued or simply missed Micheaux's use of irony and his acerbic sense of humor. Micheaux was also criticized by black elites for his stereotypical depiction of the crooked black preacher—played by Paul Robeson in *Body and Soul* in 1925.

Micheaux's earliest commercial success, *Within Our Gates*, loosely based on the Leo Frank lynching in Atlanta, was released by Capital City Studios during the

Red Summer of 1919. It was a response to the insult of the D.W. Griffiths 1915 racist epic *Birth of a Nation*, which had portrayed African American men as sexually depraved. Micheaux hired a multiracial cast, starring Evelyn Preer ("the first lady of the black screen") and Charles Lucas to reenact the lynching of an innocent black man and the attempted rape of a mulatto woman.

In *Symbol of the Unconquered* (1920), Micheaux's African American heroine Eve Mason (portrayed by Iris Hall) joined forces with Black homesteader Hugh Van Allen (Walker Thompson) to stop Klansmen from stealing their oil-rich land. Micheaux outfitted his Klansmen in white robes as Griffiths had, set them on white-sheet-covered-horses, and fitted them with what looked like plungers on their heads—flawlessly replicating *Birth of a Nation's* costuming. Then he sped up the cameras. Micheaux's clownish Klansman thrilled African American audiences, who likely cheered young Eve Mason as she chased Klansmen over the hill to save the day. In 1931 Micheaux wrote, produced, and directed *The Exile*, the first Black talkie.

Born in Metropolis, Illinois, in 1884 to former slaves, Oscar Micheaux lived in Chicago as a teenager and worked at a series of low-paying jobs. At eighteen he was hired as a Pullman porter, and his route took him west where he recognized opportunities for ambitious black men. He homesteaded for five years in Gregory, South Dakota, and self-published several novels about his experiences there. The screenplay for his first film, *The Homesteader*, was based on his novel with the same title.

Over a twenty-five-year period Micheaux wrote, produced, directed, and distributed forty-four race films. Historian Henry Louis Gates Jr. categorized Micheaux's films as "for the moment, not for the ages": "They were the kind of melodrama or farce—or often both—in which nothing succeeded like excess. But the productions were by and about black folks."[7] Micheaux portrayed a wide range of humanity—not all his stars were heroes, and he was never shy about tackling intra-racial disharmony. This brought criticism from blacks *and* whites. Whites were troubled by the vivid depictions of sex and violence, and he offended African Americans with portraits of black ministers who peddled the afterlife rather than working to make life on earth more bearable. Film historian Peter Kobel explains, "The goal of [Micheaux's] work was not to condemn the white community, but to provide a realistic and rich representation of black life and character."[8] Micheaux died in 1951, and in 1987 the film industry paid him the belated tribute of a star on Hollywood's Walk of Fame.

BUTLER'S BEACH, ST. AUGUSTINE
"The Brightest, Whitest Sand"

❖❖❖

You cannot build a house for last year's summer.
ETHIOPIAN PROVERB

A combination of land speculation, easy credit, back-to-back hurricanes, and a railroad strike that burst South Florida's 1920s real estate bubble enabled some African Americans to purchase property—land that in better times whites would never have considered selling to them. In 1927 Frank Butler, a young African American businessman, bought several lots on Anastasia Island, eight miles southeast of St. Augustine between the Atlantic Ocean and the Matanzas River.

St. Augustine's municipal parks and beaches were closed to African Americans, and black nannies who brought their white charges to the seashore were not permitted to step onto the sand with them. Butler built a seaside resort for middle-class blacks and a bathing beach for working people like those nannies on Anastasia Island. He constructed bathhouses, picnic areas, and shelters for day visitors, leased space to concessionaires and small business owners, and offered building lots to colleagues, neighbors, and friends.

LINCOLNVILLE

Frank Bertran Butler, born in Du Pont, Georgia in 1888, was twenty-five years old when he arrived in St. Augustine. Initially he worked as a clerk in S. A. Snyder's Lincolnville Market on Washington Street, a thriving African American commercial district that boasted three barbershops, six groceries, cafés, a dry cleaner, medical offices, and the Ice Berg Pharmacy and Soda Fountain.[1] The Odd Fellows Hall, built in 1908, was the social center of the city until the Jazz Age, when clubs, cabarets, theaters, and movie palaces flourished.

After President Abraham Lincoln's Emancipation Proclamation in 1863, seven hundred freedmen were released to the Union army and assigned a district in the city of St. Augustine that they named Africa. After the Great Liberator's assassination, however, they renamed the independent African American enclave Lincolnville.[2]

In 1917, when Butler was twenty-nine, he purchased a small grocery on Washington Street and offered his customers credit and free delivery. He grew it into the Palace Market, and once it was established he proposed marriage to Minnie Mae Martin, who accepted. Ten years later Butler bought the Anastasia Island property and, with several partners, incorporated as the College Park Realty Company. They advised residents: "Own Your Own Home: Pay Rent to Yourself and Provide for the Future." Butler and his partners structured affordable mortgage payment schedules and leased property to small businesses at reasonable rates. They never foreclosed unless it was absolutely the last option. Deeply committed to his community, Butler financed voter registration drives and offered his office as a polling place.[3] He would be remembered as an honest and generous man with a talent for negotiating with whites—a critical business skill. After he purchased the Anastasia Island property, the St. Augustine City Council began to drag its feet about completing a scheduled access ramp across the Matanzas River to connect the island with the mainland. It took persistence, patience, and tact to get them to proceed, but Butler managed. Like D.C.'s Lewis Jefferson, he had a knack for finding white allies. The Mary Street Ramp project went forward in 1927, and Butler's Beach opened that summer. Over the following decade, however, as white Floridians climbed out of the Great Depression, they bitterly resented African Americans owning and enjoying tracts of oceanfront like Butler's Beach.

❖❖❖

Butler built the Sea Breeze Kaseno just south of Crescent Beach, a white Anastasia Island enclave. In 1940 he added his fourteen-room Butler Inn. By that time his beach community included a subdivision of bungalows and eleven black-owned businesses. Butler's Beach offered bathing, picnicking, dancing, fireworks, barbecues, and special events. For more than a generation, day-trippers enjoyed Memorial Day and Independence Day picnics. Many maintained that the island had the brightest, whitest sand they'd ever seen. Unfortunately, little had changed on the mainland. In 1953 a black nanny, traveling to Florida with her vacationing white employers to care for their children, was arrested as she tried to enter a St. Augustine public beach to check on them.

THE ST. AUGUSTINE MOVEMENT

Early in 1964, as civil rights legislation to end segregation in public facilities was pending in Congress, Attorney General Robert Kennedy testified before the Senate Judiciary Committee, "A traveling Negro can find overnight accommodations in only one establishment in Montgomery, Alabama, and nowhere at all in Danville, Virginia, but a dog, provided it is traveling with a white man, is welcome to spend the night in at least five establishments in Montgomery and in four in Danville."[4]

On February 10, 1964, the civil rights bill passed the House but was stalled by a filibuster in the Senate. Since ending a filibuster required a two-thirds majority, the legislation was in limbo for three months. St. Augustine celebrated its four hundredth anniversary that year and became a focal point for demonstrations in support of the bill. Dr. Robert B. Hayling, a black dentist who sponsored the city's NAACP youth council, asked Martin Luther King Jr. to come to Lincolnville to encourage the demonstrators whose evening marches to the Old Slave Market were being attacked by angry whites egged on by Klansmen. When a shotgun was fired into Dr. Hayling's living room, the slugs barely missed his wife. Hayling, who had received several death threats, acknowledged, "I and the others have armed. We will shoot first and answer questions later. We are not going to die like Medgar Evers."[5] Evers was the NAACP's Mississippi field secretary who had been murdered in Jackson in 1963. When Hayling and his associates chased a Klan patrol out of Lincolnville by firing over their heads, the NAACP severed ties with him. At that point he appealed to Dr. King and the Southern Christian Leadership Conference for help.

King and his associates arrived on May 18, 1964, as Hayling was conducting a wade-in at the local whites-only beach. He was scheduled to stay at a bungalow on Crescent Beach, a whites-only Anastasia Island community. The owners were white SCLC supporters and personal friends of his family.

"[Whites] went insane at the idea of a black man staying at a white beach," historian David Nolan recalls.[6] Information about King's whereabouts was leaked, and directions to the cottage were published in the local press. Frank Butler insisted that King move to the Butler Hotel as his guest, and he eventually did so. Every night for the following week the Crescent Beach cottage was shot up and fire-bombed. Had anyone been inside, there was no way they could have survived. King subsequently marched with the Lincolnville demonstrators in support of the civil rights bill, and he commuted between St. Augustine and Atlanta.

On Friday afternoon, June 11, 1964, Dr. King and six associates attempted to enter the whites-only Monson Motor Lodge café for lunch. When the owner Jimmy Brock, president of the Florida Motel & Hotel Association, denied them entry, they refused to leave the property, and Police Chief Virgil Stuart arrested all of them. Most posted bail, but King initially refused to. He was charged with malicious trespassing, intent to breach the peace, and conspiracy, and he spent the night in the Duval County jail. J. B. Stoner, leader of the National States Rights Party, led a torchlight parade through Lincolnville that night. The following day a grand jury was assembled to investigate the violence. King and his staff were ordered to stay away from St. Augustine for a month to defuse the situation. His request for a federal mediator was denied. St. Augustine was becoming a fixture on the national evening news.

A week later, on June 18, an integrated group of young activists jumped into the Monson Motor Lodge pool to declare a "swim-in." This time Jimmy Brock poured muriatic acid into the water to scatter them. Historian Jason Sokol maintains, "This was what the fight over public accommodations had become. A 'moderate' motel owner poisoned his pool, out of which two soaked cops and seven dripping protesters emerged."[7]

King returned to the city on June 24 to support a wade-in on Anastasia Island's white Crystal Beach. As seventy-five black activists walked into the ocean, they were either prevented from going farther or pushed into deeper water. Many could not swim and had to be rescued by fellow demonstrators. When a cadre of helmeted, baton-wielding police arrived, they broke up the demonstration. It was the most violent response of that violent summer. That night five hundred angry whites attacked black protesters as they marched from Lincolnville to the downtown Slave Market, and the following day a contingent of white men entered Butler's Beach for "a counter-protest" where they harassed and beat black bathers.

Extensive media coverage of this seemingly intractable violence helped to break the Senate filibuster, and President Lyndon Johnson signed the 1964 Civil Rights Act on June 2. In July, when Jimmy Brock served black guests in his Monson Motor Lodge café, his neighbors threw a Molotov cocktail through his plate-glass window. Despite this, discrimination on the basis of race was against the law. The right to use public facilities was a right the St. Augustine activists had considered important enough to risk their lives for.

AMERICAN BEACH, ANASTASIA ISLAND
"The Negro Ocean Playground"

❖❖❖

I had to make my own living and my own opportunity.
But I made it! Don't sit down and wait for the opportunities to come.
Get up and make them.
MADAME C. J. WALKER, FIRST BLACK FEMALE MILLIONAIRE

In 1935, three years after the demise of Manhattan Beach and nearly a decade after Frank Butler established his beach on Anastasia Island, Abraham Lincoln ("A. L.") Lewis, president of the Afro-American Life Insurance Company, purchased thirty-seven acres on Amelia Island, thirty miles north of Jacksonville, to build "American Beach for Black Americans." Born in Madison, Florida, in 1865 to former slaves Robert and Judy Lewis, A. L. was eleven when his family moved to LaVilla in Jacksonville. Robert Lewis was a blacksmith, and young A. L. worked in a lumber mill. As a child he enjoyed family and church excursions to Manhattan Beach.

Bay Street, LaVilla's business district, like Northwest Second Avenue in Overtown and Lincolnville's Washington Street, was a hub of shops, service businesses, and hotels and the center of an entertainment district that later included the popular Ritz Theatre, opened in 1929, and the KP Ballroom. A. L. Lewis was a serious young man, however, and rather than waste time in theaters and ballrooms he joined the Prince Hall Masonic Lodge where he learned accounting and other business skills. He demonstrated an ability to plan, to complete projects, and to pay attention to detail. In 1888, at the age of twenty-three, he became a partner in a black-owned shoe store.[1] Lewis agreed with Booker T. Washington that black-owned businesses were critical to the economic development of his people. In 1900 he joined the National Negro Business Network and became a recruiter. A year later, he and five lodge brothers each put up $100 and applied for a corporate charter to establish the Afro-American Industrial and Benefits Association. They considered this both a financial investment and a civic responsibility since their goal was to provide affordable unemployment, health, and life insurance.

In addition to his business success, Lewis married well. He and Mary Kingsley Sammis, the daughter of Duval County justice of the peace Edward Sammis, wed when he was just nineteen. She was the great-granddaughter of Zephaniah Kingsley, a wealthy white slave trader married to a Senegalese woman. A. L. and Mary had one son, James Henry Lewis.

Unfortunately, in May 1901 a massive Jacksonville fire destroyed 146 city blocks and 2,368 buildings, including the insurance company's corporate offices, which had opened just two months earlier. The trustees subsequently worked out of Lewis's home until they were able to rebuild. Eight years later they reorganized as the Afro-American Insurance Company and added a pension bureau. In 1919 A. L., then company president, expanded the core business plan to include home mortgages. By that time satellite offices were operating in Georgia, Alabama, Louisiana, and Texas, and Lewis and his family were living on Florida Street in LaVilla's Sugar Hill. Lewis not only appreciated but rewarded loyalty. He paid his managers, salesmen, agents, and clerical staff well and offered job training for advancement. In 1926 he built the Lincoln Golf and Country Club for his executives and shareholders. During the 1920s he sponsored company picnics in Franklintown, a black oceanfront community on the north end of the thirteen-mile barrier island Amelia.[2]

In the late seventeenth and early eighteenth centuries Amelia Island's Fernandina settlement had warehoused slaves on their way for sale in Georgia. In 1862, after the Union army freed more than one hundred, the freedmen established Franklintown. Lewis's insurance company outings there were so popular that he tried to buy oceanfront property to build a company resort, but Franklintown was too small to accommodate him.

AMERICAN BEACH

In 1935 Lewis expanded the Afro-American Insurance business portfolio to include financing housing construction. He also invested in thirty-seven oceanfront acres on Amelia Island to build a corporate resort, initially for use by executives, trustees, and shareholders. He later opened up the sale of lots to Jacksonville's professionals, then to his employees, and finally to the wider African American community.

By 1946 the insurance company owned 216 contiguous acres on Amelia Island. Lewis reserved six cottages for his executives and their families. Every year his top salesman was awarded use of one for two weeks. The beach was just an hour's

FIG. 7. Postcard from American Beach, Florida, circa 1940s. The beach was built in 1935 for African American vacationers.

drive from LaVilla, and day-trippers were welcome. Tourists came from as far as Atlanta, Birmingham, Tuskegee, and Charleston, South Carolina, to bathe in the ocean, many for the first time. Some purchased land and built bungalows, while others constructed rental units and guest cottages. Over the years, annual celebrity vacationers would include Cab Calloway, Ray Charles, Joe Louis, and Zora Neale Hurston.[3] American Beach was the only oceanfront property in Florida that offered safe overnight accommodations for black vacationers.

In 1936, when he was seventy-one, A. L. Lewis retired and named his son James company president but continued on as chairman of the board. James encouraged the commercial development of American Beach, something that didn't sit well with his father or the original investors. He also permitted the Evans' Ocean Rendezvous restaurant to apply for a liquor license. One employee recalled, "By that time most of the older folks were passing away and the younger ones were looking to get rich fast."[4]

James encouraged the expansion of nightclub and juke joint establishments. After World War II, Ralph and Ada Lee built Lee's Ocean Vu Inn, with twenty-one guest rooms, a restaurant, and ballroom. They booked entertainers like Cab Calloway, James Brown, Ethel Waters, Billy Daniels, and Louise Beavers. The A. L.

FIG. 8. American Beach in the 1940s. The Ocean Vu Inn is visible in the upper right-hand corner. Visitors' cars are parked along Lewis Street.

FIG. 9. Migratory workers relax outside a Belle Glade, Florida, juke joint, 1941.

Lewis Motel (built by James Lewis), the Blue Palace, and the Scenic View were all constructed in the late 1940s. All this commercial development made A. L. uncomfortable, but his son did nothing to slow it down, and by the 1950s the island was an entrepreneur's dream.

❖❖❖

Like Suburban Gardens, Overtown, and Carr's and Edgewater Beaches, American Beach was a popular stop on the Chitlin Circuit. By 1948, a year after A. L. Lewis's death, Willie Evans, who would later manage Carr's Beach, expanded Evans' Ocean Rendezvous and featured Ray Charles, Louis Armstrong, and Billy Eckstine. The Rendezvous became the favorite haunt of James Lewis, a spoiled young man who lacked his father's talent and whom the staff referred to as "the Riverboat Gambler."[5]

The Honey Dripper Tavern came alive on Amelia Island on Monday and Tuesday nights, welcoming black workers from the Golden Isles resorts in nearby Georgia—on Jekyll, Sea Island, and St. Simons.[6] Bungalow owners, guests, and day-trippers tried to focus on their own spaces, but it wasn't always possible. The problem was similar to the one that Haley Douglass of Highland Beach and Lewis Jefferson of Washington Park experienced. Should American Beach welcome everyone, or was it a private resort for the affluent? American Beach evolved without any clear direction and a lot of alcohol during James Lewis's tenure, and journalist Russ Rymer observed, "By virtue of its popularity alone, the Rendezvous succeeded in defiling A. L. Lewis' dream of 'family friendly quietude.'"[7]

Some combination of the senior Lewis's death in 1947, the ineptness and greed of his son, the 1964 Civil Rights Act, and a series of punishing tropical storms culminating in Hurricane Dora ended American Beach's long run. Most of the businesses, hotels, and rental cottages on the island were uninsured and eventually abandoned. James Lewis retired in 1967.[8]

Much of the Amelia Island property was sold off to white developers who built gated oceanfront communities, and American Beach disappeared into mid-twentieth-century history. In 2002 a few remaining acres were placed on the National Register of Historic Places in Florida.

PARADISE PARK, SILVER SPRINGS
"The Black Silver Springs"

❖❖❖

It's not true that life is one damned thing after another—
it's one damned thing over & over.

EDNA ST. VINCENT MILLAY

After World War II, America's amusement industry grew exponentially. The postwar surge in weddings, followed by a baby boom, increased the demand for amusement parks and family-friendly vacations. This was especially true in Florida where from 1945 to 1955 the number of tourist venues increased by an incredible 50 percent. Governor LeRoy Collins maintained that the state's economic boom rested on three legs: "tourism, industrial development and agriculture."[1] Before 1950 few amusement parks were designed with families in mind.[2] More often they were set up to attract young singles. After the war, however, young families wanted playgrounds, kiddie parks, family entertainment centers, swimming pools, and affordable overnight accommodations. Racial segregation was also important to whites, who considered it synonymous with safety.[3]

At the same time America's black middle class was also prospering. A shortage of workers in northern factories during the war had increased black migration from the South, and by 1953 the average income for a northern African America family was nearly double that of those who had stayed behind.[4] Before World War II, corporations hadn't advertised in black newspapers, but after the war Coca-Cola, Pepsi, Ford, Buick, Pabst Beer, and the Safeway supermarket chain targeted black consumers. In 1949 *Sponsor*, a broadcast industry trade journal, referred to these consumers as "the forgotten fifteen million."[5]

In 1924 William "Shorty" Davidson, white owner of Union Station, a popular Ocala, Florida, café, and his friend Carl Ray, a sawmill operator, recognized an opportunity when several acres became available in Silver Springs. There, where artesian springs fed the Silver River, tourists had visited since before the Civil War. General Grant, Mary Todd Lincoln, Calvin Coolidge, and Thomas Edison were just a few of the many distinguished sightseers. At the turn of the century hundreds arrived by steamboat and rail to experience "Florida's Natural Wonder." Ray and Davidson considered investing in an amusement park.

The flamboyant Shorty Davidson was a natural promoter, and he and Ray, a seasoned businessman, designed a new Silver Springs Park. They envisioned filling it with exotic gardens, palm trees, sandy beaches, picnic areas, and bathing pavilions. They equipped the antique glass-bottom boats with gasoline engines and invited Ross Allen to bring his Reptile Institute, with all its alligators, crocodiles, and snakes, to the park. Allen's show, the glass-bottom boats, and Colonel Tooey's Jungle Cruise ride, complete with a tribe of monkeys, became their most popular attractions. *The Creature from the Black Lagoon* and six popular *Tarzan* movies were later filmed at Silver Springs—thanks to Shorty Davidson's Hollywood connections.

Ray and Davidson employed black men from nearby Ocala to captain the glass-bottom boat fleet. Unfortunately, neither these captains nor their family members could use the park. Florida was strictly segregated. The captains were required to use separate lunch and restroom facilities on the job and were ineligible for the free passes that their white coworkers enjoyed. Ray maintained that he was required to comply with Marion County's segregation statutes, and that was basically true. The captains were also responsible for turning away African Americans who attempted to enter Silver Springs. Many who made this mistake were northern tourists, and neither Ray nor Davidson felt comfortable explaining their policy. The captains complied because they wanted to keep their jobs.

PARADISE PARK

By the late 1940s, Silver Springs was welcoming nearly a million visitors annually. To their credit, this overwhelming success did not preclude Ray and Davidson from listening to the boat captains who maintained that black West Ocala was an untapped source of revenue. Families there, they insisted, were anxious to visit places like Silver Springs, and they could afford to do so. West Ocala's history was very different from Lincolnville's, LaVilla's and Overtown's. In 1912 two African American men served on Ocala's board of aldermen, and many black residents owned farms and businesses. The black proprietors of the Ocala Knitting Mills drove brand-new cars, and the Ocala Bazaar and Commercial Company, a black emporium established in 1881, was one of the city's leading enterprises. Owner Frank Gadson was a founder of West Ocala's Metropolitan Savings Bank and in 1888 was elected city treasurer and tax collector.[6]

FIG. 10. Finalists on stage in the 9th Annual Miss Paradise Park Beauty Pageant, September 2, 1957. Paradise Park, which was known as the Black Silver Springs, welcomed fifty thousand visitors during its second season. Photo by Bruce Mozert. State Archives of Florida, Florida Memory.

West Broadway, "the Black Main Street of Marion County," included a hotel, dry goods stores, meat and vegetable markets, an ice cream parlor, a pharmacy, barbers and beauty shops, a dry cleaner, and a pool hall. Its entertainment district included the Metropolitan Theatre and four nightclubs. This was a community with significant discretionary income.

Therefore, in 1948, when another opportunity arose, Ray and Davidson purchased a competitor's failed beach a mile south of Silver Springs to build Paradise Park for African Americans—a mirror image of white Silver Springs. They offered boat captain Eddie Vereen, who had been with them for two years, the position of manager of Paradise Park, "for the exclusive use of the colored people of America and the world" (Davidson had already written the brochure), and Vereen accepted. Although the bosses owned the park, Eddie would run it—that was the agreement, and they stuck to it.

Paradise Park opened on June 19, 1949, offering a river landing, food concessions, a soda fountain, picnic areas, and a dance pavilion. The Silver Springs glass-bottom boats and Colonel Tooey's Jungle Cruise made trips downriver so that black patrons could enjoy them on an "as available" basis. As a practical matter, however, the captains made sure that the boats docked frequently at Paradise Park. Ross Allen performed his reptile shows at both locations, using white and black assistants. The park, under Vereen's direction, managed its own entertainment schedule and ultimately added a summer camp, swimming areas, and a petting zoo. Flowers and palm trees were everywhere. As in Silver Springs, there were no admission or parking fees. Patrons paid by the attraction, and if they were not interested in any of them they were welcome to stroll at will. No alcohol was permitted, and, as in Silver Springs, the gates closed at sundown, so there was no nightlife. It was a family resort.

Paradise Park welcomed Boy Scout troops and summer youth basketball camps, church services, baptisms, and family reunions, as well as fraternal organization picnics. The Black American Legion sponsored an annual beauty pageant on Labor Day weekends. There was nothing like it elsewhere in all the Southeast. Encompassing thirty acres, it was modern, beautifully landscaped, safe, exciting, and managed by an African American staff. Families arrived by car or chartered bus. The parking lots were always full, and every entering vehicle was personally welcomed by a staff member.

After more than fifty thousand visitors arrived during the second season, the lack of overnight accommodations in West Ocala became painfully apparent.[7] There was only one black hotel and two motels. Churches subsequently offered their basements and sanctuaries, locals rented extra rooms, and some converted their homes into rooming houses and lived elsewhere until the season ended. No one wanted Paradise Park to fail, and everybody made a little money. By 1953 the park was attracting 150,000 guests annually. *Ebony* magazine described it as "the newest, largest recreation attraction for negroes in the South."[8] B. B. King, Lionel Hampton, Dinah Washington, and James Brown performed on the outdoor stage. Eddie Vereen proved to be a tough but fair manager, and trouble was simply not permitted on his watch.

On June 17, 1955, a fire destroyed the white Silver Springs administration building, including a gift shop and restaurant. Initially a kitchen grease fire was suspected, but there were rumors of arson. Everything was restored by opening day 1956, however, and during the next few years the park underwent several upgrades. It was a complete surprise, therefore, when in May 1962 Ray and Davidson sold Silver Springs to the ABC-Paramount Corporation.

Three years after passage of the 1964 Civil Rights Act, Silver Springs was desegregated, and black patrons were admitted for the 1967 season. By that time Paradise Park's future had been determined but not announced. Many hoped that the parks would merge. Instead, 1968 was Paradise Park's last season. Early in 1969, without further discussion, it was bulldozed.

Fifteen years later, in 1984, ABC-Paramount sold Silver Springs to Florida Leisure Activities, Inc., whose shareholders hoped the completion of Interstate 75 would make it profitable. But two years after the superhighway reached Florida, revenues had not increased. Highway construction, however, had decimated West Broadway, the heart of African American Ocala, and the historic neighborhood was destroyed. After changing ownership several times, Silver Springs Park was finally absorbed into the Florida state park system in 2013.

Dr. Dorsey Miller, a 1960s civil rights activist and Marion County NAACP official, ruminated,

> Silver Springs was not ours . . . they [took] what I felt was ours, Paradise Park. . . . They could have maintained Paradise Park and let that be integrated too. See, it was not integration that occurred for us; it was desegregation and assimilation. . . . Integration is when you bring things together . . . we never had that. It was the same with everything else, the schools and everything . . . they tried to assimilate us into theirs. They could have done some upgrading and just made Paradise Park and Silver Springs all one . . . but they didn't. They obliterated our site and wiped out our history and our culture.[9]

MISSISSIPI

GULFSIDE ASSEMBLY, HANCOCK COUNTY
"A Black Chautauqua"
◆◆◆
You can't understand it. You would have to be born there.
WILLIAM FAULKNER'S CHARACTER QUENTIN, IN *ABSALOM! ABSALOM!*

Many valued possessions, articles, souvenirs, and ephemera associated with African American amusement parks, resorts, and beaches in the South—objects like photographs, scrapbooks, and diaries—have been lost, and most of the people who built, managed, and enjoyed these places have died. Mississippi's Gulfside Assembly, established in 1923, is an exception. Bishop Robert E. Jones, the first African American superintendent of the Methodist Episcopal Church, South, kept extensive records of Gulfside, an educational, recreational, and cultural center for African Americans located on Mississippi's White Riviera.

The Methodist Episcopal Church, South, seceded from the mother church in 1844 over the issue of slavery. In 1939 they reunited, and a separate "Central Jurisdiction" was established for African American congregations in Louisiana, Mississippi, and East Texas. Bishop Jones, editor of the *Southwestern Christian Advocate*, was appointed administrator of the jurisdiction, which would be abolished in 1968, eight years after his death.

As in nearby New Orleans, Mississippi's Gulf Coast had a substantial Creole population, and, while not by any measure liberal, it was a more relaxed environment than inland in terms of race relations. Because of this New Orleans influence, it was arguably the most likely place to establish an African American retreat in the area if one was determined to do so. The bishop's colleagues were mostly white clergymen and advocates for the Social Gospel—the call to a progressive religious agenda that included prison reform, industrial safety, and abolition of child labor. They argued that the church's mission had to be extended to confront problems in the temporal world. Jones therefore felt confident in proposing a Chautauqua-like resort and retreat center for his Central Jurisdiction. Chautauqua was a popular adult education movement founded in New York State in 1874 by John Heyl Vincent, superintendent of the Methodist Sunday School Society, and philanthropist Lewis Miller, the father-in-law of Thomas Edison. Bishop Jones maintained that a black Chautauqua would be a welcome alternative to traditional camp meetings, assemblies, and revival centers and amenable to wider educational pursuits.

Traditional Chautauqua organizations offered healthy living programs, exercise, spiritual development, cultural events, and family recreation and entertainment. These facilities were generally white, middle-class, and Protestant and tended to promote democracy, female suffrage, and political and economic (if not social) equality for African Americans.[1] Chautauqua values were amenable to Booker T. Washington's "racial uplift" ideology as they stressed respectability, frugality, refinement, and the pursuit of education. President Teddy Roosevelt described Chautauqua as the "most American thing in America."[2]

In 1920 white Methodist minister Will Alexander invited Bishop Jones and Robert Moton, Booker T. Washington's successor at Tuskegee Institute, to become founding members of a Commission on Interracial Cooperation (CIC), his response to the bloody rioting of Red Summer 1919, when African American servicemen, anticipating first-class citizenship for their wartime service, were attacked by white mobs determined to maintain white supremacy. Alexander actively recruited board members from the "better classes" of both races in an attempt to assign a white and a black representative to each southern state and build committees of mediators to work on improving race relations. The CIC promoted educational, political, and economic advancement for African Americans and endorsed state-based anti-lynching legislation—with the understanding that all was to be accomplished within the limits of the segregated system. Historian John Egerton maintains that the CIC "developed a curious image of liberal activism within the bounds of cautious and proper respectability."[3] It effectively sanctioned African American second-class citizenship.

In 1921 Bishop Jones requested financial support from the CIC and the church to create a new kind of "Methodist Assembly" for the Central Jurisdiction. It would be similar to the white Sea Shore Campground in Biloxi, Mississippi, which had a conference center, retreat houses, and summer camps. After obtaining the church's blessing, it took him a year to raise the $4,000 required to purchase an abandoned three-hundred-acre Mississippi plantation on the Gulf, fifty-five miles east of New Orleans. He had received financial assistance from Atlanta's Gammon Theological Seminary, the Julius Rosenwald Foundation, and Dr. George Vincent of the Rockefeller Foundation (Rev. John Heyl Vincent's son). This old plantation, once owned by President Andrew Jackson's nephew, was completely overgrown, and Jones required the services of fourteen local preachers and their congregations to put it in order.

Between 1923 and 1931 Bishop Jones oversaw construction of a twenty-five-room hotel, a chapel, auditorium, classroom building, library, theater, two dormitories, and several guest cottages. His black "Chautauqua on the Gulf" became a center for clergy training, and for conferences, summer schools, teacher workshops, stage productions, lectures, concerts, tennis tournaments, and YMCA programs. In 1929 Jones moved the Central Jurisdiction's headquarters from New Orleans to Gulfside and afterward welcomed ten thousand visitors annually. Metropolitan Opera star Leontyne Price, a native of Laurel, Mississippi, performed there—it was the only auditorium in her home state where black audiences could enjoy her beautiful voice. Jones also offered affluent black families from New Orleans rental cabins where they could spend the summer.

Unfortunately, Jones's guests were required to walk behind the property and through the woods to access their beach since they were not permitted on the public roads that led to the gulf. Living in such close proximity to white resorts was not always comfortable and at times dangerous. The Clermont Harbor Hotel, where President Woodrow Wilson vacationed during his White House years, was just three miles south of Gulfside, and Poplarville, Mississippi, a center of Klan activity, was forty-six miles to the north. Gulfside experienced several cross burnings during its early years, and more than a decade later, at midnight on September 30, 1935, a fire destroyed the administration building. Under the bishop's watch however, the community not only endured but prospered. How did he manage?

A diplomat and a gifted orator, Bishop Jones, like NAACP national secretary Walter White, had the physical appearance of a white man. While visiting congregations in East Texas he had been threatened with arrest for fraternizing as he walked with his wife Valena, who was visibly black. Although the bishop never admitted passing for white, it is likely that he did so when he contracted with lumber baron John DeBlieux for the Gulfside property. He purchased 100 waterfront acres and secured a long-term lease for another 326 and an option for 150 more. The thought that they were negotiating with a black man apparently never occurred to either DeBlieux or his attorney. Jones purchased everything in his own name and subsequently transferred it to the Gulfside Association where he served as president.[4] He correctly assumed that it was advisable to close the deal in the simplest and quickest way.

Gulfside Assembly was dedicated on April 16, 1923, with a mission to build "strong black minds in strong black bodies." It was, to paraphrase the bishop's words, a healthy-living community based on education, physical exercise, and spiritual nourishment. His greatest challenge was ensuring that Mississippi's Jim Crow statutes were observed. That was critical to retaining Gulfside, and it required making compromises that he might not have been willing to make under different circumstances.

Visitors were not permitted to leave the Gulfside grounds until it was time for them to return home, and they were counseled never to provoke their white neighbors in any way, including by playing loud music. For many who came to relax and recreate, and for children who were exposed to many new and exciting experiences, this was not a problem, but making so many accommodations to white supremacy was unacceptable for others.

While the Commission on Interracial Cooperation praised Gulfside as the epitome of successful race relations, historian Andrew Kahrl maintains that what it really exemplified was "the type of institution white Southerners saw as a small, incremental improvement to race relations that did not fundamentally alter the asymmetry of power."[5] The April 7, 1926, *Amsterdam News* described it as "the only project of its kind that has ever been launched in America." That was entirely accurate.[6] Gulfside ran weekly summer camps for black residents from as far away as New Orleans and vacation getaways for the more affluent, funded a boys school, provided jobs for the black residents of nearby Waveland, and provided many visitors with their first access to a coastal beach.

Two decades earlier Lewis Jefferson had lost customers at Washington Park by refusing to accommodate to middle-class propriety. He had also had the audacity to confront the white D.C. police when they targeted black men for exhibiting the same behaviors that in whites were considered "rowdy" but harmless. Bishop Jones chose not to make waves, and as a result many of his guests chose not to return to Gulfside. His strictness limited and often spoiled their good times. While Jones took their criticism seriously, he continued to follow a course that he believed was necessary to maintain a sanctuary for black people—especially black Mississippians. He felt a responsibility to protect this space inside the Deep South where recreation and relaxation, for a week, a month, or even a summer was actually feasible.

By the late 1950s, black activists increasingly disdained the bishop. In Biloxi, just forty miles northeast, protesters were being beaten and jailed for attempting to desegregate the gulf beaches that were constructed by the Army Corps of Engineers and were being maintained with tax revenues.[7] The Biloxi activists were led by Gilbert Mason, M.D., a doctor who had returned to his native Mississippi in 1955. Four years later, fed up with being denied access to the local "white beaches," he and eight friends decided to "gain access to God's Gulf Coast Beaches," which had always been public. As they waded into the gulf, they were dispersed by police, and subsequently organized the Harrison County Civic Action Committee to call for community participation in "Operation Surf," a wade-in scheduled for Easter Sunday, April 17, 1960. When Dr. Mason reached the beach that morning, he was the only one there. Those who had agreed to participate failed to show up. Undaunted, he carried out the first wade-in protest as a solo march into the gulf and was promptly arrested.

The courtroom was packed as Mason was tried and convicted of disturbing the peace. But following Sunday, 125 protesters showed up on Biloxi Beach and were so viciously attacked by a white mob that two of them died. Mason subsequently petitioned the U.S. Department of Justice to sue Biloxi for denying African Americans access to federally funded public facilities.[8] White Biloxi maintained that the beachfront was privately owned and delayed court proceedings for years. In 1967, however, a federal appeals court ruled that Biloxi's beaches were indeed public since Harrison County maintained them, and the city was ordered to desegregate. The young activists of the Student Nonviolent Coordinating Committee (SNCC) and the Congress of Racial Equality (CORE) admired that kind of pushback. Dr. Mason was a man of his times. Bishop Jones was a product of the passive past.

❖❖❖

When Bishop Jones retired, Bishop Robert N. Brooks, also African American, succeeded him. Jones lived on the Gulfside campus until he died on May 18, 1960, at the age of eighty-eight. By that time nearly fifty years had passed since his Chautauqua was hailed as the flagship program of the Methodist Episcopal Church, South. It had been reduced to a retreat center leased by nonprofit organizations for conferences and training. Ironically, in the late 1960s Gulfside became a sanctuary for the black and white SNCC activists. That was possible only because its white neighbors never considered it a threat. The young activists were able to live and work there undercover—just as Bishop Jones had a half century before. In 1993 SNCC activist Hollis Watkins of Jackson, Mississippi, recalled, "There were only three places where blacks could meet in Mississippi during the movement—Tougaloo College, Rusk College, and Gulfside."[9]

In 1968 the Central Jurisdiction was dissolved, and the African American Methodist churches folded into their local Methodist conferences. Early in 2005 Gulfside was purchased by developers who planned a two-story hotel complex at a cost of $2.8 million. The project was completed in July that year, and the hotel was officially opened on August 13. Two weeks later Hurricane Katrina hit the coast. All fourteen buildings on the property, including the hotel and hundred-year-old trees, were leveled. In 2010, plans were developed to adapt the great Gulfside for use as a nonprofit retirement community, but those plans fell through.

FARISH STREET, JACKSON
"Crossroads of the South"

❖❖❖

Farish Street was the artery of Jackson. We could shop there, eat there, everything.... There were stores on Capitol Street we couldn't go in.
DOROTHY DAVIS

Farish Street in Jackson, Mississippi, was a classic "stroll"—a black business, cultural, and entertainment district. Five railroad lines intersected Jackson, and by the turn of the twentieth century the city boasted thirteen lumber companies and several cottonseed oil mills. In 1908 half the black residents of the Farish district owned their own homes. This was a self-sustaining community of lawyers' and doctors' offices, loan associations, grocery stores, funeral homes, schools, restaurants, a hospital, countless blues and jazz clubs, and almost as many churches. Medgar Evers, the NAACP Mississippi field secretary, kept an office on Farish, as did Percy Green, editor of the black *Jackson Advocate*.

In 2004 Scott Barretta, a reporter for the *Jackson Free Press*, noted, "Four or five decades earlier Farish Street was hopping, and on Saturdays it was always crowded. Much of that crowd included country folk who took special buses to Farish Street to stock up on dry goods and to visit the cafés where inexpensive beer flowed and jukeboxes blared out the latest R&B sounds."[1] Merlie Evers, Medgar Evers's widow, recalled Farish Street as "this composit006 community, where you come together, where you could be treated with dignity and where you could learn entrepreneurship with the hope of spreading further."[2]

Farish Street was a mecca for the blues. In 1923 the Edwards Hotel served as a temporary recording studio for Okeh Records, which cut demos for Robert Williams, Joe McCoy, Isaiah Nettles, and the Mississippi Sheiks. In 1926 Henry Columbus (H. C.) Speir quit his job assembling phonographs and opened a music shop on North Farish Street. A white man and a devotee of Delta Blues music, Speir sold 78 rpm recordings on the Okeh, Gennett, Victor, and Paramount labels. He subsequently petitioned those companies to permit him to represent them as an A&R (artist and repertoire) man—a talent agent. They agreed to try him out while his wife Rosa ran the store.

Okeh Records generally promoted white country music artists like Mamie

Smith and the Carter family, while the Gennett label featured Jelly Roll Morton, Blind Lemon Jefferson, King Oliver's Creole Band, and Louis Armstrong. Paramount introduced Robert Johnson, said to have sold his soul to the devil in exchange for his guitar virtuosity, and Charley Patton, "the voice of the Delta."

Speir is said to have discovered Skip James, Tommy Johnson, Ishman Bracey, Son House, the Mississippi Sheiks, Bo Carter, and Uncle Dave Macon. He apparently had a good ear for the blues. The Speirs retired in 1943, and H.C. died in 1972. He was posthumously inducted into the Blues Hall of Fame in Memphis in 2005.

TRUMPET RECORDS

The first Mississippi record label to achieve national recognition was Trumpet Records thanks to Willard and Lillian McMurry, a white couple who owned a furniture and music store on North Farish. In 1950 stores that sold "Victrolas" were expected to stock records as well, and Lillian quickly discovered that records were her best-selling items. She had Willard build a recording studio in the storeroom, and like H. C. Speir she began to scout talent. Lillian claimed not to know much about music, but she knew what she liked. Her early recruits included Sonny Boy Williamson, Elmore James, Willie Love, and Wynonie Harris. The McMurry demos were featured on the local white radio station WRBC, "Rebel Radio." Lillian, a natural entrepreneur, contracted with Ivan Scott's Radio Service (also located on Farish) to assist her with the purchase of state-of-the-art recording equipment.

She established the Trumpet label, which became the fifth largest in the nation.[3] Although Lillian was the powerhouse behind the project, she went to great lengths to keep her women's club friends from discovering it. She gave Willard all the credit, fearing that she would be shunned if her friends found out that she had been working with black men.

NIGHT SPOTS

Farish Street's celebrated African American clubs included the Art Deco Crystal Palace Ballroom, which featured Duke Ellington, Cab Calloway, Louis Armstrong, Fletcher Henderson, Count Basie, and Fats Waller, many of whom stayed overnight at the Edward Lee Hotel. The ballroom took up the entire second floor of the Crystal Palace. Other clubs included the Alamo, the Masonic Temple, the Elks

Lodge, and the College Park Auditorium. For those seeking grittier entertainment there was East Jackson's infamous Gold Coast, where gambling, bootleg liquor, and ladies of the evening were available in every juke joint on Fannin Road. Joints (or "juke houses") were those bars with juke boxes rather than live music. Fannin Road was home to the Blue Flame, the Rocket lounge, and the Heat Wave, all owned and operated by African Americans.

Today, while 79 percent of Jackson's residents are black, only 25 percent of its businesses are black-owned. Maati Jone Primm, proprietor of Marshall's Music and Bookstore, maintains that this is because "integration did not mean access to capital."[4] Journalist Boyce Uphold adds that many "blame the Civil Rights Act of 1964 for Farish Street's decline. When black shoppers suddenly had more choices about where to spend their money they went to white stores, while white shoppers generally did not patronize black-owned businesses."

Geno Lee, owner of the Big Apple Inn, the last surviving restaurant of Farish Street's heyday (and whose specialties remain pig ear sandwiches and hot tamales, agreed Desegregation was great for the black race, but it was "horrible for the black businessmen."[5]

"It didn't work both ways," Dorothy Steward, a native Jacksonian, confirms. "We wanted the open access and we got the open access, but no one came back to do anything with the places. We almost threw the baby out with the bath water. And so when we left everything fell apart."[6]

White journalist Russ Rymer explains, "The immediate tangible commercial benefits of integration accrued exclusively to white businesses. Integration represented the greatest opening of a domestic American market in the nation's history, but the windfall worked only one way. Black customers flocked to white stores, restaurants—and beaches—where they had formerly been prohibited and forsook the black businesses where they'd been confined. Whites, however, did not storm across the same open border to spend their money in black establishments."

In 2014 the Southern Foodways Alliance and the Southern Documentary Project joined forces to establish the Farish Street Project to study "what happened to the black mecca of Mississippi?" Some maintain that "in many ways, the story of Farish Street—and other communities like it—is a counter narrative to the celebratory accounts of the successes of the Civil Rights Movement."

ALABAMA

TUXEDO JUNCTION, ENSLEY
"Where the Town Folks Meet"

❖❖❖

There was nothing but clubs and bars all up and down the street.
Mama didn't allow us in Tuxedo Junction."

LELAR SPEARS

Music was central to just about every African American entertainment or amusement, whether founded by blacks or owned by whites and operated by blacks. Tuxedo Junction in Ensley—now a neighborhood in Birmingham, Alabama—was an exception. The district fanned out from a streetcar hub later designated as the Pratt City Carline Historic District at the beginning of the twentieth century. It was where all the trolley lines ended, and the cars were turned around to start over again.

Ensley, a company town, was founded in 1887 for employees of the Tennessee Coal and Iron Company and named for Enoch Ensley, president of the company. In 1898 Ensley built two hundred cottages for black workers, and two hundred more were added in 1900. Incorporated in 1899 as a suburb of Birmingham, Ensley became part of the city in 1909 at the height of the region's iron production. It was surrounded by the black communities of Fairfield, Wylam, Bush Hills, and Pratt City, all located along the trolley routes. Between 1920 and 1950 "the Junction" served as a quitting time and weekend gathering place. Bars, pool halls, juke joints, and cafés came alive, offering sweet relief from workday problems and challenges.[1] The district included the Palace Theatre and several nightclubs.

Tuxedo Park, a few blocks away from the Junction, was a small black amusement area built in the 1920s and upgraded in 1944. It offered a pool and bathhouse, a skating rink, a shooting gallery, and a dance pavilion. But the jewel of Tuxedo Junction was the African American Woodmen Fraternal Society ballroom located on Ensley Avenue. On Friday nights and weekends it became both a dancehall and a practice venue for up-and-coming black musicians. The African American Woodmen Fraternal Society leased the ground floor to Andrew Belcher, a black dentist, and several black doctors, but on weekends the ballroom, which filled the second floor with its polished wooden floor and high ceilings, pulsated with workingmen, friends, neighbors, and musicians. Locals maintained that it was the only place in Birmingham where African Americans could dance freely and without fear.[2]

The ballroom was a mecca for jazz, blues, and swing artists. Aspiring musicians joined all-night jam sessions and sat in with entertainers like Lionel Hampton, Eubie Blake, Ella Fitzgerald, B.B. King, and Nat King Cole. It's credited as the birthplace of "jive dancing." There was no need to dress up for a night in the Junction if you were heading to a bar, lounge, or joint, but the ballroom was someplace else. There men arrived in zoot suits and two-tone shoes or in a tuxedo if they were lucky enough to own one. If not, one could be rented at Johnson's Cleaners around the corner. In 1939 African American band leader Erskine Hawkins, a Birmingham native who began playing at the ballroom when he was fourteen, wrote "Tuxedo Junction," the district's anthem.

> Way down south in Birmingham
> I mean south in Alabam'
> There's an old place where people go
> To dance the night away

During World War II, white bandleader Glenn Miller heard that song while entertaining white troops at Maxwell Air Force Base in Montgomery. He purchased the rights from Hawkins, and his recording "Tuxedo Junction" sold 3.5 million copies.

For years the Junction offered African American workingmen and workingwomen good times and provided young musicians with a chance to jam with some of the best in the South. Paul Williams and Eddie Kendricks, who had honed their skills in the ballroom, left for the North in 1957 first to Cleveland, and then to Detroit. In the early 1960s they became founding members of the Temptations.

The Junction was not without its critics. Birmingham's white mayor Jimmy Morgan who served from 1953 to 1961, called it "the filthiest thing" he had ever seen. "Crime and illness are bound to come from nasty holes like that," he maintained.[3] During his administration Birmingham embarked on series of slum clearance projects, and a subsequent urban renewal program created hard times for the black population.

In 1963 the city commissioner closed Tuxedo Park, the children's amusement park, to circumvent court-ordered integration. When it reopened a year later, integration was the law, and many former customers did not return. Birmingham's steel plants began shutting down in the 1970s, and the trolley routes were eventually discontinued. By the end of the decade the last of the open hearth furnaces had closed.

The American Woodmen's Auditorium is now the Belcher-Nixon Building, named for the two dentists who had rented the offices on the first floor. Dr. Andrew Belcher was a member of the American Woodmen fraternity, and he chaired the board of directors of the Jones Valley Finance Company. Dr. John Nixon served as president of the local NAACP chapter and later chaired the Alabama Conference of NAACP Branches.

As of early 2024 Tuxedo Junction is being restored as a tourist destination. A former resident recalls it fondly as "our little Negro Town, somewhere we could be off to ourselves and where we wanted to remain."[4]

BLACK MARDI GRAS, MOBILE

❖❖❖

If, as a child, you saw, every Mardi Gras, the figure of Folly chasing Death around the broken column of Life, beating him on the back with a Fool's Scepter from which dangled two gilded pig bladders; or the figure of Columbus dancing drunkenly on top of a huge revolving globe of the world; or Revelry dancing on an enormous, upturned wine glass—wouldn't you see the world in different terms, too?

EUGENE WALTER

In 1703 Mobile, Alabama, hosted its first Carnival, a traditional celebration of Boef Gras—the slaughter of the "fatted calf"—the last feast before the Lenten season's abstinence. French soldiers were stationed in Mobile, at that time capital of the French Louisiana Territory. In 1704 Nicholas Langlois, a wealthy French expatriate, founded the Société de Saint Louis and began the tradition of a masked ball—the "Masque de la Mobile."

The Big Easy's Carnival may have been bigger, but Mobile's was—and still is—impressive. Journalist Michael Harriot maintains, "While Bourbon Street is a tourist destination in New Orleans, the entire city of Mobile transforms into one big, black homecoming [for Mardi Gras] ok."[1] Carnival begins on Twelfth Night, celebrated in January with galas sponsored by the "mystic" or secret societies, and it culminates in a feast to kick off Lent on Mardi Gras ("Fat Tuesday").

A Colored Carnival Association was organized by Mobile's black mystic societies in 1939. Like their white counterparts, these were social clubs whose membership lists were kept secret. They designed colorful floats for the grand parade and marched to the accompaniment of jazz bands. A black "King and Queen of Misrule" were crowned at a formal masquerade ball featuring skits, music, dancing, and, of course, dining. The Colored Carnival Association eventually became the Mobile Area Mardi Gras Association, and a celebration of Africatown was later added to the annual Spirit of Our Ancestors Festival in February.

AFRICATOWN

Africatown, established as Plateau, Alabama, is an unincorporated town three miles north of Mobile. Generations of survivors of the last slave ship, the *Clotilda*, created and sustained a community of freedpeople there. In 1808 importation of enslaved people was banned in the United States and two years later declared an act of piracy punishable by death. Buying and selling enslaved people inside the nation, however, remained legal.

Timothy Meaher, a white Mobile shipbuilder who modified vessels for blockade runners, had grown rich since slave traders continued to stockpile and sell human chattel. A notorious gambler, in the spring of 1860 Meacher made a wager that he would be able to bring one hundred Black Africans into Mobile from West Africa without getting caught (and subsequently hanged). Several of his friends took him on.

Meaher asked a colleague, Captain Bill Foster, to partner with him on an expedition to Africa, in the *Clotilda*, a fast schooner capable of carrying 190 adults. Foster agreed, and they sailed to Ouidah, a coastal village in Dahomey, West Africa, where Meaher purchased 110 black men and women before heading back to Mobile. His cruel mission was successful, as the *Clotilda* returned on July 8, 1860, with its cargo intact. Foster anchored in Grand Bay, and a tugboat hauled the ship up the Alabama River to Twelve Mile Island, where African men and women were transferred onto the *Czar* and taken farther upriver for sale. Ten Africans were presented to Captain Foster as payment, and Meaher kept thirty for himself. Foster subsequently burned and sank the *Clotilda* to destroy the evidence of this last documented voyage of enslaved Africans brought to the United States, nearly four hundred thousand people.[2]

For the next three years the Dahomey men and women were enslaved—thirty of them on Meaher's property. On January 11, 1861, Alabama seceded from the Union, and when Emancipation came in 1863 the Africans had no way of getting back to Dahomey. Their leader Cudjo Lewis confronted Meaher with the fact that he had enslaved them, saying that since they were now free and had no place to go, he owed them land. Meaher was furious, but he agreed to rent them land until they could buy it outright, and with it they established Africatown in 1866. There they built homes, farmed, and raised their children. Some later worked in Mobile's shipyards or in its mills and factories. They were granted U.S. citizenship in 1868 and two years later petitioned the American Colonization Society to fund their passage home but were refused. They would never see Africa again.

In the 1930s Zora Neal Hurston, a black anthropologist celebrated for her novel

Their Eyes Were Watching God, completed a series of interviews with Cudjo Lewis, who by then was the last survivor of the *Clotilda*. Lewis described his life from his kidnapping in Africa at the age of nineteen through his enslavement and the long years as a freedman, raising his family and trying to make ends meet. All the while he had longed to get back home. Hurston's manuscript *Barracoon: The Story of the Last Black Cargo*, Cudjo's story, was subsequently rejected by Viking Press and other white publishers who had no interest in the subject, and by black publishers who feared that it might expose black African involvement in the slave trade. *Barracoon* was finally published in 2018 by Amistad Press, eighty-seven years after Hurston wrote it and long after both she and Cudjo Lewis had died.

Hurston developed a relationship with Lewis over the many months of their interviews. She chose *Barracoon* as her book's title because it is the African word for stockade—the enclosure in which kidnapped black men and women were confined while awaiting transport to America.

On May 22, 2019, the wreckage of the *Clotilda* was discovered in the lower Mobile-Tensaw River Delta near Twelve Mile Island just where Captain Foster said he had sunk it.

THE ORDER OF MYTHS

In 2008 Margaret Brown, a young white Mobile native, produced and directed a documentary film about the history of the city's two Mardi Gras celebrations, one black and one white. In *The Order of Myths* she explored how it all came to be.[3] Two separate kings and queens. Two Grand Balls and two parades. Focusing on the 2007 Mardi Gras celebration, Brown's documentary commemorates the black King and Queen of Misrule attending the coronation of the white king and queen for the first time. Unfortunately, it did not signal the start of a shared tradition.

THE BEN MOORE HOTEL AND THE LAICOS CLUB, MONTGOMERY
Montgomery Nightlife

> I have walked into the palaces of kings and queens and into the houses of presidents. And much more. But I could not walk into a hotel in America and get a cup of coffee, and that made me mad.
>
> JOSEPHINE BAKER

On September 23, 1951, the Ben Moore Hotel celebrated its grand opening on Centennial Hill in Montgomery, Alabama, a middle-class black neighborhood adjoining the business district. The first licensed black hotel in Montgomery, the Ben Moore was a twenty-eight-room, four-story structure within view of the historic Dexter Avenue Baptist Church. Three years later, when Martin Luther King Jr. was appointed pastor there, the hotel provided a back room in its Majestic Café for him to meet with other civil rights activists and colleagues. Like Benjamin Beamon's Atlanta Café, the Ben Moore supported the activist community during the 1954 Bus Boycott and became a meeting place for the Montgomery Improvement Association. It also provided shelter for beaten and bruised Freedom Riders in 1961 and offered respite for many of the Selma marchers four years later. Entertainment and survival were linked in Montgomery.

D. C. Moore built his hotel in September 1951 and named it for his father, Ben F. Moore, the last enslaved person born in Montgomery. D. C. Moore, who worked on a farm in Tuskegee, had invented a new water filtration technique and subsequently enjoyed a comfortable living.

The Malden Brothers Barbershop and the Majestic Café rented space on the hotel's ground floor. A false floor in the café's pantry opened to a staircase leading down to a separate basement, awaiting use in case hiding became necessary. The second and third floors included guest rooms that were small—designed for utility rather than comfort—and the top floor housed the Afro Club, where Tina Turner, Clarence Carter, Ray Charles, and B. B. King entertained, and the Rooftop Garden Restaurant. A Montgomery resident recalled, "During the day it was the Roof Garden and at night it was the Afro Club."[1]

After D. C. Moore died in the late 1950s, his widow Maggie leased the hotel for the next decade. The Afro Club continued to attract entertainers like Duke

Ellington and Little Richard. They generally spent the night there and played in Montgomery's Club Delisa, the West Tavern, the Esquire, or the Blue Flame. After passage of the 1964 Civil Rights Act, however, the black hotel business slowed, and the Ben Moore was unable to compete with the integrated Holiday Inn and Marriot chains.

Edward Clinton Davis, a teacher at Montgomery's Booker T. Washington and George Washington Carver High Schools, purchased the Ben Moore from Ellen Sloan, D. C. Moore's daughter, in 1979 and continued to lease the restaurant and nightclub. Before Davis died in 2014, representatives from the City of Montgomery approached him with a restoration plan to revitalize the hotel and three street corners surrounding it, and to widen those streets at a cost of $3 million. City officials proposed funding $2 million of the project and offered to lend Davis the other $1 million, with the stipulation that the property would be seized if he were unable to repay the loan. Davis declined the offer, and his son, Ed Davis Jr., rejected a later offer from Alabama State University to use the old hotel as the site of a radio station. He maintained that he would rather see it landmarked and protected as a historic site, as he feared that it would eventually become another cheap clothing store or fast food outlet. Above all, he didn't want them to tear it down.

Michael Driver, a white Montgomery resident and author of an article titled "Discovering the Ben Moore Hotel," accepts that places like the Ben Moore are "destined never to be the hottest and happiest spots in town again." But, he explains,

> The Ben Moore is a structural celebration of black history in exactly the same way that the antebellum plantations represent white supremacy... For this reason, any business occupying space in the Ben Moore Hotel should be owned and operated by African Americans. Let white clients dine in the Majestic Café with black clients do business with professionals in offices above exactly as black clients and are served today by white owned businesses in a legally and culturally appropriate manner. But it would be an unpardonable affront to Ben Moore himself, and to all the other black men and women of history to allow white domination of this important landmark.[2]

THE LAICOS CLUB

In 1961 Montgomery's vaudeville palace, the Carver Theatre, a popular stop on the Chitlin Circuit, was renovated, and the Laicos Club was established. "Laicos" is simply "social" spelled backwards. The club quickly became *the* place for dancing in West Montgomery. In 2021 Brad Harper, a white reporter for the daily *Montgomery Advertiser*, interviewed Coleman Woodson Jr., president of the Alabama Jazz & Blues Federation, who assured him, "To get into the Laicos Club was quite an accomplishment . . . it never scheduled anyone who wasn't really good." Woodson noted that local talent like Bennie "Buckwheat" Payne, a trumpet player with the Sheiks, and Bobby Moore & The Rhythm Aces, who had toured with Sam Cooke and Ray Charles, played there.

Roscoe Williams, an electrician by day, managed the club on Friday, Saturday, and Sunday nights from 1965 to 1968. He and his wife, Mary Lucy, were members of Martin Luther King's Dexter Avenue Baptist Church. Williams served as a deacon, and the couples were close friends. On January 30, 1956, Mary Lucy was sitting in the parsonage living room with Coretta King and her new baby daughter Yolanda when the Klan dynamited the house. It was one of the few "black events" covered in the *Advertiser*. The next day Williams installed floodlights on the front lawn of the parsonage.

In 1965, one year after Mississippi Freedom Summer's massive drive to register black voters ended, a group of white northern journalism students began publishing the *Southern Courier* in Montgomery. This was a weekly newspaper described as "an independent paper giving blacks a voice." Some reporters were veterans of Freedom Summer, and all were required to live in the communities they reported on. Coeditors Peter Cummings and Ellen Lake recruited and trained the integrated staff to "cover the stories of the civil rights movement that usually went unreported." For this they were paid between $20 and $75 a week. The paper survived on grants, donations, and support from several wealthy backers.

Jim Peppler, the *Courier*'s photographer, took a series of photos inside the Laicos that have been preserved. He recalls walking into the club one Friday night and being welcomed by Roscoe Williams. When Peppler asked if he could take photos, Williams told him it would be fine. But "he was warned not to photograph the few other white men who came in, most of whom sat at the bar to try to pick up women."[3] Whites trespassed freely and repeatedly returned, but they did not want their friends, neighbors, and especially their employers to know about it. Blacks may have been curious about white entertainment, but if they trespassed in white facilities the repercussions could be dire.

Peppler subsequently enjoyed a long career with the New York *Newsday*, and when he retired he donated more than eleven thousand photos to the Alabama Department of Archives and History in Montgomery, many of them taken inside the Laicos. Before the *Southern Courier* folded in December 1978, it published 177 issues.[4]

LOUISIANA

CONGO SQUARE AND STORYVILLE, NEW ORLEANS
"The Beat of the Big Easy"
♦♦♦
Jazz was not only built in the minds of the great ones,
but on the backs of the ordinary ones.
CAB CALLOWAY

In antebellum Louisiana, French and Spanish slaveholders, unlike the English or Anglo-Irish, permitted enslaved people a day off on Sundays. Never required to accept Christianity or to assimilate, these slaves gathered in New Orleans's Congo Square on Sundays to meet with others from the Caribbean as well as free people of color to socialize, enjoy music, dance, play games, and sell their wares. Musicians fashioned homemade drums, called "bamboulas," from bamboo covered with animal skins. They made saxophones out of gourds, wooden xylophones, and a variety of stringed instruments. Contemporary musicians maintain that the rhythms heard in Congo Square continue to reverberate in New Orleans jazz funeral music and in Mardi Gras parades.

In 1879 white novelist George Washington Cable, a native of New Orleans and a former reporter for the *Picayune*, published his memoir, *Old Creole Days*, in which he vividly described Sundays at Congo Square. "The hour was the slave's term of momentary liberty," Cable wrote.

> The booming of African drums and blast of huge wooden horns called to the gathering.... And then there was that long-drawn human cry of tremendous volume, richness, and resound, to which no instrument within their reach could make the faintest approach . . . [And] the dance! There was constant, exhilarating novelty—endless invention—in the turning, bowing, arm-swinging, posturing, and leaping of the dancers. Moreover, the music of Congo Plains was not tamed to mere monotone. The strain was wild. Its contact with French taste gave it often great tenderness of sentiment. It grew in fervor, and rose and sank, and rose again, with the play of emotion in the singers and dancers....
>
> See! Yonder brisk and sinewy fellow has taken one short, nervy step into the ring, chanting with rising energy. Now he takes another, and stands and sings and looks here and there, rising upon his broad toes and sinking and rising again, with what wonderful lightness! How tall and lithe he is. Notice his brawn shining through his rags. He too is . . . by the three long rays of tat-

tooing on each side of his face, a Kiamba. The music has got into his feet. He moves off to the farther edge of the circle, still singing, takes the prompt hand of an unsmiling Congo girl, leads her into the ring, and, leaving the chant to the throng, stands her before him for the dance.[1]

Music historian Robert H. Cataliotti describes the polyrhythms, syncopation, and pulse beats that filled Congo Square as "the heartbeat of the musical forms that emerged from New Orleans: ragtime, jazz, rhythm and blues, and funk." "The music made there," he maintains, "was founded on African-based cultural retentions: call and response, improvisation, and rhythmic sophistication. Eventually, these building blocks of expressive, black folk culture absorbed elements of the cultures they encountered and created something distinctly American."[2]

Today only 2.2 acres of Congo Square remain as part of Louis Armstrong Park. Congo Square was added to the National Register of Historic Places in 1993, and the Congo Square Preservation Society placed a historical marker at the site in 1997.

STORYVILLE

New Orleans's Faubourg Tremé District, an integrated working-class neighborhood that incorporated Congo Square and Storyville, was located just north of the French Quarter. In 1897 the Storyville district was carved out by the city council as New Orleans's red-light and gambling quarter. It was called Storyville because Alderman Sidney Story had proposed the ordinance. Believed to be the birthplace of jazz, it was home to Lulu White's Mahogany Hall, an "octoroon brothel" with a marble staircase and fifteen bedrooms. There on Basin Street, Lulu employed parlor pianist Jelly Roll Morton and forty female entertainers. Spencer Williams, who wrote "Basin Street Blues" and the "Mahogany Hall Stomp," was Lulu's nephew. Her regular guests included Babe Ruth, John L. Sullivan, and P. T. Barnum.

At 25 Basin Street was the four-story mansion in which Josie Arlington, a white madam, presided over Chateau Lobrano d'Arlington, a high-class—or at least expensive—brothel, which could provide a live sex circus for an extra fee.

The Big 25 Lounge, with resident musicians "Big Eye" Louis Nelson, Kid Ory, Joe "King" Oliver, and his protégé, a young Louis Armstrong, was another Storyville high spot. It was common at that time for black jazz musicians to play in white brothels, and at its height Storyville employed over two thousand prostitutes and generated millions of dollars. The district produced some of the most innovative musicians of the twentieth century, including Charles "Buddy" Bolden, remembered as King Bolden, a cornetist who raised ragtime to new heights with an improvised style fusing blues and gospel rhythms. Bolden is believed to have been inspired by both the Congo Square dances and the music of the Black Baptist Church. He played cornet by ear and insisted that "everything must be felt to be played."[3] Jelly Roll Morton and Louis Armstrong recalled Bolden as the most talented of the early jazz musicians.

Storyville was shut down in November 1917 by Secretary of War Newton Baker. It shared the fate of every red-light district within five miles of a military base. Lulu White tried to rebrand Mahogany Hall as a hotel and restaurant, but that didn't fly, and in 1918 she sold everything for $100,000 and moved on.[4] The party was over. By 1937 most of the structures in the district had been demolished, and by 1940 the Iberville Housing Project was being constructed on the site.

CRESCENT STARS STADIUM, NEW ORLEANS
"Downriver from the French Quarter"

◆◆◆

If you keep your eye on the ball you can accomplish anything.
HANK AARON

New Orleans's Crescent Stars' Stadium, home to the 1933–34 Negro Southern League champions, the Crescent Stars, was built in 1921 by and for the residents of the city's Seventh ("Creole") Ward. The project was launched by Wallace Marine, manager of the Crescent Stars and president of the Autocrat Social & Pleasure Club, organized in 1907 by "several colored men who'd been harassed by the police for gathering on a street corner." They applied for a poker club charter, rented clubhouse space, and in 1914 incorporated as the Autocrat Club. They would sponsor athletic competitions and later lavish Mardi Gras balls.

A charter club member, Wallace Marine, owner of the Belkoma Cigar Company, navigated the Crescent Stars stadium proposal through the City bureaucracy. In this he was ably assisted by Walter L. ("Cap") Cohen, New Orleans's comptroller of customs and chair of the Louisiana Republican Party.[1]

Cohen, whose father was Jewish, was a gambler who owned the Pinchbacks, Louisiana's first black semipro baseball team. He arranged a meeting with Mayor Andrew McShane to discuss purchasing property in the Seventh Ward, then called Faubourg Tremé.[2] During Reconstruction, free people of color could buy land there, and it developed into "a cultural rendezvous" for blacks and whites.

After Marine, Cohen, and C. C. Dejoie Sr., editor of the black *Louisiana Weekly*, were granted a charter for their Crescent Park Corporation, they recruited a board of directors whose fourteen members each purchased $1,000 in stock.[3] These included Albert Workman, vice president of the local International Longshoremen's Association; professional photographer Arthur Bedou; jazz drummer Alex Bigard; and Edwin "Beansie" Fauria, a music promoter and "Numbers King of the South." Fauria owned the Astoria and Pelican Clubs, several bars and dance halls, and all the slot machines in the Seventh Ward. A man of mixed race, he was light-skinned like his cousin Ernie Cagnolatti, a New Orleans trumpeter. F. T. Jones, a respected surgeon, later served on the board, as did Walter Bemiss, pastor of the Fifth African Missionary Baptist Church and a musician in his own right.

The corporation sold $50 stock shares to raise the $45,000 needed to cover the cost of building a stadium with a baseball diamond and grandstands that could accommodate four thousand spectators, a dance pavilion, and refreshment booths. Crescent Park Stadium opened in April 1921 with the Crescents challenging the New Orleans Black Pelicans. Pelicans star Leroy "Satchel" Paige pitched. A decade later in the 1933 Dixie Series the Stars defeated Nashville's Elite Giants and took the Negro Southern Leagues pennant. The Big Easy celebrated them as heroes and looked forward to their defeating Chicago's American Giants in the Black World Series scheduled to be played in Crescent Park that fall. According to the *Louisiana Weekly*, the Black World Series had the largest attendance ever recorded for an African American sporting event. Marine rented additional bleacher seats to accommodate the demand. As in other black recreation venues, many whites crossed the line without fear to attend the Negro Southern League games. Nobody asked them to leave.

"The crowd alone furnished a thrill," the *Weekly* reported. "Thousands of persons representing every walk of life filed into the stands proper, into temporary bleachers, out into the field and into every nook and corner which provided points of vantage... There were men, women, kids and even pets on the house tops, men in the treetops, on fences, sheds, and posts." Although Chicago won the Series (5–0), the Crescent Star fans were loyal—and not all of them were black.[4]

The white *Times-Picayune* covered every Crescent Stars game leading up to the World Series and for several seasons after that until the team disbanded in 1937.[5] The stadium made space available for community fund-raising events, circuses, fraternal and church picnics, outdoor concerts, and cultural and artistic performances. In 1938 the Crescent Park board gifted the land to the city to establish (and maintain) an African American municipal park. In 1941 Hardin Park opened at the site where it remains.

SEABROOK AND LINCOLN BEACHES, EAST NEW ORLEANS
"The Ninth Ward Shoreline"

❖❖❖

Rejoice at the death and cry at the birth:
New Orleans sticks close to the scriptures.
JELLY ROLL MORTON

East New Orleans, one of the poorest districts of the Big Easy, remains the largest and most diverse of its seventeen wards. For decades white fishermen built cabins, (more like sheds on stilts) called "camps," along the south shore of Lake Pontchartrain. By 1922 they numbered 230. The land was owned by the Orleans Levee Board, and in 1926, after the city completed a paved two-lane road along the shoreline, dance halls and cafés began springing up in what became "the Poor (White) Man's Miami Beach." As a teenager, Louis Armstrong, a New Orleans native, played jazz trumpet in several of these clubs. In 1932, however, the Levee Board reclaimed its property, cleared out the fishing camps, and evicted the squatters.

African American community leaders had always been anxious to acquire some lakefront property. During New Orleans's famously hot summers the black Ninth Ward residents suffered from the lack of recreation amenities—public or private. In 1938 delivery came from an unexpected quarter when Sam Zemurray, a Russian Jewish immigrant and CEO of the United Fruit Company, donated 2.3 acres of Lake Pontchartrain shoreline to the Levee Board for the specific purpose of creating a "Negro beach." A self-made millionaire, Zemurray had expressed concern about the number of African American children who drowned every summer while attempting to swim in lonely unsupervised areas of the giant lake. In the summer of 1931 when six boys drowned, the *Louisiana Weekly* referred to them as "a sacrifice for the failure of the local municipalities to provide the Negro citizenry with an adequate bathing beach."[1]

The Levee Board cleared Zemurray's land, constructed Seabrook Beach, and equipped it with a few picnic tables. After the CCC added a bathhouse and the Works Progress Administration provided additional funding, the white *Times-Picayune* described it as "a barren sand beach with a lone unimpressive building." For more than a decade Seabrook was the only African American beach in the city, and from the outset there were problems.

Seabrook was located twelve miles from downtown New Orleans, and three bus transfers were required to get there. In a 2020 article for *Antigravity Magazine*, journalist James Cullen described it as "a deathtrap."[2] The combination of a seawall and an industrial canal in the area caused sinkholes to form, and several people drowned. There were no lifeguards and no lights at night. In addition, Cullen explained, the white community complained that Seabrook was located too close to white beaches and subdivisions and that the sight of black swimmers was hurting both the tourism trade and real estate prices. By 1943 swimming was banned at Seabrook Beach.

By contrast, Pontchartrain Beach, a private white amusement park built in 1928 by entrepreneur Harry Batt, was situated closer to the city and served by a municipal bus line. It had Art Deco bathhouses, offered summer shows and concerts, and boasted the Zephyr and Ragin' Cajun roller coasters, a "Scrambler," bumper cars, and several restaurants.

After years of pressure by the NAACP and the Urban League, in 1938 the Orleans Levee Board set aside 2.3 acres of lakefront on the southern shore to create Lincoln Beach for the ward's black residents. This was fourteen miles from the city, with no public transportation, and the water was polluted. Mayor Chep Morrison agreed to add two swimming pools and provided lifeguards.

Lincoln Beach was upgraded through the efforts of Ernest Wright, a black CIO labor organizer and Ninth Ward resident. In 1941 he had founded the People's Defense League to encourage voter registration and to protest police brutality. Wright knew not to expect much from either the state or the municipal government (or any white political organization, for that matter), so it was a leap of faith when he approached the politician he considered the lesser of many evils: Earl K. Long, brother of the infamous senator and former Louisiana governor Huey Long. White supremacists had by and large aligned with the Dixiecrat Party, but Long was not a white supremacist. He supported African American voter registration, and Wright could work with that.

In the 1947 governor's race the People's Defense League backed Earl Long, and he won the election. Governor Long is believed to have subsequently used his influence with the Levee Board to fund a million-dollar upgrade of Lincoln Beach.[3] In 1953 the shoreline was extended by seventeen acres, and a new bathhouse with two thousand lockers was added. The Levee Board contracted with Paul J. Lacassin Amusements, Inc., to construct and to manage an amusement park with a Ferris wheel, roller coaster, kiddie rides, and a penny arcade. The new Lincoln Beach Park opened on May 8, 1954. Black entrepreneurs added the Carver House Restaurant and the Terrace, which offered dancing under the stars, and a municipal bus route was finally extended to the park's entrance. Families, church organizations, fraternal groups, and day-tripper all enjoyed the amenities. On Thursday nights WMRY-FM's black disc jockey Larry McKinley hosted midway dances, and on weekends he broadcast live from the beach, featuring artists like Fats Domino, the Ink Spots, Earl King, Sam Cooke, Ike and Tina Turner, Little Richard, the Neville Brothers, and Ray Charles. The first season ended with a Miss Lincoln Beach Contest, which became a tradition. Lincoln Park advertised in the *Louisiana Weekly* as "the Coney Island of the South," and in 1958 it hosted the Negro State Fair.

Irma Phillips, who had visited Lincoln Beach as a child, recalled, "My family and I, we were able to go to Lincoln Beach and shed ourselves of racism. [It] was a shelter of calm, peace, and laughter, for us. Family picnics, rides, dances—just having fun. And we didn't have to worry about people throwing rocks at us and calling us filthy names."[4]

New Orleans historian Keith Weldon Medley notes, "With the passage of the Civil Rights Bill in 1964, Lincoln Beach met the fate of segregated lunch counters and water fountains. . . . Historical and market forces prevailed. Attendance dropped dramatically, and Lincoln Beach closed in the autumn of 1964."[5]

When Pontchartrain Beach was ordered to desegregate, the Batt family instituted a gate fee and required tickets for each ride to discourage black patrons, but they were helpless to stem the tsunami of white flight. Despite staggering losses, the Batts held on until September 1983 when competition from theme parks and the upcoming 1984 World's Fair finally made it untenable.

ARKANSAS

WILEY JONES PARK AND RACE TRACK, PINE BLUFF
"Second to None in the South"

❖❖❖

I've missed more than nine thousand shots in my career. I've lost almost three hundred games. Twenty-six times, I've been trusted to take the game-winning shot and missed. I've failed over and over and over again in my life. And that is why I succeed.

MICHAEL JORDAN

Wiley Jones Park opened in 1899 in Pine Bluff, Arkansas, offering a harness racing track, fifty-five acres of recreation space, and "The Colored People's Fair Grounds"—it was a gift to the African American community by a formerly enslaved person. A successful black entrepreneur, Walter ("Wiley") Jones had developed a passion for harness racing, and he owned twenty-four horses who competed against some of the finest "trotters" in Jefferson County, Arkansas.

Jones, born in Georgia in 1848, was one of six children of George Jones, a white plantation owner and an enslaved woman named Ann. He was named Walter after the doctor who delivered him but was called "Wiley" due to his precociousness (he was "wily"). In 1858, when Wiley's father died, the family was sold to General James Yell, a prominent attorney and planter in Pine Bluff. Wiley was subsequently gifted to Yell's son, Fountain Pitts Yell, on his wedding day.

After Emancipation, Jones worked as a farm laborer, hotel porter, and ultimately as a barber in his brother-in-law Ben Reed's shop. For eight years he saved his money, invested in land, and entered the liquor distribution business. By 1876 was able to open a saloon, the Jones Casino at 207 Main Street in Pine Bluff. Determined to achieve respectability, Jones joined the Prince Hall Masons, the Oddfellows, the Black Knights of Pythias, and the Republican Party and befriended Ferdinand ("Ferd") Havis, a black millionaire who served as a Third Ward alderman and chair of Jefferson County's new Black Republican Party. In 1880 Havis and Jones served as delegates to the Chicago Republican Convention that nominated James A. Garfield for president.[1]

Six years later Jones applied to the Pine Bluff City Council to secure a franchise to operate a mule-drawn streetcar line. When he was awarded it, he put his older brother Matthew in charge of construction. By 1890 the "Jones Line" was operating between downtown Pine Bluff and the city line, and it eventually merged with the Citizens Street Railway. Jones was simultaneously working with Edward Houston, a white investment banker to rebuild a defunct pre-Civil War spa at Sulphur Springs, two miles south of Pine Bluff. They began refurbishing the twenty-room hotel in 1889, and when it burned to the ground they rebuilt the following spring. In August 1893 it went up in flames again. Undaunted, they rebuilt a second time, finally advertising a hotel complex with billiard parlors, bowling allies, a dance hall, and a swimming pool. This effort survived, and they subsequently added twenty summer rental cottages.[2]

In 1899 Jones built the first city park for black people. It was time. He had made a fortune providing goods and services for white people, and while he'd always given generously to black causes and philanthropic organizations, at forty-seven he wanted to do something more tangible for his own. This was Wiley Jones Park, fifty-five acres adjoining his racetrack and fairgrounds, and it included a baseball stadium with a grandstand that could accommodate eight hundred people. He subsequently purchased a African American semipro baseball team, the Pine Bluff Owls.

Jones offered amusements and thrill rides, hosted traveling shows, and sponsored sporting events. In the early 1900s he added bicycle racing, a popular sport at the time. One of its biggest stars, and the only black one, was Marshall "Major" Taylor, hailed in France as the "Flying Negro." Between 1898 and 1899 Taylor broke seven world short-distance records and was choked into unconsciousness by a white competitor when he became the first black American world champion. Ice cubes and nails were thrown under his tires during races, and many American hotels and restaurants refused to serve him. In 1996 the *Los Angeles Times* called Taylor "one of the greatest sports stars that no one knows."

Jones's last project was the Southern Mercantile Company, a wholesale farm supply business in which he partnered with Ferd Havis. It was the largest operation of its kind owned by African Americans in the South. Havis was named company president, and Jones appointed his own brother James to manage daily operations so that he could concentrate on Jones Park. At the time of his death in 1904 Wiley Jones was respected by both the black and white communities of Pine Bluff. At his funeral his Oddfellow lodge brothers offered a "Resolution of Respect" that read, in part: "God blessed Wiley Jones with the touchstone of success, common sense, perseverance, energy, lofty spirit and a public disposition possessed by none other in so great a measure... Whatever his magic hand touched turned to gold... He was the first man of his race to commence commercial businesses, to build and maintain a street railway, to operate a sawmill, and to establish a city park.... [He] set the example before the Negro and turned it to the possibility of success."[3]

BATHHOUSES AND SPRING TRAINING, HOT SPRINGS
"It's Different Here"

❖❖❖

There must be quite a few things that a hot bath won't cure,
but I don't know many of them.
SYLVIA PLATH

In 1832, during President Andrew Jackson's administration, Congress for the first time set aside land for recreation, establishing the Hot Springs Reservation in the Ouachita Mountains of Arkansas. His intention was to preserve public access to the therapeutic hot mineral spring waters in what Native Americans of the area called "the valley of the vapors."[1] Fed by underground geysers, the springs released water heated by molten rock from were was believed to be dormant volcanoes. Hydrotherapy, especially hot bath therapy, was routinely prescribed to treat lead poisoning, rheumatoid arthritis, psoriasis, syphilis, and polio. The Department of the Interior was charged with leasing this public land so that poor people could bathe without charge.

It didn't take long for entrepreneurs to arrive and build hotels, bathhouses, clinics, infirmaries, and spectacular homes for themselves. After the Civil War, Confederate veterans made their way to the springs seeking relief from the pain of infected wounds and from illnesses they had contracted, including syphilis and tuberculosis. Initially the baths were not segregated, and Ral Spring, the largest of the outdoor facilities was used African Americans and white people. "Ral" was supposedly short for "neuralgia," but it was also slang for syphilis.[2]

By 1877 more than four hundred squatters were living in Ral City, along the western edge of Hot Springs Mountain. That year retired U.S. Army officer Benjamin F. Kelley was appointed superintendent of the Hot Springs Reservation and charged with removing them. Kelley gave the order to evacuate within thirty days, but many were too sick or disabled to move, and most had no place to go. Kelley subsequently built the Government Free Bathhouse and an infirmary that was also free of charge and eventually named the Army-Navy Hospital.

It was not until the early 1880s and the coming of Jim Crow legislation that the baths were racially segregated. Hot Springs became a popular white vacation and resort community, often compared with European spas like Carlsbad (Karlovy

Vary). As new bathhouses were privately built and exorbitantly expensive, Congress charged Superintendent Kelley with maintaining a "sufficient number of free baths" to assist poor people.

After the Ral settlement was vacated, an epidemic of yellow fever swept Hot Springs, and many paying customers stayed away, fearing the fever but also rumors that the mineral water was infected with syphilis. By the turn of the century most of the private bathhouses were updated and sanitized, and luxurious hotels along Bathhouse Row were being constructed. During the Jazz Age the Arlington was a favorite of Andrew Carnegie, F. W. Woolworth, and celebrities like Sarah Bernhardt, Rudolph Valentino, and Gene Autrey.

Earlier, in 1881, Albert G. Ingalls opened the Palace Hotel and Bath House in Eureka Springs two hundred miles north of Hot Springs, to welcome black guests who were likely affluent since the Palace wasn't cheap. Two years later, however, the Supreme Court overturned the 1875 Civil Rights Act, which had required equal treatment for all Americans in public spaces, and Jim Crow statutes were passed by southern state legislatures in 1890. The Hot Springs bathhouses were already segregated by then, and the pressure on Ingalls to do likewise became so intense that he sold the Palace in 1901.

BLACK BATHHOUSES

African Americans could work as attendants or therapists in the white bathhouses but could not use them before the Civil Rights Act of 1964. The first Hot Springs bathhouse built for African American paying guests was the Crystal, constructed in 1904 on Malvern Avenue near the city's black business district. It was designed by W. T. Baily, chair of the Architecture Department at Tuskegee Institute. Unfortunately, fire destroyed it in 1913, but it was rebuilt by the Black Knights of Pythias, and a hotel was added in 1914. When popular black vaudeville entertainer Bill "Bojangles" Robinson visited in 1944, he tap-danced from the downtown Hot Springs railroad station to the Pythian Bathhouse and Hotel, with admirers following along.[3]

The cost of running bathhouses that offered clinics or hospital services required assistance, and black fraternal organizations and insurance companies stepped up. More affordable guest houses were built in the black section of town on Cottage Street. These included the Claridy House, the Crittenden Hotel, and the Reed House, all listed in *The Negro Motorist Green-Book*.

In 1923 the grandest of the black bathhouses opened in the Woodmen of the Union Building near the Pythian Temple. It was a first-class hotel, with a two-thousand-seat theater, a six-hundred-seat auditorium, a beauty parlor, a barbershop, and a gymnasium as well as a medical facility. Guests included Count Basie, Duke Ellington, Joe Louis, and Jackie Robinson. When the Woodmen of the Union baths closed in 1935, its medical clinic was transferred to the Pythian Bathhouse. In 1948 the National Baptist Convention purchased the Woodmen of the Union Building, renovated it, and opened a new bathhouse, which flourished until 1983 when the convention relocated to Nashville. Famous guests there included Diana Ross and Thurgood Marshall. The advent of modern medicine eventually lessened the demand for healing waters, and Hot Springs morphed into a vacation spa and a spring training camp for professional baseball teams.

THE NEGRO LEAGUES AND SPRING TRAINING

In 1886 the Chicago White Stockings baseball franchise scheduled spring training in Hot Springs. The climate, the healing water, and the resort environment made it a perfect choice. Gradually other major league teams, including the Pittsburgh Pirates, Boston Red Sox, and Cincinnati Reds, followed suit. This required a minimum of four baseball fields—the Majestic, the Whittington, Sam Guinn Field, and the Fogel. All were located within a half mile of the baths. Black players stayed at the National Baptist Hotel while whites checked into the Eastman, Majestic or Arlington Hotels on Bathhouse Row.

Baseball players were America's heroes, and tourists, black and white, flocked to Hot Springs each spring to enjoy watching their favorite players—Bill Dickey, Buck Ewing, Mel Ott, Stan Musial, Rogers Hornsby, and Babe Ruth from the major leagues, and Satchel Paige, Buck O'Neil, "Bullet" Rogan, Oscar Charleston, "Smokey" Joe Williams, and Josh Gibson from the "Negro leagues."

The players loved Hot Springs, and many spent their days off at the Essex Park and Oaklawn Park racetracks. Gambling was illegal in the city, but since a good number of underworld figures like Al Capone, Lucky Luciano, and Owney Madden (manager of Harlem's Cotton Club) enjoyed it, authorities tended to look the other way.

By the 1920s several white major league teams had moved spring training to Florida, Arizona, or California, where the climate was warmer and there was less rainfall. By the early 1940s the Hot Springs days as a professional spring training center and mecca for black and white fans were over, but Hot Springs National Park remained an integrated destination for black and white vacationers.

MISSOURI

DEEP MORGAN, ST. LOUIS
"Ragtime and the Sporting Life"

❖❖❖

Part of it went on gambling, and part of it went on women.
The rest I wasted.

W. C. FIELDS

St. Louis, a midwestern city in a former Confederate state, was situated at the confluence of the Missouri and Mississippi Rivers. In 1894, it was the only U.S. city where prostitution was still legal. Deep Morgan's red-light district was located in north St. Louis near Biddle Street in the city's "Bloody Third Ward," which was filled with gaming halls, saloons, and brothels. All of them employed piano players to provide the new ragtime music, so named because of its "ragged" or syncopated rhythms.

Scott Joplin and a young W. C. Handy played at Tom Turpin's Rosebud Café. In 1914 Handy wrote "The St. Louis Blues," and on June 14, 1925, Bessie Smith, accompanied by Louis Armstrong, recorded it for Columbia Records. With a voice that could evoke unbearable sorrow, Bessie Smith became one of the greatest blues singers in American musical history.

Tom Turpin sponsored piano-playing contests at the Rosebud. Six feet tall and three hundred pounds, he could only play piano standing up. As a young man he had entertained in his father's Silver Dollar Bar and in 1897 composed and published "Harlem Rag." His father owned both Honest John's Bar and the Booker T. Washington Theatre where Ethel Waters and Bessie Smith performed and a very young Josephine Baker enthusiastically danced on the sidewalk outside. At fifteen Baker joined the Dixie Steppers, a traveling vaudeville troupe, and never look back.

Tom Turpin's Rosebud, established in 1901, spanned nearly a city block and boasted two bars, a gambling parlor, a sportsmen's club, a wine room, a pool hall, and a brothel upstairs. The brothel was very successful, especially during the 1904 St. Louis World's Fair. Blacks were admitted to the fair if they had the price of a ticket but were not welcomed at any exhibit, nor were they served at any restaurant. One popular exhibit was "a human zoo" with "specimens" from Japan, South America, Africa, the Philippines, and Australia, all of whom lived on site. The great Apache chief Geronimo posed for "nickel-apiece souvenir photographs" and played the part of the Sioux chief Sitting Bull in daily reenactments of the Battle of the Little Bighorn.[1]

Perhaps most chilling was the exhibition of Ota Benga, a Mbuti "pygmy" brought from the Congo. St. Louis historian Angela da Silver explains, "Some anthropologists of the time maintained that pygmies were the missing link between men and monkeys."[2] When the fair ended, Ota Benga went to live in the Bronx Zoo, where he was exhibited in the Monkey House. He was later released to Rev. James H. Gordon in New York City who arranged for him to relocate to Lynchburg, Virginia, where he attended school and worked in a tobacco factory to earn his passage back to Africa. In 1914 when World War I started in Europe, travel was restricted, and he was unable to arrange passage. Two years later he committed suicide.[3]

STAGGER LEE

Tom Turpin's chief competitor was Bill Curtis's saloon, the scene of the 1885 Christmas Day murder of Billy Lyons by "Stagger Lee" Sheldon. On December 26, 1885, the *St. Louis Globe-Democrat* reported: "William Lyons, 25, coloured, a levee hand, living at 1410 Morgan Street, was shot in the abdomen yesterday evening at 10 o'clock in the saloon of Bill Curtis, at Eleventh and Morgan streets, by Lee Sheldon (Stagger Lee), also coloured."

Both parties, it seems, had been drinking and were feeling exuberant. Lyons and Sheldon were friends and were talking. The discussion drifted to politics, and an argument started, during which Lyons snatched Sheldon's hat from his head. Sheldon indignantly demanded its return. Lyons refused, and Sheldon drew his revolver and shot Lyons in the abdomen. When his victim fell to the floor, Sheldon took his hat from the hand of the wounded man and coolly walked away.

The ballad of Stagger Lee, written in 1911, was recorded in 1923 by white band leader Fred Waring and his Pennsylvanians. Lloyd Price, who was black, would make it a hit in 1959. Folklorists John and Alan Lomax maintained that "Stagger Lee" (Lee Shelton) was a pimp who had gotten his nickname from the riverboat "Stack Lee," on which he provided prostitutes.

MADAME BABE'S

The Curtis Saloon, Henry Bridgewater's, Jim Ray's Falstaff Club, Bill Walker's Alcove Café, and Madame Babe's White Castle Club all flourished in the Deep Morgan district at the turn of the century. In 1898 Madame Babe set up business in the heart of Chestnut Street's red-light district in a three-story bright-white building. Originally Sarah Connors of Nashville, she was born enslaved in 1857 and worked on her father's plantation. As a teenager she arrived in St. Louis, shared an apartment with several "working girls," and eventually joined them in the trade.

Madame Babe promised her customers genuine New Orleans Creole companions, and she delivered. She was famous for dressing in "gowns from Paris, with feather boas" and "putting diamonds in her teeth." The parlor in her Castle Club had a mirrored floor, on which her girls danced sans underwear. Club membership was fifty dollars annually, and members received gold coins as admission tokens. "Everything else was a la carte."[4]

Madame Babe's brothel featured "Mama Lou" (Letitia Lu Lu Agatha Fontaine), who performed in French maid costumes and calico dresses. Mama Lou was a very large, very black, very energetic performer who belted out bawdy songs in a husky voice and hurled mock insults at the audience. Tom Turpin usually accompanied her on the piano. Lou spoke with a clipped English accent and is believed to have come from Santo Domingo. Maxwell Marcuse, author of *Tin Pan Alley in Gaslight*, maintains that the popular 1880s cancan numbers "Ta! Ra! Ra! Boom De Ay" and "A Hot Time in the Old Town Tonight" were Mama Lou's compositions that were stolen. Since she "didn't bother with musical notation, white songwriters who scribbled down the melodies and registered them reaped the profits."[5] Lou was never credited with authorship, nor did she receive any royalties, but she didn't let that bother her. Eventually she opened a bordello of her own and retired a very wealthy woman.

RUNNING THE BASES

Deep Morgan was almost as famous for its black pro baseball as for its saloons and bordellos. In 1882 Henry Bridgewater and his partner Charles Tyler organized the St. Louis Black Stockings and reportedly paid their pitchers a whopping $50 a week. Not just a successful saloon keeper, Bridgewater was also a liquor distributor, political boss, gambler, and real estate developer who could pass for white. Negro League teams were incredibly popular locally and an ongoing source of entertainment and excitement in other black communities.

By 1883 the Black Stockings became "Bridgewater's Champions" after successfully completing four tours of the United States and Canada. They had attracted huge crowds in Louisville, Cincinnati, and Detroit. In 1906 Charlie Mills, owner of Deep Morgan's Keystone Café and Cabaret, organized a new team: the St. Louis Giants. He was financially backed by Conrad Kuebler, a white man who made Kuebler Park available to them. This was no act of charity. Kuebler had organized a "stock company" whereby the Giants were jointly owned by sixteen white businessmen, with himself as chief stockholder. Charlie Mills continued to manage the team, and Kuebler Park eventually attracted five thousand fans over a single season. Almost decade and a half later, as the 1920 season approached, Andrew "Rube" Foster, black owner of the Chicago American Giants, established the Negro National League. The St. Louis Giants became one of eight franchise teams, though not one of the best. In their first season they finished in sixth place. On March 31, 1922, Dr. Samuel Shepard and Dick Kent, both black, purchased the franchise, renamed the team the St. Louis Stars, and built Stars Park, which opened in September 1930.[6] The Stars attracted a record number of fans and clinched Negro National League pennants in 1928, 1930, and 1931. By mid-century baseball would be one of America's most popular pastimes.

FAIRGROUND PARK POOL, ST. LOUIS
"Contested Waters"

❖❖❖

This life is like a swimming pool. You dive into the water,
but you can't see how deep it is.

DENNIS RODMAN

Attempts by black urban residents to use public beaches and especially municipal park swimming pools produced some of the angriest battles of the civil rights movement, North and South. During demonstrations like the April 17, 1960, wade-in at Biloxi Beach led by Dr. Gilbert Mason to integrate its bathing facilities, violence was provoked by angry whites. Four years later, Jimmie Brock, owner of the Monson Motor Lodge in St. Augustine, Florida, poured muriatic acid into his swimming pool where an integrated "swim-in" was taking place.

Between 1920 and 1940 nearly two thousand pools were constructed across the United States as competitive swimming became very popular. Children and young adults, black and white, generally learned to swim in local YMCA pools, in church clubs, or in schools where physical exercise was encouraged. In the South, swimming pools were segregated and became, as author Jeff Wiltse notes in his study *Contested Waters*—"another example of contested amusement space."

In 1949 St. Louis desegregated its municipal pool in Fairground Park in response to a federal court ruling that "prohibiting blacks from using public golf courses was a violation of the 14th Amendment."[1] On opening day, June 21, 1949, thirty black children arrived planning to swim in the Fairground Park pool, a grand, ornate structure built in 1913. It was rumored to be able to accommodate 12,000 swimmers at any one time. An angry white crowd subsequently arrived and became so threatening that the police removed the approximately thirty black children from the pool and police were called to escort them out of the park for their safety.

That evening local whites armed with clubs and bricks ran every black person out of Fairground Park and rioted in the downtown. Wiltse describes the rage of a white man who during the riot "encouraged white boys to 'get bricks and smash their heads.'"[2] The press reported that it took between 150 and 400 policemen to quell the melee, and a dozen people were hospitalized. Mayor Joseph Darst reinstituted the pool's segregation policy, and the NAACP subsequently filed suit and won. One year later a federal judge ordered the City of St. Louis to open its pools to all. This case would be cited in part as the basis for the Supreme Court's ruling to desegregate schools in the 1954 *Brown v. Board of Education* decision.

Professor Virginia Walcott of the University of Buffalo maintains that many whites argued that swimming pools were intimate spaces. Gender integration that began in the 1920's made them uncomfortable—men and women clad in scanty attire splashing about in the water troubled them. Mixing races and genders like that seemed to them like playing with fire. In addition, many whites also believed that blacks carried diseases like syphilis that they thought could be passed on in water.[3]

Many urban whites never returned to municipal pools after they were integrated and instead joined or formed their own private swimming clubs. In 1954 St. Louis closed Fairground Pool, and by that time the city was well on its way to becoming one of the most segregated cities in the nation.

TEXAS

COUNTY LINE / UPSHAW, EAST TEXAS
"A Freedmen's Settlement"

❖❖❖

I had crossed the line. I was free; but there was no one there to welcome me to the land of freedom. I was a stranger in a strange land.

HARRIET TUBMAN

"Freedmen's settlements" were communities of formerly enslaved people or black squatters who, after emancipation, avoided the sharecropping system that was just another version of bondage. These freedmen were independent farmers who provided services like blacksmithing or milling. In 1887 an early settlement of freedpeople in Mound Bayou, Mississippi, was established by cousins Isaiah and Joshua Montgomery and Benjamin Green, who had been enslaved on the Davis Bend Plantation owned by Jefferson Davis's brother. The Mound Bayou settlement eventually produced three cotton gins, a sawmill, and several small businesses. Other settlements include Eatontown and Rosewood in Florida; Roanoke Island, North Carolina; Promised Land, South Carolina; and Unionville, Maryland. Whites sometimes referred to them as "free nigger patches."

Although many of these settlements were established across Florida, South Carolina, Georgia, Alabama, and especially Mississippi, the highest concentration were in East Texas on hundreds of wild acres and swampland that periodically flooded. Whites considered it of no value, but freedpeople cleared the land, settled on it, and worked to make it produce.

On May 8, 1967, when Martin Luther King Jr. was interviewed by journalist Sander Vanocur on the issue of black poverty, he reflected,

> America freed the slaves in 1863, through the Emancipation Proclamation of Abraham Lincoln, but gave the slaves no land, and nothing in reality . . . as a matter of fact, to get started on. At the same time, America was giving away millions of acres of land in the West and the Midwest. Which meant that there was a willingness to give the white peasants from Europe an economic base, and yet it refused to give its black peasants from Africa, who came here involuntarily in chains and had worked free for [244] years, any kind of economic base.[1]

❖❖❖

County Line, or Upshaw, was an East Texas freedmen settlement established by Guss, Jim, and Felix Upshaw, three brothers from Tennessee who in 1870 obtained formal title to this swampland by registering it with Nacogdoches County. It was not a simple process, however, and most freedmen simply squatted on unwanted land and quietly farmed it.

In these settlements the church became the center of community life and leisure. Preachers provided spiritual guidance, leadership, and a safe place to express ideas and share information. Congregations built schools, sponsored picnics and sports activities, and celebrated baptisms and weddings. Harvard professor Henry Louis Gates Jr. asserts, "The importance of the role of the black church at its best cannot be gainsaid in the history of the African American people. Nor can it be underestimated."[2] It was the first American institution to be controlled by black people.

As freedmen settlements expanded, shacks hidden away in wooded areas became gathering places for men and women to enjoy music, dancing, gambling, and drinking "likker." These were the "juke joints," later compared with white honky-tonks. "Juke" is believed to be a derivative of the Gullah Geechee word "joog," meaning "wicked conduct."

In her 2002 study "Roomful of Blues: Juke Joints and the Cultural Landscape of the Mississippi Delta," historian Jennifer Nardone explains, "Juke joints were seldom built, but rather appropriated previous spaces. They had different layouts, but all included elements that redefined the previous space. All joints had a bar of some sort (even if only a few cases of beer and a garbage can full of ice), a pool table, a stage area, seats for patrons, and the interior walls were often roughly painted with scenes of celebration (people drinking, dancing, and singing) or with idyllic magazine photos of paradise (palm trees and islands). Celebratory decorations of various kinds often adorned the walls—*Happy Birthday*, Christmas lights, confetti, and tinsel." Nardone explains that juke joints required only the lowest common denominators of celebration, relying on basic decorations and design elements like the bar to establish themselves.[3] In freedmen settlements, juke joints became the testing and proving grounds for new music and dance innovations.

THE VICTORY GRILL, EAST AUSTIN
Austin's Blues Scene

❖❖❖

When white folks want you gone, you gone.
JAMALA ROGERS

A case can be made for East Texas having more in common with the Deep South than the Wild West. Austin, the state capital, had Jim Crow statutes in place by the turn of the century, and in 1928 the city council established a distinct Negro District. At the time, the majority of African American Texans lived in fifteen former freedmen communities—places like Clarkesville, Gregory Town, Pleasantville, and Wheatville. The new Negro District relocated them to East Austin, a working-class black community.

East Austin's downtown was a center of black business ownership, including Dr. Ulysses Young's Hillside Drug Store, Rhambo's Barbershop, the Parisienne Beauty Shop, Arnold's Bakery, Lawson's Ice Cream Parlor, and the Crescent Business School. East Eleventh Street boasted the Deluxe and Driskell Hotels, Charlie's Playhouse, and the Southern Dinette. A community of single-family homes, churches, and schools fanned out beyond the downtown.[1]

In 1929 the Austin City Council passed an ordinance declaring that only those African Americans who lived within the borders of the Negro District would be able to access utilities, sewer lines, garbage collection, paved roads, libraries, schools, and other amenities. The city of Austin would refuse to hook up or maintain utility lines for black residences outside the district. Historian Andrew Busch writes, "In 1930 there were African Americans scattered all over the city but ten years later they were all on the East Side."[2]

Austin set aside seventeen acres in the district for Rosewood Park, "for the exclusive use of African Americans."[3] It was an effort to demonstrate what a modern "separate but equal" neighborhood could look like. Rosewood Park had state-of-the-art playgrounds and picnic areas, tennis courts, a swimming pool, and later baseball fields and a bandstand.

In June 1933 the federal Home Owners' Loan Corporation began offering long-term self-amortizing mortgages. Between 1935 and 1937 it developed a property appraisal system that divided neighborhoods into regions and assigned each a grade. The most desirable areas were designated by green on maps. A once-desirable neighborhood that had reached its peak was blue, yellow signified a district in decline, and red was applied to those said to be in active decline. In 1935, six years after the Negro District was established, it was redlined, making the residents ineligible to apply for government-guaranteed mortgages.[4] In March 2018 a *Washington Post* investigative report revealed that in Baltimore nearly 70 percent of formerly redlined communities remained predominantly minority and lower-income areas.[5]

THE VICTORY GRILL

Johnny Holmes, a black man who ran a juke joint in an old East Austin icehouse, expanded it in 1942 to accommodate African American servicemen on leave from nearby Camp Swift and Fort Hood. They were routinely refused admission to Austin's white establishments and were not welcome in the United Service Organization (USO) cantinas on their own bases. African Americans in uniform were routinely denied the comforts and amusements provided to white soldiers in southern military towns, many of them funded by the USO. Volunteers established black USOs in Hattiesburg, Mississippi, and in Montgomery and Birmingham, Alabama. They used community centers, churches, Masonic and other fraternal temples, and even libraries. Segregated audiences were required on armed forces bases when USO performers toured.

Black vocalist Lena Horne walked off an air base stage in Arkansas when she noticed German prisoners of war sitting in front of black soldiers. She went over to the black GIs, sang to them, and never toured with the USO again. Horne toured on her own or with other black performers for the duration of the war.

Because black servicemen spent so much time in East Austin, the Civilian Conservation Corps agreed to build them an auditorium in Rosewood Park. After the war the park was rededicated to the memory of Dorie Miller, an African American sailor who, without formal training, manned an antiaircraft gun during the 1941 attack on Pearl Harbor. He became the first African American to be awarded the Navy Cross.

Johnny Holmes's success during the war permitted him to expand, and on August 16, 1945, "VJ Day" ("Victory over Japan"), when the Victory Grill. Black soldiers celebrated their discharges there, and by 1947 Holmes had added an outdoor stage and a rooming house for Chitlin Circuit performers like Louis Armstrong, B. B. King, Bobby "Blue" Bland, Ella Fitzgerald, Ike and Tina Turner, Chuck Berry, and later Janis Joplin who all performed on his outdoor stage. Johnny Holmes is remembered as the founder of Austin's blues scene.[6]

Harrison Eppright, former manager of the Austin Convention and Visitors Bureau, recalls the Victory Grill as "a place where black Austinites could enjoy themselves in a way they couldn't any place else in town without suffering the indignities of racial segregation. This gave it an air of pride, and it prospered. . . Everybody thinks we didn't have live music until [Willie] Nelson and [Waylon] Jennings came along, but that's not true. There was a thriving scene in the city long before then—and the Victory Grill was its focal point."[7]

URBAN RENEWAL

After the 1968 Federal Fair Housing Act banned racial discrimination, redlining became illegal. In November 1968, however, East Austin began a program of urban renewal. Most of the old stores, clubs, and businesses along East Eleventh Street (including the Deluxe Hotel) were demolished. Many long-time East Austin residents were forced into the suburbs, where rents kept rising and private homes were impossible to afford or to maintain.

Austin became one of the fastest-growing and trendiest of American cities. Ironically, it is both the most liberal and the most racially segregated municipality in Texas. While public funds were used to attract investment and subsidize its development, virtually no investment was made in affordable housing.[8] Gentrification began in the late 1990s.

The uneasy history of East Austin includes both forced relocation in 1930 and removal by gentrification sixty years later. The legacy that cannot be stolen or denied, however, is the music.

BLACK RODEOS AND TRAILBLAZERS, WEST TEXAS

❖❖❖

> They numbered thousands, among them many of
> the best riders, ropers and wranglers.
> **PHILIP DURHAM,** *THE NEGRO COWBOYS*

The word "cowboy" evokes the image of a "hero," a "tough guy," or a "superstar," yet it was once a pejorative term. The white men who herded cattle, broke horses, and worked on ranches were "cowhands." Black men who did these same things, and there were many of them, were "cowboys," branded with a term that diminished them, despite the fact that historians report one in four American cowhands were black.[1]

The earliest evidence of black cattle herders in North America was in colonial South Carolina in 1724 when enslaved "stock grazers" or "cow hunters" from Senegal in West Africa were sought because of their skills. Carolina planters often raised livestock, including cattle, hogs, and horses. One especially large stock herd was located on James Island, South Carolina. Enslaved Africans managed, branded, and slaughtered the stock, allowing planters to produce salted beef for export to the British West Indies.[2]

By the early 1850s, "slave cowboys" were being sent to Texas, and after emancipation many found work there as trail hands, horse breakers, and trainers in the Arizona Territory, California, Nevada, and the New Mexico Territory.

THE WILCOX RANCH

Near Seguin, in Guadalupe County, Texas, Jakes Colony, a freedmen's settlement much like Upshaw (County Line) in East Texas, and Africatown near Mobile, was established in 1870. Four years earlier, in 1866, the Texas Homestead Act had offered 160 acres of public land to every white settler. This benefit was not extended to black people, and so, as in the other former states of the old Confederacy, blacks were forced to settle on unincorporated and by definition inferior land. Researchers have discovered more than 550 settlements of freedpeople in Texas.[3]

Jakes Colony was organized by Henry Wilcox, born in Guinea, enslaved, and emancipated in 1863. The Jakes colonists built Wilcox Ranch, a settlement that included seventy black-owned working ranches and a self-sufficient central community with schools, churches, and a cemetery. There they raised horses, pigs, and chickens, grew a variety of crops, and maintained fruit orchards. Henry Wilcox died in 1922. Lola Wilcox-Moore, a descendent, told the *San Antonio Express News* in 2022, "This is a part of American history most of us never learn. This is an opening for us to step up and edit American history."[4]

Wilcox Ranch, in Jakes Colony, reflected the spirit of black movers and shakers in the early twentieth century who opened businesses and offered services to provide people with basic needs as well as public and private amusements, entertainment, and sports.

BLACK WRANGLERS AND RODEO STARS

Mexican vaqueros taught Anglo ranch hands how to break horses and move cattle, and these skills were eventually tested in competitions between ranches, which later became "rodeos."[5] Nat Love, born a slave in 1854, was an early black rodeo cowhand who had learned to ride and to groom horses on a Tennessee plantation. He left in 1869 at age sixteen to "go west," and almost forty years later wrote and self-published his autobiography, *The Life and Adventures of Nat Love, Better Known in the Cattle Country as Deadwood Dick, by Himself.* Describing his journey, he wrote:

> I at once struck out for Kansas of which I had heard something. And believing it was a good place in which to seek employment. It was in the west, and it was the great west I wanted to see, and so by walking and occasional lifts from farmers going my way and taking advantage of everything that promised to assist me on my way, I eventually brought up at Dodge City, Kansas, which at that time was a typical frontier city, with a great many saloons, dance halls, and gambling houses, and very little of anything else. When I arrived, the town was full of cow boys from the surrounding ranches, and from Texas and other parts of the west. As Kansas was a great cattle center and market, the wild cow boy, prancing horses of which I was very fond, and the wild life generally, all had their attractions for me, and I decided to try for a place with them. Although it seemed to me I had met with a bad outfit, at least some of them, going around among them I watched my chances to get to speak with them, as I wanted to find someone whom I thought would give me a civil answer to the questions I wanted to ask, but they all seemed too wild around town, so the next day I went out where they were in camp.[6]

At the camp the trail boss told Love that he would hire him if he could break the horse known as Good Eye, the wildest of the lot. Love apparently succeeded because he got the job. In 1872 he delivered a herd of cattle to Deadwood in the Dakota Territory, and while there he won $200 in a "cowboy contest" for his roping, throwing, tying, bridling, saddling, and bronco riding skills. He was subsequently known as "Deadwood Dick," a reference to a popular dime novel cowboy hero. Love made a good living working on ranches and competing for prize money, but by the late 1880s cattle drives had become fewer due to the increasing enclosure of private property and the growing number of railroad tracks. In 1889 he built a home in Denver, married, became a Pullman porter on the Denver and Rio Grande Western Railroad, and wrote his memoir.

The old West was more racially diverse than most Americans realize. Mexican vaqueros, Native Americans, Chinese immigrants, African Americans, and European Americans all had a role in its development.

"THE BULLDOGGER"

Bill Pickett, the first national black rodeo cowboy star, was of African American, white, and Cherokee descent. Born in Travis County, Texas, in 1870, he perfected by the age of eighteen a method for wrestling steers down. Pickett enjoyed performing this stunt, which he called "bulldogging," at local county fairs, and he and four of his brothers subsequently established the Pickett Brothers Bronco Busters and Rough Riders Association, a horse-breaking service and rodeo.

In 1905 Pickett was recruited by the 101 Ranch in Ponca City, Oklahoma, 110,000 acres of Indian land covering four Oklahoma counties. The ranch was leased by cattle baron George W. Miller, who had established breeding ranches there as well as an oil refinery, a meatpacking plant, and a vacation community. Miller's sons Joe and Zachary saw Pickett perform that year and hired him on the spot for their rodeo.

Pickett made his first tour with the 101 Ranch Wild West Show in 1907, performing as "The Dusky Demon" along with Buffalo Bill Cody, Will Rogers, Hoot Gibson, and Tom Mix. His "bulldogging" event was one of the most popular on the circuit. In 1922 white silent film maker Richard Norman cast him in *The Bull-Dogger*, which was shot in Oklahoma. It thrilled African American audiences, most of whom had never conceived of, let alone seen, a black rodeo cowboy. Advance publicity for the film included assurance from President Theodore Roosevelt: "Bill Pickett's name will go down in Western history as being one of the best trained ropers and riders the West has produced."

The 101 Ranch Wild West Show thrived until World War I but declined during the Jazz Age and closed in the late 1930s at about the time Bill Pickett died, eleven days after a wild mare kicked him in the head and fractured his skull. He was buried on the grounds of the ranch. The first black cowboy film star, Pickett was inducted into the National Cowboy Hall of Fame in Oklahoma City in 1971.

White rodeo organizations rarely featured black cowboys, and across the 1920s South and all over Texas a resurgent Klan was re-forming, expanding, and sponsoring its own rodeos, circuses, and carnivals.

Decades later, in 1967, shortly after the 1964 Civil Rights Act became law, Myrtis Dightman, a thirty-one-year-old black bull rider from East Texas participated in a Rodeo in Edmonton, Alberta, where he was ranked number one bull rider in the world by the Rodeo Cowboys Association. Sportswriters there, and later in the United States, referred to him "the Jackie Robinson of Rodeo."

Dightman grew up around horses—feeding, branding, and tending herds of cattle to help his father, a cowhand who worked on a sprawling ranch near Crockett, Texas. Myrtis left school in the seventh grade to work there. At eighteen he moved to Houston, accepted a series of opportunities with small rodeos, and eventually carved out a role as a rodeo clown. The clown's job is to keep the bull from injuring a cowboy who gets thrown off a bronco or a bull. It was neither a safe nor an easy job, but he was good at it.

Eventually Dightman became a bull rider and traveled with regional rodeos across the South and the West. Life on the road was not easy. While white riders booked themselves into hotels, he slept in his car and was never sure how white audiences would receive him. Ultimately he won his way to the National Finals Rodeo and became the first African American to compete in the World Series of Rodeo, where he placed second. By 1964 he was ranked seventeenth in the world.

In 1983, Lu Vason, a wealthy black talent promoter and producer whose clients included Prince, Stevie Wonder, and the Pointer Sisters, attended a Cheyenne Frontier Days Celebration in Wyoming where no black cowboys performed—not even Bill Pickett. Infuriated, Vason vowed to create his own black rodeo circuit. His Bill Pickett Invitational Rodeo, which debuted in Denver in 1984, is still held annually in thirty cities across the United States and celebrated its thirty-fifth anniversary in 2019. Two years later it was picked up by network television. "Everybody," Vason said, "told me that I was crazy."

When Vason died in 2015 his widow Valaria Howard-Cunningham became the first black woman to run a rodeo association. "As black audiences were introduced to the Bill Pickett Invitational Rodeo, black cowboys were embraced and in turn have taken pride in this otherwise overlooked piece of their history," she said.[7]

In 1997 Myrtis Dightman was inducted into the Rodeo Hall of Fame in Oklahoma City and subsequently installed into the Professional Bull Riders' Ring of Honor as well. "I've had a good life," Dightman said that night. "I was a cowboy."[8]

STATE AND COUNTY FAIRS AND NATIONAL PARKS

COLORED STATE AND COUNTY FAIRS

❖❖❖

It won't be long before another day / and we're gonna have
a good time / And no one's gonna take that time away /
You can stay as long as you like.

JAMES TAYLOR

The first American state fair opened in Syracuse, New York, in the spring of 1841. Essentially an agricultural exposition, it offered displays of new farming techniques and practices, horse racing competitions, and music—and black people were excluded.

NORTH CAROLINA

In 1879 twenty-two African American residents of Raleigh, North Carolina, organized the Colored Industrial Association to raise funds for a black state fair similar to the one that whites had been enjoying since the 1850s. Charles N. Hunter, a respected black educator, advertised the fair in both the black press and in church bulletins as "an opportunity for our farmers, mechanics, artisans, and educators to come forward and place on exhibition their best productions."

On November 1, 1879, Raleigh's first Colored Fair opened in the city's white fairgrounds, with a parade, brass bands, competitions, and speeches delivered by black and white dignitaries. The white *Charlotte Daily Chronicle* reported that it "was very successful and displayed great advancement in Negro industrial pursuits and many of the higher arts."[1] The Colored Fair continued annually as funds permitted from 1879 through 1930.

Most black fairs in the South developed along similar lines. Local community leaders organized the likes of South Carolina's Negro State Fair Association, planned festivities, raised funds, and scouted locations. They scheduled industrial, agricultural, and artistic demonstrations, offered competitions and prizes, and added entertainment, including children's rides and sometimes circuses and freak shows. While these fairs were popular, they seldom broke even financially.

SOUTH CAROLINA

In 1904 Rev. Richard Carroll of Columbia, South Carolina, black editor of the *Plowman*, chaplain of the Tenth Regiment of Spanish-American War Veterans,

FIG. 11. Newsboys treated to a day at the annual Palmetto State Fair, Columbia, South Carolina, summer of 1955. The fair offered rides, games, and midway entertainment for African Americans.

FIG. 12. Ferris wheel at the Palmetto State Fair in 1966.

and founder of the South Carolina Industrial Home for Small Children, engaged the South Carolina Negro State Fair Association to help establish a state fair tradition. In the summer of 1908 the Palmetto State Fair opened. Well-funded and well-attended, by the 1950s the fair was offering a four-lane midway filled with amusements and rides leased from Prell's Side Shows, including a "Wild Mouse and Trooper" ride. The white *State News* reported that it offered "the largest wild animal show on the road, an astonishing freak show, a minstrel show, and many other entertaining amusements." Attendance approached one hundred thousand during the 1959 season.

This was progress, since in 1917 the South Carolina legislature had required black and white people to be seated in separate sections when the circuses came to town. "Tent shows," the legislation specified, were to maintain separate and clearly marked entrances and exits. Failure to comply was punishable by a $500 fine. It was particularly cruel since circuses were one of the most beloved entertainments of the children of both races.[2]

In 1965 when South Carolina's white state fair desegregated, the Palmetto Fair Association chose to continue independently, and it remained in business until 1971.

TEXAS

Little evidence of any black state fairs survives in Texas, but thanks to Tom Scott, former director of the Fannin County Museum in Bonham, we know that there was at least one held in 1911. Scott queried his counterpart at the Amon Carter Museum in Fort Worth after locating a photograph of black cowboys and trying to identify the source. Searching early editions of the *Bonham Daily Favorite*, the Carter Museum director discovered that the photo was part of a series taken by cowboy photographer Erwin E. Smith at the 1911 Negro State Fair at the Fannin County Fairgrounds.

This black fair was held August 23–27, 1911, with participants and visitors from Texas and Oklahoma. Apparently the organizing committee invited white cowboys to participate in the Saturday night rodeo, but there is no record of whether or not they accepted. The fair was entirely funded by African Americans through the Colored State Fair Association of Texas.[3]

Scott later discovered that a white state fair had also been held in Houston in 1870, and a decade later two others competed for the title of the "Dallas State

Fair." In 1889 the fairs merged to become the Dallas State Fair and subsequently offered a "Colored People's Day." That was eliminated in 1910, followed in 1923 with "Klan Day." African Americans would not be invited back to the Dallas fairgrounds until 1936 when the Texas State Centennial Committee encouraged them to exhibit in a Hall of Negro Life. The exhibit was visited by four hundred thousand people, 60 percent of whom were white. When the exposition ended, the Hall of Negro Life was the first building razed. The Texas Centennial celebrated at "The State Fair of Texas" served as the model for the 1962 Rogers and Hammerstein musical *State Fair*.

CHESTERFIELD COUNTY, VIRGINIA

On October 25, 1911, the first Chesterfield County Fair was held in Virginia, on the courthouse grounds. The whites-only event ran for two days. A colored fair was organized eight years later. Since no written record of that event exists, Richard Griset, a staff writer for the *Chesterfield Observer*, set himself the task of finding out about it. In 2017 he located eighty-seven-year-old Maceo Jones, whose father, R. F. Jones, a farm agent, had managed the black fair. It ran, Maceo said, one week after the white fair using the same grounds. In the early years both fairs were more focused on agriculture than entertainment.

Maceo's son, Marshall, a county extension agent, added that from 1952 to 1975 the black community sponsored four farming clubs and encouraged students to exhibit crops that were judged on both quality and visual display. His neighbor, a retired teacher concurred. "We had science projects, the kids would build things, and the fair was their showtime," she said.

Debra A. Reid, an Eastern Illinois University history professor, explains that the 1910's and '20's were the heydays of black fairs and black owned businesses in the South. After that, the Great Migration—the massive northward and westward movement of blacks to escape southern segregation and lynching, and to pursue economic opportunities—drained people from every other sphere of southern black life.

"Integration with the white fair began sometime in the 1960's, 'best as anyone can remember," Maceo added. When asked about the lack of records and written history of the black fairs Dr. Reid explained that sadly it wasn't unusual. "It's the history of black America that's never discussed, history seemed to leap over [the fairs] and go from the Civil War to Reconstruction then strait to Civil Rights. These farmers worked hard constantly, and against great odds to create the things that they then celebrated at the fair."

When researcher Richard Griset published his findings in the *Chesterfield Observer* on August 30, 2017, during the 104th Chesterfield County Fair, he described the integrated fair as "a symbol of American values and togetherness": "[it] comes on the heels of racially charged violence in nearby Charlottesville, at a time when America's fractured racial history has been brought to the forefront of the national conversation."[4]

THE NATIONAL PARK SERVICE
"Entrusted with the Care of Our National Treasures"

❖❖❖

The food of the soul is light and space.
HERMAN MELVILLE

The National Park Service was established by a 1916 act of Congress to support President Theodore Roosevelt's national parks initiative. Five years later the Park Service was charged with preserving state parks as well—significant landscapes that fell short of national park standards.[1] During the Great Depression the CCC put unemployed men to work constructing state parks, and by 1942 there were 150 in the South alone. Unfortunately, only seven permitted use by African Americans, and their options were limited to visiting a "Negro area" of a national or state park or finding one of the few "Negro parks" generally located near a white one. In either case, African Americans, unlike whites, were not permitted overnight stays.

The "Negro areas" of national and state parks had separate entrances for black people and were little more than picnic grounds. Some had swimming facilities, a few had baseball diamonds, but none included nature trails or other outdoor facilities.[2]

THE TVA

In May 1933 the Tennessee Valley Authority, a public corporation, was established as an instrumentality of the federal government to alleviate flooding in the Tennessee Valley, a region that included parts of Tennessee, Alabama, Mississippi, and Kentucky. The TVA generated cheap electric power, replanted forests, and built "reservoir parks." The Wilson Dam on the Tennessee River near Florence, Alabama, was the first to come under TVA supervision. It consisted of four hundred acres of Muscle Shoals State Park (for whites) and the one-hundred-acre Wilson Negro Park built on land earlier used as a dumping ground. Muscle Shoals Park offered overnight cabins, a nature study center, a lookout tower, nature trails, and access to the riverfront.[3] Historian Nancy Grant notes that while the TVA treated white reservoir parks as financial "pass throughs," African American parks like Wilson or park areas reserved for black people required feasibility studies because they were considered "additional cost outlays."[4]

T. O. FULLER STATE PARK, MEMPHIS

In 1933 Greater Memphis, which included the Arkansas Delta, West Tennessee, and northwestern Mississippi, set aside one thousand acres for "recreation space for negroes." After four years without a plan, the Memphis NAACP petitioned the National Park Service to build a black facility comparable to the white Shelby Farms State Park that had recently been constructed in East Memphis. Shelby had sheltered picnic grounds, tennis courts, barbeque pits, basketball courts, and a baseball diamond. Robert Church Jr. was a member of the NAACP national board of directors at that time. Local NAACP chapters and national NAACP secretary Walter White offered support. E. W. Hale, white chair of the Shelby County Commission, and First Lady Eleanor Roosevelt asked Secretary of the Interior Harold Ickes to intercede after Mrs. Roosevelt was briefed during her 1937 visit to Memphis. Together these provoked a response, if not immediate action.

Secretary Ickes explained to Walter White that because funding for the federal Civilian Conservation Corps had been cut, no new projects were being considered. Commissioner Hale subsequently requested that the Park Service transfer a black CCC crew from Shelby Farms to construct the African American county park that had been added to the schedule in 1932. Construction finally got underway in 1939, but remains of a Native American village were discovered during excavation for a swimming pool. University of Tennessee archaeologists estimated that they dated back to 1000 CE, and the "Fuller Mounds Project" ended park construction. The 188-acre site was fenced off, and in 1952 it was opened as Chucalissa Village Archaeological Park.

In 1938 Shelby County Park for Negroes was finally completed and dedicated as the Rev. Thomas O. Fuller County Park and was re-named Thomas Oscar Fuller State Park in 1942 for an African American editor, pastor and politician who had worked with the Memphis NAACP and the Shelby County commissioners to make the park a reality. Camping facilities, lodges, and hiking trails were completed the following year, a swimming pool was added in 1954, and a golf course and nature center followed in 1957.

CHEROKEE LAKE STATE PARK, AURORA, KENTUCKY

The TVA's Cherokee Lake State Park in Aurora, Kentucky, the only "colored park" in the state, opened in 1951. Camping facilities were added two years later. A 1955 state highway map lists it as "the finest colored vacation site in the South," and it may well have been. National Park Service records document tourists visiting from St. Louis, Chicago, Memphis, and Birmingham, and former Cherokee Park lifeguard James Stubblefield recalled, "[It] attracted people from miles and miles around." "There was people come from as far away as New York," he said, "and they said it was really great because there was nowhere to go like this. They wanted someplace where they could more or less feel at home, with their own kind."[5]

Cherokee Lake State Park's 360 acres included ten vacation cottages with screened-in porches and outfitted with electrical appliances. There were fishing docks, rental canoes, a bathhouse, and a restaurant. Between 1951 and 1963, African American superintendent L. G. Mimms and a staff of thirteen African American men maintained it. While its white sister park Kenlake was four times larger and had a fifty-eight-room Lodge, Joe Creason, a white Louisville *Courier Journal* columnist noted in 1952 that "it would amaze many folks" that such a place as Cherokee existed in Kentucky. "Before Cherokee," he explained, "except for a picnic area near the Kentucky Dam, the state had done nothing in the recreation line for its Negro citizens and travelers. . . . It would be difficult to convince most skeptics that such a park had been built and set aside for Negro Kentuckians."[6]

It *would* indeed be difficult to imagine, but Cherokee Lake was likely part of the border states' last-ditch effort to demonstrate that "separate but equal" parks were viable, and that federal intervention to impose integration was unnecessary.[7] This was the infamous "equalization strategy." Cherokee Lake closed in 1963 after Kentucky governor Bert T. Combs issued an executive order to desegregate the state's public recreation facilities.

Unlike the majority of southern "Negro parks" Cherokee Lake, (despite the questionable intention of its creators), offered visitors a safe and pleasant experience. It was one of the last black parks in the United States. By 1948 the NAACP's Legal Defense Fund was working almost exclusively with plaintiffs bringing suit for desegregation—not equalization, and on November 14, 1955, the U.S. Supreme Court extended the 1954 *Brown* decision to cover public recreation facilities.

JOHNSON BEACH, PERDIDO KEY, FLORIDA

Manhattan Beach in Jacksonville, Florida, was one of several African American recreation facilities in the South that were absorbed by state or county park systems. It became part of Duval County's Kathryn Abbey Hanna Park in the 1970s. Butler's Beach on Anastasia Island also became a state park in 1980.

Less well known were places like Johnson Beach on Florida's Perdido Key, built in 1947 as a whites-only county park and originally called Gulf Beach. Simon W. Boyd, an African American Pensacola dentist, leased the land in 1954 on behalf of the Sunset Riding Club for "the sole use [as] a bathing beach and recreational facilities for colored citizens." The lease was likely approved because Gulf Beach was so isolated. It had been occupied for only three seasons as a Kiwanis summer camp for underprivileged children. "Perdido" means "lost" in both Spanish and Portuguese.

Dr. Boyd was a well-known figure in the civic, political, and social life of black Pensacola. In the 1930s he had purchased a defunct turpentine factory, renovated it, and opened as the Royal Entertainers Club for black Pensacolans (a forerunner of his "Sunset Riding Club").[8] He renamed Gulf Beach "Rosemond Johnson Beach" in honor of army private Rosemond Johnson Jr., a seventeen-year-old African American soldier killed in action on July 26, 1950. Johnson was Escambia County's first casualty of the Korean War. He had carried two wounded soldiers to safety while under fire and was killed as he returned for a third. On April 21, 1950, Johnson was posthumously awarded a Purple Heart. A childhood friend of Boyd's son Simon Jr., Johnson had lied about his age to join the army at fifteen and served with the Twenty-Fourth Infantry Regiment.

In 1956 the Escambia County Commission canceled Boyd's lease, apparently due to his involvement with the Pensacola NAACP Youth Council's civil rights demonstrations supporting the *Brown* decision. Pensacola's white community charged Boyd with using the isolated beach as a staging area for demonstrations.[9] Despite loss of his lease, the name Johnson Beach stuck, and four years later Pensacola's downtown stores lost over 50 percent of their business as the result of African American boycotts, protests, and sit-ins.

On May 8, 1973, Rosemond Johnson Beach became part of the Gulf Islands National Seashore. More twenty-three years later, on June 10, 1996, a monument to Private Johnson was erected by the community. Veterans groups continue to petition the U.S. military to award him a posthumous Silver Star for "gallantry in action."

EPILOGUE
Litigation, White Flight, and Theme Parks
❖❖❖
I swear to the Lord / I still can't see /
why democracy means / everybody but me.
LANGSTON HUGHES

Kevin Kruse, an American historian who specializes in urban and suburban studies, maintains that the most successful segregationist response to the moral demands of the civil rights movement and to the legal authority of the courts, was white flight.[1] During the 1960s nearly sixty thousand whites abandoned Atlanta. Another one hundred thousand left Atlanta proper for the suburbs during the next decade.[2]

Intractable bitterness was a legacy of racial desegregation. Many white working-class Americans believed that integration had been achieved at their expense. They lost amusement parks, playgrounds, golf courses, tennis courts, and swimming pools, while more affluent whites never suffered as they did. *Their* country clubs remained segregated, while courts forced the working class to mix. Integrated swimming pools were seen as especially heinous since they required "interracial intimacy," and pools were the first facilities to close "for the public good." After Atlanta's Candler Park Pool desegregated in 1964, 850 residents signed a petition to close it as "a menace to the peace and tranquility of the community."[3] Mayor Ivan Allen, a former segregationist, disagreed. By the mid-1960s he had become convinced that the South would never prosper with a segregated economy, and he ordered the removal of all "white" and "colored" signs from inside city hall and desegregated its cafeteria. During his two terms in office spanning 1962 and 1970, he desegregated the city. Mayor Allen was the only southern elected official who endorsed the Civil Rights Act of 1964. After Candler Park Pool desegregated, he and his family received death threats.

Whites in major cities (those who could afford to) fled to the suburbs, established homeowner associations, and built private pools, golf courses and tennis courts. Those who remained petitioned municipal governments to close public parks and services or privatize them. Many who had joined the middle class during the postwar economic boom opposed fair housing programs, busing, welfare, and affirmative action. In 1964 British journalist Godfrey Hodgson, on assignment in Atlantic City, New Jersey, to cover the Democratic Convention that year noted, "Those who have most to thank the Democrats for, can most afford to vote Republican. Economically, these working-class groups have prospered. Emotionally and socially, they are insecure. Far more than the mythology of the melting-pot would suggest, they have already chosen segregation for themselves. Poles cling to Polish neighborhoods, Italians tend to marry Italians. And now along comes the Negro, moving into beloved neighborhoods, threatening jobs, and stirring up unsuspected prejudice."[4]

Suburban secessionists defended their right to "free association" and expressed hostility to the federal government. Many joined the conservative revolution that supported school tuition vouchers, privatization of public services, and a tax revolt.[5] Historian Victoria Wolcott points out that, in larger cities, the "[formerly] segregated parks, theaters, and other venues, however popular, were [suddenly] no longer considered premium recreation sites by whites." After whites fled, many municipal governments ceased funding or even maintaining them.[6] In 1968 the U.S. Commission on Marine Science, Engineering and Resources reported a "growing tendency by counties and municipalities adjoining large urban areas to restrict access to local residents . . . [and] to discriminate against low-income groups and racial minorities."[7] They achieved this by imposing beach fees, limiting parking, and passing resident-only ordinances.

In 1950, Robert Dawson, who was black, filed suit in *Dawson v. Mayor and City Council of Baltimore* after he was denied use of a public beach in Baltimore's Fort Smallwood Park. The park, owned by the city since 1927, had never admitted African Americans. In 1952, Dawson prevailed, and Smallwood was ordered to cease discriminating. The decision imposed a "separate but equal" remedy. Specific days were set aside when black people could swim at the park. When the NAACP objected, U.S. district court judge Rozel Thomsen maintained that he had been "persuaded that violence would ensue if segregated recreation was outlawed." While the judge did not have authority to dismiss the *Dawson* suit, he could (and did) appeal to custom. "Swimming" he said, "was more sensitive than schools." He cited State Attorney Edward Harlan's argument: "It is better for public safety in any activity involving physical contact that the races be separated." Judge Thomsen concurred with the state attorney that Maryland's primary responsibility was to "keep order and prevent riots."[8]

In 1955 the U.S. Fourth Circuit Court overturned Judge Thomsen's decision, and the following year the U.S. Supreme Court extended the *Brown* decision to include state facilities, effectively making public park segregation unconstitutional. The City of Baltimore was ordered to open its public recreation facilities to all the public.[9] Five years later, the chairman of the Charlotte (North Carolina) Park and Recreation Commission, while conceding that "all people have a right under the law to use public facilities including swimming pools," still maintained that "swimming pools put the tolerance of white people to the test," and concluded that "public order is more important than rights of Negroes to use public facilities."[10] This determination was based, at least in part, on a cultural fallacy—that the demand for equal access arose from the desire of African Americans to interact socially with whites and ultimately to intermarry. Black playwright and activist Lorraine Hansberry argued that to the contrary integration was "the removal of all barriers to the construction of solidarity among the children of the American working class—both white and black." Integration, she maintained, was "not a sign that African Americans wish to be absorbed into this house, but rather that 'the Negro people would like to see this house rebuilt.'"[11] Writer James Baldwin was more blunt. "I do not know many Negroes who are eager to be 'accepted' by white people," he wrote in *The Fire Next Time*, "and still less to be loved by them; they, the blacks, simply don't wish to be beaten over the head by the whites every instant of our brief passage on this planet."

"Segregation," "desegregation," and "integration" had very different connotations across America's social, political, and racial divides. African Americans, for example, considered segregated public amusement facilities a denial of their constitutionally protected right to access public accommodations. Parks, pools, beaches, and playgrounds invited public participation, and they, after all, were members of the public. For many whites, integration signified little more than trespassing, and desegregation meant the devaluation of their property.

THEME PARKS

As amusement parks declined, theme parks were established for the class that could afford them. They were designed to minimize an African American presence. Most were difficult if not impossible to reach by public transportation and charged high admission fees. They were either walled in or gated to preclude the free strolling that was a hallmark of the older parks that charged by the ride.

Theme parks were advertised as "cleaner" and "safer." places. Architect Michael Sorkin describes them as presenting "happy regulated vision[s] of pleasure—all those artfully hoodwinking forms—as a substitute for the democratic public realm, and [doing] so appealingly by stripping troubled urbanity of its sting, of the presence of the poor, of crime, of dirt, of work."[12]

In July 1955 Walt Disney transformed the amusement park industry when he opened Disneyland in Anaheim, California, to offer a completely new and focused series of experiences. Visitors could escape into nostalgia, fantasy, or the future. John Hench, then creative director for the Disney Company, explained, "What we create is a 'Disney Realism,' sort of Utopian in nature, where we carefully program out the negative, unwanted elements and program in the positive."[13] In truth, black life was whitewashed with the assistance of a sanitized and avuncular Uncle Remus.

Historian Eric Avila maintains that Disneyland provided "a suburban alternative to the disordered chaos of modern city culture," adding that "it was the very antithesis of Coney Island." There were no freaks, no sideshows, no penny arcades or hangouts, no vulgarity. Disneyland was all about order, homogeneity, and predictability, with a nostalgic emphasis on family.[14]

In the June 7, 1958 issue of *The Nation*, screenwriter Julian Halevy published a scathing description of his trip to Disneyland. "As in the Disney movies," he wrote, "the whole world, the universe, and all man's striving for dominion over self and nature, have been reduced to a sickening blend of cheap formulas packaged to sell. Romance, Adventure, Fantasy, Science are ballyhooed and marketed; life is bright-colored, clean, cute, titillating, safe, mediocre, inoffensive to the lowest common denominator, and somehow poignantly inhuman. . . . But the overwhelming feeling that one carries away is sadness for the empty lives which accept such tawdry substitutes."

NOTES

PREFACE

1. Charles Denson, *Coney Island Lost and Found* (Berkley: Ten Speed Press, 2007), 134.
2. Martin Tolchin, "Coney Island Slump Grows Worse," *New York Times*, July 2, 1964.
3. Denson, *Coney Island Lost and Found*, 135
4. Ibid., 14.

INTRODUCTION

1. Robert McKay, "Segregation and Public Recreation," *Virginia Law Review* 40, no. 6 (October 1954): 703.
2. William O'Brien, *Landscapes of Exclusion: State Parks and Jim Crow in the American South* (Amherst: University of Massachusetts Press, 2015), 6.
3. Nancy McArdle and Dolores Acevedo-Garcia, "Consequences of Segregation for Children's Opportunity and Well Being," presentation at "A Shared Future: Fostering Communities of Inclusion in an Era of Inequality," symposium hosted by the Harvard Joint Center for Housing Studies, April 2017.
4. Forrester B. Washington, "Recreation Facilities for the Negro," *Annals of the American Academy of Political and Social Sciences* 140 (November 1928): 276–77.
5. Myrdal, Gunnar Myrdal, *An American Dilemma: The Negro Problem and American Democracy*, first published 1962 (New York: Routledge, 1995),
6. C. Vann Woodward, *The Strange Career of Jim Crow* (New York: Oxford University Press, 1974), 7.
7. Robin D. G. Kelley, *Race Rebels: Culture, Politics and the Black Working Class* (New York: Free Press, 1996), 45.

SUBURBAN GARDENS, DEANWOOD

1. Deanwood History Commission, *Washington D.C.'s Deanwood* (Charleston, S.C.: Arcadia, 2008), 6.
2. *Deanwood 1880–1950: A Model of Self-Sufficiency in Far Northeast Washington, D.C.* (Washington, D.C.: Deanwood History Project, 2005).
3. Deanwood Historic Project, 104.
4. Preston Lauterbach, *The Chitlin' Circuit and the Road to Rock 'n' Roll* (New York: Norton, 2011), 9–12.
5. Ibid., 10.

BLACK MINSTREL AND VAUDEVILLE SHOWS

1. Edwin S. Grosvenor and Robert Toll, "Blackface: The Sad History of Minstrel Shows," *American Heritage*, Winter 2019, https://www.americanheritage.com/blackface-sad-his.

2. Zaron Burnett III, "The Complex Legacy of Black Comedians in Blackface," *MEL*, n.d., https://melmagazine.com/en-us/story/black-comedians-blackface-minstrel-show-history.

3. W. C. Handy, *Father of the Blues: An Autobiography* (New York: Da Capo, 1969), 13–16.

4. Marc Kirkeby, "The Brightest Days of the Marshall," NYC Department of Records & Information services, April 4, 2017, https://www.archives.nyc/blog/2017/4/20/the-brightest-days-of-the-marshall. Ellipses in original.

5. Richard Snow, "Bert Williams," *American Heritage*, August/September 1980, https://www.americanheritage.com/bert-williams.

THE THEATRICAL OWNERS BOOKING AGENCY

1. Nadine George-Graves, *The Royalty of Negro Vaudeville: The Whitman Sisters and the Negotiation of Race, Gender, and Class in the African American Theater, 1900–1940* (New York: Palgrave MacMillan, 2000), 104, 127.

2. David Nasaw, *Going Out: The Rise and Fall of Public Amusements* (New York: Basic, 1993), 50–51.

3. Nadine George-Graves, "Spreading the Sand: Understanding the Economic and Creative Impetus for the Black Vaudeville Industry," *Continuum: The Journal of African Diaspora, Drama, Theatre and Performance* 1, no. 1 (June 2014), https://continuumjournal.org/index.php/spreading-the-sand.

4. Jason E. Ellerbee, "African American Theaters in Georgia: Preserving an Entertainment Legacy," master's thesis, University of Georgia, 2004, 16.

5. *Baltimore Afro-American*, January 19, 1929.

6. Timothy J. Fisher, "You Must Be This to Ride: Class, Gender and Race in the American Amusement Park," master's thesis, Washington and Lee University, 2015.

"BLACK BROADWAY," GREATER U STREET

1. *The Story of Black Broadway Before Harlem*, https://blackbroadwayonu.com/.

2. Jessica Weiss, "A Portrait of a Community: The Life of Shaw," *University of Maryland Undergraduate History Journal*, Fall 2004, 10–12.

3. *Washington Star*, October 22, 1966.

HIGHLAND BEACH, ANNE ARUNDEL COUNTY

1. W. E. B. Dubois, "Reconstruction and Its Benefits," *American History Review*, no. 15 (July 1910), 786.

2. Adel Logan Alexander, *Homelands and Waterways: The American Journey of the Bond Family, 1846–1926* (New York: Pantheon, 1999), 450.

3. Ibid., 446.

4. Andrew W. Kahrl, *The Land Was Ours: How Black Beaches Became White Wealth in the Coastal South* (Chapel Hill: University of North Carolina Press, 2012), 102.

5. Ralph Matthews, "Heard and Seen in Baltimore" *Baltimore Afro- American*, August 21, 1926.

6. *New York Times*, September 4, 2009.

7. Kahrl, *The Land Was Ours*, 108.

8. Patsy Moss Fletcher, *Historically African American Leisure Destinations around Washington D.C.* (Charleston, S.C.: History Press, 2015), 155–56.

9. Ibid., 157.

10. Michael Andrew Fitzpatrick, "Shaw, Washington's Premier Black Neighborhood: An Examination of the Origins and Development of a Black Business Movement, 1880–1920" (master's thesis, University of Virginia, 1989), 73–75.

11. "African-American Sites along the Patuxent River: Eagle Harbor," Maryland Park Service, https://web.archive.org/web/20091018114156/www.dnr.maryland.gov/publiclands/aapaxeagle.html.

12. "The Cedar Haven Documents," University of Maryland Archives and Manuscript Collection, McKelden Library, College Park, Maryland.

13. Karl, *The Land Was Ours*, 94.

14. "Protest Tax Raise in Prince Georges," *Baltimore Afro-American*, February 11, 1928. See also Karl, *The Land Was Ours*, 94–95.

WASHINGTON PARK, PRINCE GEORGE'S COUNTY

1. Les Washington, *Generations: A Commentary on the History of African American Immigrants and Their American Descendants* (Bloomington, Ind.: iUniverse, 2002), 53.

2. Kahrl, *The Land Was Ours*, 39.

3. Ibid., 40.

4. Fletcher, *Historically African American Leisure Destinations around Washington D.C.*, 67.

5. "Out of the Attic: Collingwood Beach: An Early African American Resort," *Alexandria (Va.) Times*, August 8, 2018.

6. Kahrl, *The Land Was Ours*, 43.

7. "Mr. Jefferson's Boats," *Washington Bee*, July 17, 1909, 4.

8. "The River Queen: Col. Lewis Jefferson Now in Charge. The Colored People Have Purchased the Entire Interest of Mr. Bessinger," *Washington Bee*, May 13, 1911, p. 1.

9. Andrew Kahrl, "The Slightest Semblance of Unruliness: Steamboat Excursions, Pleasure Resorts and the Emergence of Segregation Culture on the Potomac River," *Journal of American History* 94, no. 4 (March 2008): 1119.

10. Ibid., 1130.

11. Ibid., 1120.

12. Fletcher, *Historically African American Leisure Destinations around Washington D.C.*, 74.

BROWN'S GROVE, ROCK CREEK

1. James Roland Coates Jr., "Recreation and Sport in the African American Community of Baltimore, 1890–1920" (PhD diss., University of Maryland, 1991), 2.

2. Ibid., 191–92.

3. "Baltimore's Colored Parks," *Billboard*, July 5, 1924, 7–8.

4. Gilbert Sandler, *Small Town Baltimore* (Baltimore: Johns Hopkins University Press, 2002), 82–83.

5. "The Great Colored Resort," *Baltimore Afro-American*, July 19, 1904.

6. Mandy Melton, *Anne Arundel County's Historic Beach Resorts* (Annapolis, Md.: Anne Arundel County Trust for Preservation, 2017), 42.

7. Sandler, *Small Town Baltimore*, 83.

8. Kahrl, "The Slightest Semblance of Unruliness," 1136.

9. Gilbert Sandler, "When Brown's Grove Went Up in Smoke," *Baltimore Sun*, August 22, 1995.

EDGEWATER BEACH PARK, TURNER STATION

1. Linda Zeidman, "Sparrows Point, Dundalk, Highland Town, Old West Baltimore: Home of Gold Dust and the Union Card," in *The Baltimore Book New Visions of Local History*, edited by Elizabeth Fee, Linda Shopes and Linda Ziedman (Philadelphia: Temple University Press, 1991), 175–203.

2. Ibid., 183.

3. Woodward, *The Strange Career of Jim Crow*, 100.

4. Louis Diggs, *From the Meadows to the Point: The Histories of the African American Community of Turner Station and of Sparrows Point* (Baltimore: L. Diggs, 2003), 219–22.

5. Robyn N. Smith, "Life on the North Side: The African American Community in Sparrows Point," *Reclaiming Kin: Taking Back What Was Once Lost*, March 2018, https://www.reclaimingkin.com/wp-content/uploads/2018/03/Sparrows-Point-Article.pdf.

CARR'S AND SPARROW'S BEACHES, ANNAPOLIS

1. Ronald J. Stephens, "Carr and Sparrow's Beach, Annapolis, Maryland (1926–1974)," *BlackPast*, April 23, 2004, https://www.blackpast.org/african-american-history/carr-and-sparrow-s-beach-annapolis-maryland-1926-1974.

2. Carr's Beach Community, www.carrsbeach.com/.

3. Ann Powell, "Remembering Carr's Beach: The Most Popular African American Beach and Music Venue on the Chesapeake," *Annapolis Discovered*, March 26, 2021, https://www.visitannapolis.org/blog/stories/post/remembering-carrs-beach-the-most-popular-african-american-beach-and-music-venue-on-the-chesapeake.

4. Robyn-Denise Yourse, "Carr's Beach Parties On in Hearts of Area Blacks," *Washington Times*, July 4, 2007.

5. Theodora Aidoo, "Remembering the Carr Sisters Who Created Beaches Exclusively for Blacks during the Segregation Era," *Face2Face Africa*, January 29, 2020, https://face2faceafrica.com/article/remembering-the-carr-sisters-who-created-beaches-exclusively-for-blacks-during-the-segregation-era.

WILMER'S PARK, PRINCE GEORGE'S COUNTY

1. "Wilmer's Park," Maryland Historical Trust Inventory of Historical Properties Form, no. PG 86B-037, prepared by Stacy Patterson, architectural historian, March 5, 2009, https://www

.mncppcapps.org/planning/HistoricCommunitiesSurvey/Documentations/86B-037/86B-037_Wilmers%20Park_MIHP%20Form.pdf.

2. Natalie Hopkinson, "Music, Memories at Wilmer's," *Washington Post*, August 18, 1999.

THE CHITLIN' CIRCUIT

1. Preston Lauterbach, *The Chitlin' Circuit and the Road to Rock 'n' Roll* (New York: Norton, 2011), 147.

2. Ibid., 266.

3. Ibid., 265–68.

4. Andrew Read, "Jazz Speaks for Life: M.L.K. at the Berlin Jazz Festival in 1964," *Portside*, January 21, 2019, https://portside.org/2022-04-02/jazz-speaks-life-martin-luther-king-berlin-jazz-fest-1964.

SEAVIEW BEACH RESORT AND AMUSEMENT PARK, NORFOLK

1. Earl Lewis, *In Their Own Interests: Race, Class and Power in Twentieth-Century Norfolk, Virginia* (Berkeley: University of California Press, 1991), 83.

2. "A Plea for Fair Play," *Journal and Guide* (Norfolk, Va.), August 4, 1923.

3. Lewis, *In Their Own Interests*, 85.

4. Ibid., 90.

5. Quoted in Denise Watson, "More than a 'Little Place for Coloreds,'" *Virginian-Pilot*, July 8, 2018.

6. "Resort Operators Prepare for Gala Season: Opening Set," *Journal and Guide* (Norfolk, Va.), May 29, 1948.

7. Andrew W. Kahrl, *The Land Was Ours: How Black Beaches Became White Wealth in the Coastal South* (Chapel Hill: University of North Carolina Press, 2012), 82.

8. "Sea View Attracts Negro Society," *Life*, August 18, 1947, https://oldlifemagazine.com/august-18-1947-life-magazine.html.

9. Ibid.

10. O. McColum, "Looking in on Norfolk," *Journal and Guide* (Norfolk, Va.), November 6, 1945.

11. Ibid.

SHELL ISLAND RESORT, WILMINGTON

1. Andrew Morgan Benton, "The Press and the Sword: Journalism, Racial Violence and Political Control in Postbellum, North Carolina" (master's thesis, North Carolina State University, 2016), 61.

2. Quoted in LeeAnn White, "Rebecca Latimer Felton and the Wife's Farm: The Class and Racial Politics of Gender Reform," *Georgia Historical Quarterly* 76, no. 2 (Summer 1992): 354–72.

3. Glenda Gilmore, *Gender and Jim Crow: Women and the Politics of White Supremacy in North Carolina, 1896–1920* (Chapel Hill: University of North Carolina Press, 1996), 105–7.

4. David W. Blight, "An American Pogrom," review of David Zucchino's *Wilmington Lie: The*

Murderous Coup of 1898 and the Rise of White Supremacy, New York Review of Books, November 19, 2020, 25.

5. Cripps quoted in Leon A. Prather, *We Have Taken a City: Wilmington's Racial Massacre and Coup of 1898* (Rutherford, N.J.: Fairleigh Dickinson University Press, 1984), 166.

6. Kahrl, *The Land Was Ours,* 158.

7. Ray McAllister, *Wrightsville Beach: The Luminous Island* (Winston-Salem: John Blair, 2007), 67–68.

8. Ibid., 68.

9. Ibid.

10. Caleb Crain, "What a White Supremacist Coup Looks Like," *New Yorker,* April 20, 2020, 42–46.

11. "Pine Crest Inn, Negro Amusement Center, Destroyed by Explosion," *Roanoke Times,* September 7, 1926.

12. Kevin Maurer, "White Sand, Shell Island: The 20th Century 'Negro Atlantic City' That Never Was" *Port City Daily* (Wilmington, N.C.), February 10, 2022.

SEA BREEZE AND BOP CITY, NEW HANOVER COUNTY

1. Elaine Blackman Henson, *Carolina Beach* (Charleston, S.C.: Acadia, 2007), 8.

2. Kahrl, *The Land Was Ours,* 157.

3. Susan Block, *Cape Fear Beaches* (Charleston, S.C.: Arcadia, 2000), 112.

4. Elizabeth Hines, "Sea Breeze to Sherbet Town: An Historic African American Beach Resort Lost to Affluenza," *North Carolina Geographer,* no. 19 (2000), 9–10.

5. Susan Block, *Along the Cape Fear River* (Charleston, S.C.: Arcadia, 1998), 99.

6. Herbert L. White, "Ocean Divide," *Our State,* November 3, 2013, accessed August 14, 2019, www.ourstate.com/.

7. "Malcolm Ray 'Chicken' Hicks," *Wilmington Star-News,* July 6, 2004, https://www.starnewsonline.com/story/news/2004/07/06/malcolm-ray-chicken-hicks/30555858007. For more on Sea Breeze, see Rebecca Taylor, "Sea Breeze: A History," parts 1 through 5, Federal Point Historic Preservation Society, http://federal-point-history.org/.

8. Assata Shakur, *Assata: An Autobiography* (Chicago: Chicago Review Press, 2001), 25.

CHOWAN BEACH, WINTON

1. George Farrell and Rawl Gelinas, "The History of Chowan Beach," Chowan Beach Recreation Association, http://www.chowanbeach.com/cb-history-preface.html.

2. Marvin T. Jones, "The Leading Edges: The Tri-Racial People of the Winton Triangle," in *Carolina Genesis: Beyond the Color Line,* edited by Scott Withrow (Palm Coast, Fla.: Backintyme, 2010), 187–89.

3. Ibid., 216.

4. Dudley Flood and Ben Watford, *You Can't Fall Off the Floor,* (Bloomington, Ind.: AuthorHouse, 2009), 94.

5. Norma Cromwell Fields, "Blacks in Norfolk, Virginia during the 1930's" (Master's thesis, Old Dominion University, 1979).

6. Frank Stephenson, *Cowan Beach: Remembering an African American Resort* (Charleston, S.C.: History, 2009), 18.

MOSQUITO BEACH, JAMES ISLAND

1. Ramon Jackson, "A Trip Back in Time: Mosquito Beach," in *Discover South Carolina: 2022 Vacation Guide* ([Columbia]: [South Carolina Department of Parks, Recreation & Tourism], 2022), 15.

2. Oral histories of Richard Brown (April 24, 2019), Cassandra Roper (February 14, 2019), and Russell Roper and Cubby Wilder (2019). All were conducted and recorded by Michael and Latanya Allen in support of a National Register nomination for Mosquito Beach. Voices of Mosquito Beach, https://www.historicmosquitobeach.com/home/faces-and-places/voices-of-mosquito-beach.

3. "Beaches, Black, Jim Crow Era," in *The New Encyclopedia of Southern Culture*, vol. 16, edited by Harvey H. Jackson (Oxford: University of Mississippi, 2011), 46.

ATLANTIC BEACH, HORRY COUNTY

1. Susan Hoffer McMillan, *Myrtle Beach and the Grand Strand* (Charleston, S.C.: Arcadia, 2004), 12–24.

2. Catherine Lewis, *Horry County, South Carolina, 1730–1933* (Columbia: University of South Carolina Press, 1995), 13.

3. Sherry Shuttles, *Atlantic Beach* (Charleston, S.C.: Arcadia Press, 2009), 10.

4. Ibid., 23.

5. P. Nicole King, *Sombreros and Motorcycles in a Newer South: The Politics of Aesthetics in South Carolina's Tourism Industry* (Jackson: University Press of Mississippi, 2012), 115.

6. Lewis, *Horry County, South Carolina*, 84.

7. Elizabeth Leland, *The Vanishing Coast* (Durham, N.C.: Blair, 1996), 73.

8. King, *Sombreros and Motorcycles in a Newer South*, 115.

9. Ronald Smothers, "Black Resort in South Splits over Developing," *New York Times*, August 16, 1989.

10. Leland, *Vanishing Coast*, 73.

11. Barbara Stokes, *Myrtle Beach: A History 1900–1980* (Columbia: University of South Carolina Press, 2007), 192–96.

12. Ibid., 195–96.

13. Ibid., 198.

14. Smothers, "Black Resort in South Splits."

15. Ibid.

16. King, *Sombrerosand Motorcycles in a Newer South*, 152.

17. *Oaks News* (Orangeburg, S.C.), February 1, 2009.

18. King, *Sombreros and Motorcycles in a Newer South*, 186.

CHURCH'S PARK, MEMPHIS

1. T. H. Watkins, "If Beale Street Could Talk, *American Heritage*, February/March 1979, 52–53.
2. Thomas E. Young, *Memphis World*, "Picnics Forty Years Ago," May 12, 1933.
3. *North and South Magazine* (Montgomery, Ala.), vol. 2 (1901).
4. Henry T. Sampson, *Blacks in Blackface: A Sourcebook on Early Black Musical Shows* (Lanham, Md.: Scarecrow Press, 1980), 22, 66.
5. Nadine George-Graves, "Spreading the Sand: Understanding the Economic and Creative Impetus for the Black Vaudeville Industry," *Continuum: The Journal of African Diaspora Drama, Theatre and Performance* 1, no. 1 (June 2014): 1.
6. Preston Lauterbach, *Beale Street Dynasty: Sex, Segregation, and the Struggle for the Soul of Memphis* (New York: Norton, 2015), 122.
7. Lauterbach, *Beale Street*, 1.
8. *Memphis Watchman*, January 1888.
9. Lauterbach, *Beale Street*, 72.
10. Grace Hale, *Making Whiteness: The Culture of Segregation in the South 1890–1940* (New York: Pantheon, 1998), 208–9.
11. Ibid., 210.
12. Lauterbach, *Beale Street*, 65.
13. Hale, *Making Whiteness*, 208–9.
14. Andrew Kahrl, "On the Beach: Race and Leisure in the Jim Crow South" (PhD diss., Indiana University, 2008), 176.
15. *Memphis Commercial Appeal*, February 20, 1911.
16. Darius Young, *Robert R. Church Jr. and the African American Political Struggle* (Gainesville: University Press of Florida, 2019), 24–27.
17. Roger Biles, *Memphis and the Great Depression* (Knoxville: University of Tennessee Press,1986), 45.
18. Annette and Roberta Church, *The Robert R. Churches of Memphis: A Father and Son Who Achieved in Spite of Race* (Ann Arbor: Edwards Brothers, 1974), 3.
19. *Memphis Commercial Appeal*, October 23, 1956.
20. Richard Wallace, "Defeat Comes to Boss Crump," *National Civic Review* 37, no. 8 (September 1948): 410.

1. N1>Greenwood Park, Nashville

1. *Iowa State Bystander*, September 29, 1905.
2. August Meier and Elliott Rudwick, "Negro Boycotts of Jim Crow Streetcars in Tennessee," *American Quarterly* 21 no. 4 (Winter 1969): 757.
3. Jae Jones, "Greenwood Park, Nashville's First Recreation Park for African Americans," *Black Then: Discovering Our History*, April 30, 2022, https://blackthen.com/greenwood-park-nashvilles-first-recreation-park-for-african-americans.

THE ATLANTA COTTON STATES AND INTERNATIONAL EXPOSITION

1. Dorothy Berry, "Black America, 1985," *Public Domain Review*, February 24, 2021, https://publicdomainreview.org/essay/black-america-1895/.

2. Theda Perdue, *Race and the Atlanta Cotton States Exposition of 1895* (Athens: University of Georgia Press, 2010), 1.

3. Charles L. Lumpkins, *American Pogrom: The East St. Louis Race Riot and Black Politics* (Athens: Ohio University Press, 2008), 53.

4. Perdue, *Race and the Atlanta Cotton States Exposition*, 3.

5. Stephen Tuck, *We Ain't What We Ought to Be: The Black Freedom Struggle from Emancipation to Obama* (Cambridge, Mass.: Belknap Press of Harvard University Press, 2011), 104

6. Elizabeth Hale, *Making Whiteness: The Culture of Segregation in the South 1890–1940* (New York: Pantheon, 1998), 149.

7. Mabel O. Wilson, *Negro Building: Black Americans in the World's Fairs and Museums* (Berkeley: University of California Press, 2012), 74.

8. Louis R. Harlan, *Booker T. Washington: The Making of a Black Leader, 1856–1901* (New York: Oxford University Press, 1972), 227.

9. Ibid.

KING'S WIGWAM COUNTRY CLUB, KENNESAW

1. Edward Randolph Carter, *The Black Side: A Partial History of the Business, Religious and Educational Side of the Negro in Atlanta* (Atlanta, 1894), 157–62.

2. Arica L. Coleman, "How a Court Answered a Forgotten Question of Slavery's Legacy," *Time*, September 11, 2017, https://time.com/author/arica-l-coleman.

3. Ibid.

4. John Dittmer, *Black Georgia in the Progressive Era, 1900–1920*, (Urbana: University of Illinois Press, 1977), 5.

5. Nina K. Miller obituary, *Atlanta Constitution*, September 16, 1983.

6. Kenneth Janken, *White: The Biography of Walter White, Mr. NAACP* (New York: New Press, 2003), 13.

7. Wyn Craig Wade, *The Fiery Cross: The Ku Klux Klan in America* (New York: Oxford University Press, 1987), 139.

8. Pete Daniel, *Standing at the Crossroads: Southern Life in the Twentieth Century* (New York: Hill & Wang, 1986), 81.

9. Ursula Wolfe-Rocca, "The Red Summer of 1919 Explained," *Teen Vogue*, April 8, 2019, https://www.teenvogue.com/story/the-red-summer-of-1919-explained.

10. Edgar Webster, *Chums and Brothers* (Boston: Badger, 1920), 51–52.

11. Stephen Birmingham, *Certain People: America's Black Elite* (Boston: Little, Brown, 1977), 182–85.

SWEET AUBURN/ATLANTA'S STROLL

1. Clifford M. Kuhn, Harlon E. Joye, and E. Bernard West, *Living Atlanta: An Oral History of the City, 1914–1948* (Athens: University of Georgia Press, 1990), 6.

2. Herman Mason Jr., *Black Atlanta in the Roaring Twenties* (Charleston, S. C.: Arcadia, 1997), 6.

3. Ibid., 7.

4. Candice Dyer, "The Royal Peacock: Atlanta's 'Club Beautiful,'" *Candice Dyer's Writing: The Offbeat from the Lowbrow to the High-End*, May 11, 2010, https://anticsincandyland.files.wordpress.com/2010/05.

5. Quoted in Connor Towne O'Neill, "Nightclubbing: Royal Peacock," *Red Bull Music Academy*, August 18, 2016.

OVERTOWN, MIAMI-DADE COUNTY

1. David Leon Chandler, *Henry Flagler: The Astonishing Life and Times of the Visionary Robber Baron Who Founded Florida* (New York: MacMillan, 1986).

2. Ibid.

3. Roderick Waters, "Dr. William B. Sawyer of Colored Town," *Tequesta* 57 (1997), 72.

4. Jordan Levin, "Miami's Overtown Was Once a Mecca of Music," *Miami Herald*, January 31, 2009

5. Raymond Mohl, "Shadows in the Sunshine: Race and Ethnicity in Miami," *Tequesta*, vol. 62 (1989), 76.

6. Ira De A. Reid, *The Negro Immigrant: His Background, Characteristics and Social Adjustment 1899–1937*" (New York City: Columbia University Press, 1938), 189.

7. "500 Greatest Albums List," *Rolling Stone*, 2003, https://www.rollingstone.com/music/music-lists/500-greatest-albums-of-all-time-156826.

8. Robin Faith Bachin, ed., *Race, Housing, and Displacement in Miami* (Coral Gables: University of Miami, 2020).

9. Paul S. George and Thomas K. Petersen, "Liberty Square: 1933–1987, The Origins and Evolution of a Public Housing Project," *Tequesta* 48 (1988), 54.

10. Marvin Dunn, "Bygone Days: The Sweet Music of Miami's Overtown," *Miami Herald*, February 1, 2009.

MANHATTAN BEACH AND JACKSONVILLE'S MOVIES

1. Matt Soergal, "Manhattan Beach, a Resort for African Americans Once Flourished in Hanna Park Dunes," *Florida Times Union*, May 4, 2008, p. 8.

2. Ennis Davis, "The Line: Jacksonville's Notorious Red Light District, *The Jaxon*, Jacksonville, Florida, April 15, 2019.

3. Gregory Waller, "Another Audience," in *Exhibition: The Film Reader*, ed. Ina Rae Hark (London: Routledge, 2001), 31.

4. Thomas Cripps, *Slow Fade to Black* (New York: Oxford University Press, 1977), 170.

5. Ibid., 173.

6. Robert Cassanello, *To Render Invisible: Jim Crow and Public Life in New South Jacksonville* (Gainesville: University Press of Florida, 2013), 147.

7. Gates, "The Chitlin Circuit," *New Yorker*, February 3, 1997.

8. Peter Kobel, *Silent Movies: The Birth of Film and the Triumph of Movie Culture* (New York: Little Brown, 2007), 36.

BUTLER'S BEACH, ST. AUGUSTINE

1. "The Forgotten History of Lincolnville," *Florida Memory*, August 8, 2016, https://www.floridamemory.com/items/show/322317.

2. James G. Smith, "Before King Came: The Foundation of Civil Rights Resistance and St. Augustine Florida, 1900–1960" (master's thesis, University of North Florida, 2014).

3. "St. Augustine Treasures Its African American History," *St. Augustine Blade*, February 15, 2004.

4. "The Negro in America," *Newsweek*, July 29, 1963, 36.

5. David Garrow, *Bearing the Cross: Martin Luther King, Jr., and the Southern Christian Leadership Conference* (New York: Vintage Books, 1988), 316–18.

6. Jessica Clark, *First Coast News* (Jacksonville, Fla.), transcript of April 3, 2018, broadcast.

7. Jason Sokol, *There Goes My Everything: White Southerners in the Age of Civil Rights 1945–1975* (New York: Vintage, 2007), 200.

BUTLER'S BEACH, ST. AUGUSTINE

1. Phelts, *An American Beach for African Americans*, 28.

2. Ibid., 37–38.

3. Ibid., 67.

4. Russ Rymer, *American Beach: A Saga of Race, Wealth and Memory* (New York: Harper Collins, 1998), 225.

5. Ibid., 241

6. Phelts, *An American Beach for African Americans*, 88.

7. Rymer, *American Beach*, 241.

8. Ibid., 101.

PARADISE PARK, SILVER SPRINGS

1. Gilbert King, *Devil in the Grove: Thurgood Marshall, the Groveland Boss and the Dawn of a New America* (New York: Harper, 2012), 343.

2. Timothy J. Fisher, "You Must Be This to Ride: Class, Gender and Race in the American Amusement Park" (master's thesis, Washington & Lee University, 2015), 20.

3. Virginia Wolcott, *Race Riots and Roller Coasters: The Struggle over Segregated Recreation in America* (Philadelphia: University of Pennsylvania Press, 2012), 3.

4. Abigail Thernstrom and Stephan Thernstrom, "Black Progress: How Far We've Come, and How Far We Have to Go," *Brookings*, March 1, 1998. https://www.brookings.edu/articles/black-progress-how-far-weve-come-and-how-far-we-have-to-go.

5. Robert C. Weems, *Desegregating the Dollar: African American Consumerism in the Twentieth Century* (New York: New York University Press, 1998), 41.

6. City of Ocala website, www.ocalafl.org/.

7. Lu Vickers and Cynthia Wilson-Graham, *Remembering Paradise Park: Tourism and Segregation at Silver Springs* (Gainesville: University Press of Florida, 2015), 150.

8. Vickers, *Remembering Paradise Park*, 162.

9. Ibid., 189–90.

GULFSIDE ASSEMBLY, HANCOCK COUNTY

1. Elizabeth Cole and Safiya Omari, "Race, Class and the Dilemmas of Upward Mobility for African Americans," *Journal of Social Issues* 59, no. 4 (2003): 788.

2. Andrew Rieser, *The Chautauqua Movement: Protestants, Progressives and the Culture of Modern Liberalism* (New York: Columbia University Press, 2003), 123.

3. John Egerton, *Speak Now against the Day* (New York: Knopf, 1994), 48, 49.

4. Andrew Kahrl, "On The Beach: Race and Leisure in the Jim Crow South" (PhD diss., University, 2008), 190.

5. Ibid., 210.

6. Cleveland G. Allen, "Bishop Jones Establishes Negro Chautauqua at Waveland Mississippi," *Amsterdam News*, April 7, 1926.

7. Gilbert Mason, *Beaches, Blood, and Ballots: A Black Doctor's Civil Rights Struggle* (Jackson: University Press of Mississippi, 2007), 65–87.

8. *Biloxi Sun Herald*, May 1960.

9. Raymond R. Breaux, "Gulfside: Seventy Years of Service," *New World Outlook*, April 1993, 18.

FARISH STREET

1. Boyce Upholt, "Up All Night on Farish Street," *Bitter Southerner*, August 2016, bittersoutherner.com/up-all-night-on-farish-street.

2. "The Farish Street Project," Southern Foodways Alliance and the Southern Documentary Project, https://olemiss.edu/projects/sfa/farish-street-project.

3. Robert Mcg. Thomas Jr., "Lillian McMurry, Blues Producer, Dies at 77," *New York Times*, March 29, 1999.

4. *Bitter Southerner* no. 27 August 2016, 27.

5. "The Farish Street Project."

6. Ibid.

TUXEDO JUNCTION, ENSLEY

1. Glen Eskew, *But for Birmingham: The Local and National Movements in the Civil Rights Struggle* (Chapel Hill: University of North Carolina Press, 1997), 64.

2. Donald E. Rohar, "Tuxedo Junction, Where the Townsfolk Meet," *Alabama Heritage*, no. 76 (Spring 2005), 45.

3. David B. Schneider, *Downtown Ensley and Tuxedo Junction: An Introductory History* (Birmingham: City of Birmingham, 2009), 15.

4. Rohar, " Tuxedo Junction," 45.

BLACK MARDI GRAS, MOBILE

1. Michael Harriot, "Fat Tuesday in Mobile: Like Regular Mardi Gras . . . but Blacker," *The Root*, March 5, 2019, https://www.theroot.com/fat-tuesday-in-mobile-like-regular-mardi-gras-but-bl-1833074861.

2. Catherine Roth, "Clotilda (Slave Ship)," *BlackPast*, December 19, 2009, https://www.blackpast.org/african-american-history/clotilda.

3. Margaret Brown, dir., *The Order of Myths* (New York: Cinema Guild, 2008).

THE BEN MOORE HOTEL AND THE LAICOS CLUB, MONTGOMERY

1. Candacy Taylor, "Interview with Dr. Edward Clinton Davis, Ben Moore Hotel, Montgomery, Alabama," *Montgomery Advertiser*, December 31, 2018.

2. Michael Driver, "Discovering the Ben Moore Hotel," *Medium*, July 19, 2018, https://medium.com/@mdmichaeldriver/discovering-the-ben-moore-hotel-a3bc5d022e77.

3. Brad Harper, "Inside the Laicos: Legends, Friends, and a Respite from Jim Crow," *Montgomery Advertiser*, January 31, 2021.

4. Scotty E. Kirkland, "The Southern Courier," in *Encyclopedia of Alabama*, December 7, 2010, https://encyclopediaofalabama.org/article/the-southern-courier.

CONGO SQUARE AND STORYVILLE, NEW ORLEANS

1. George Washington Cable, "The Dance in Place Congo," in Maurice Garland Fulton, ed., *Southern Life in Southern Literature* (Boston: Atheneum, 1917), 314–17.

2. "Some Kind of Something Is Going on down There: Crossroads at Congo Square," *Folkways*, Winter/Spring 2015, https://foodways.si.edu/aritcle/smithsonian.

3. Frederick Turner, "Congo Square," *American Heritage*, February/March 1982, https://www.americanheritage.com/congo-square.

4. *Times-Picayune* (New Orleans), April 29, 2010.

CRESCENT STARS STADIUM, NEW ORLEANS

1. James Gill, *Lords of Misrule: Mardi Gras and the Politics of Race in New Orleans* (Jackson: University Press of Mississippi, 1997), 176.

2. "Both Organizations Enjoy an Unrivaled Reputation in the World of Colored Sport," *Baseball History Daily*, baseballhistorydaily.com/tag/new-orleans-pinchbacks

3. John H. Ingram and Lynne Feldman, *African American Business Leaders: A Biographical Dictionary* (Westport, Conn.: Greenwood, 1994), 176.

4. *Louisiana Weekly*, September 30, 1933.

5. Kevin G. McQueeney, *Playing with Jim Crow: African American Private Parks in Early 20th Century New Orleans* (master's thesis, University of New Orleans, 2015), 43–44.

SEABROOK BEACH AND LINCOLN BEACH, EAST NEW ORLEANS

1. "Recent Dredging of Lake Proves Costly," *Louisiana Weekly*, June 13, 1931, 1.

2. James Cullen, "Keeping the Peace at Lincoln Beach, *Antigravity Magazine*, September 2020, https://antigravitymagazine.com/feature/keeping-the-peace-at-lincoln-beach.

3. Keith Weldon Medley, "Bittersweet Memories of Lincoln Beach," *Preservation in Print* 28, no. 7 (September 18, 1999): 18.

4. Cullen, "Keeping the Peace at Lincoln Beach."

5. Keith Weldon Medley, "Lincoln Beach Was a Haven for Black Families during Oppressive Jim Crow Era," *Preservation in Print*, September 2020, https://prcno.org/lincoln-beach-was-a-haven-for-black-families-during-oppressive-jim-crow-era.

WILEY JONES PARK AND RACE TRACK, PINE BLUFF

1. James W. Leslie, "Ferd Harris, Jefferson County's Black Republican Leader," *Arkansas Historical Quarterly* 37, no. 3 (1978): 250.

2. Bettye J. Williams, *The Pioneers: Early African American Leaders in Pine Bluff* (Bloomington, Ind.: Archway, 2020), 105–9.

3. "Resolution of Respect for Wiley Jones," *Pine Bluff Daily Graphic*, December 9, 1904.

BATH HOUSES AND SPRING TRAINING, HOT SPRINGS

1. "Hot Springs Guest Guide," Arkansas Business Publishing Group, February 27, 2020, https://www.hsguestguide.com/post/129965/hot-springs-guest-guide-shopping-showcase

2. "Uncovering Ral City: Discover How a Large Squatters' Camp Called Ral City Influenced Hot Springs to Become Spa City, a 20th Century Health Destination," Hot Springs National Park, https://www.nps.gov/articles/000/uncovering-ral-city.htm.

3. "The African-American Experience in Hot Springs National Park," Old State House Museum, October 29, 2019, YouTube, https://www.youtube.com/watch?v=yTOUtymzdB8.

DEEP MORGAN, ST. LOUIS

1. Walter Johnson, *The Broken Heart of America: St. Louis and the Violent History of the United State* (New York: Basic, 2020) 205–7.

2. Walter Johnson, " The Largest Human Zoo in World History: Visiting thee 1904 World's Fair in St. Louis," St. Louis Public Library, April 14, 2020.

3. Mikelle Howard, "Ota Benga (1883–1916)," *Black Past*, September 22, 2018.

4. Jeanette Cooperman, "Babe and Priscilla," *St. Louis Magazine*, September 19, 2014.

5. Maxwell Marcuse, *Tin Pan Alley in Gaslight* (Watkins Glen, N.Y.: Century House, 1959), 192.

6. Layton Revel, *Early Pioneers of the Negro Leagues: Charles Mills* ([Carrolton, Tex.]: [Center for Negro League Baseball Research], 2017), https://www.cnlbr.org/.

FAIRGROUND PARK POOL, ST. LOUIS

1. Emma Newcombe, "The Legacy of the St. Louis Municipal Pool Race Riots," State and Local Politics and Policy, August 15, 2021, https://www.governing.com/now/the-legacy-of-the-st-louis-municipal-pool-race-riots.

2. Jeff Wiltse, *Contested Waters: A Social History of Swimming Pools in America* (Chapel Hill: University of North Carolina Press, 2007), 171.

3. Virginia W. Wolcott, "Here's the Disturbing History of Segregated Swimming Pools and Amusement Parks," *Huffington Post*, July 21, 2019.

COUNTY LINE/UPSHAW, EAST TEXAS

1. Joshua Dance, "Source of MLK 'Cruel Jest to Say to a Bootless Man' Interview Quote," *Medium*, January 21, 2019, https://joshdance.medium.com/source-of-mlk-cruel-jest-to-say-to-a-bootless-man-interview-quote-4b71105dee35.

2. Henry Louis Gates Jr., *The Black Church: This Is Our Story, This Is Our Song* (New York: Penguin, 2022), 45.

3. Jennifer Nardone, "Roomful of Blues: Juke Joints and the Cultural Landscape of the Mississippi Delta," *Perspectives in Vernacular Architecture* 9 (2003): 166–75.

THE VICTORY GRILL, EAST AUSTIN

1. Sharon Hill, "The Empty Stairs: The Lost History of East Austin," *Intersections: New Perspectives in Texas Public History* 1, no. 1, (Spring 2012): 14–16.

2. Andrew M. Busch, *City in a Garden: Environmental Transformations and Racial Justice in Twentieth-Century Austin, Texas* (Chapel Hill: University of North Carolina Press, 2017), 56–58.

3. Ibid.

4. Kenneth T. Jackson, *Crabgrass Frontier: The Suburbanization of the United States* (New York: Oxford University Press, 1985), 198–99.

5. Frank Mills, *Remembering Johnny Holmes and the Victory Grill*, CultureMap Austin, https://austin.culturemap.com/news/city-life/09-05-11-11-48-johnny-holmes-and-the-victory-grill.

6. Tracy Jan, "Redlining Was Banned Fifty Years Ago: It's Still Hurting Minorities Today," *Washington Post*, March 28, 2018.

7. David Leffler, "The Victory Grill's Revival," *Austin Monthly*, August 2020, https://www.austinmonthly.com/the-evolution-of-victory-grill.

8. Jan, "Redlining Was Banned Fifty Years Ago."

BLACK RODEOS AND TRAILBLAZERS, WEST TEXAS

1. Ronald Davis, "Black Cowboys: An American Story," *Not Even Past*, https://notevenpast.org/black-cowboys-an-american-story.

2. Christine Bell, "Cow Hunters of Colonial South Carolina," Lowcountry Africana, https://lowcountryafricana.com/cow-hunters-of-colonial-south-carolina.

3. Thad Sitton, "Freedmen's Settlements," July 17, 2007, *Handbook of Texas*, https://www.tshaonline.org/handbook/entries/freedmens-settlements.

4. Vincent T. Davis, "That's Those Spirits Talking: Freed Slaves' Descendants Preserve 150-Year-Old Ranch in Seguin," *San Antonio Express News*, April 24, 2022.

5. Tracy Owen Patton and Sally M. Schedlock, "Let's Rodeo: African Americans and the History of the Rodeo," *Journal of African American History*, 96, no. 4 (Fall 2011), 503–21.

6. Nat Love, *The Life and Adventures of Nat Love, Better Known in the Cattle Country as Deadwood Dick* (Lincoln: University of Nebraska Press, 1995).

7. Keith Ryan Cartwright, "Lu Vason's Rodeo Dream Celebrates the Place of Black Cowboy in American History," Wrangler Network, June 9, 2021, https://wranglernetwork.com/pbr-blog/lu-vasons-rodeo-dream-celebrates-the-place-of-the-black-cowboy-in-american-history.

8. Christian Walling "The Jackie Robinson of Rodeo," *Texas Monthly*, July 2018, 32.

STATE AND COUNTY FAIRS AND NATIONAL PARKS

1. Jim Sumner, "The African American State Fair," *Tar Heel Jr. Historian* 42, no. 1 (Fall 2002): 16–18.

2. Margaret D., "Remembering the Palmetto State Fair," Richland Library (South Carolina) blog, https://www.richlandlibrary.com/blog/2021-10-14/remembering-palmetto-state-fair.

3. Mandy Leonard, "Fannin County Uncovers First Records of Negro State Fair, Held 1911 in Bonham," *North Texas e-News*, August 25, 2021, http://www.ntxe-news.com/cgi-bin/artman/exec/view.cgi?archive=86&num=125779.

4. Richard Griset, "The History behind the County's Forgotten Fair, *Chesterfield Observer* (Midlothian, Va.), August 30, 2017, https://web.archive.org/web/20220517221803/www.chesterfieldobserver.com/articles/the-history-behind-the-countys-forgotten-fair.

THE NATIONAL PARK SERVICE

1. William O'Brien, *Landscapes of Exclusion: State Parks and Jim Crow in the American South* (Amhurst: University of Massachusetts Press, 2015), 6.

2. Ibid., 37.

3. Ibid., 11.

4. Nancy Grant, *TVA and Black Americans: Planning for the Status Quo* (Philadelphia: Temple University Press, 1990), 86.

5. "Cherokee State Park," Angela Hatton, WKMS, February 13, 2009, https://www.wkms.org/2009-02-13/cherokee-state-park.

6. Joe Creason, "A Honey of a Park for Negro Citizens," *Louisville Courier*, 1952, cited in O'Brien, *Landscapes of Exclusion*, 107.

7. William O'Brien, "State Parks and Jim Crow in the Decade before *Brown v. Board of Education*," *Geographical Review*, 102, no. 2 (April 2012): 166.

8. *Pensacola News Journal*, June 21, 1967.

9. Harvey H. Jackson III, *The Rise and Decline of the Redneck Riviera: An Insider's History of the Florida-Alabama Coast* (Athens: University of Georgia Press, 2012), 68–70.

EPILOGUE

1. Kevin M. Kruse, *White Flight: Atlanta and the Making of Modern Conservatism* (Princeton: Princeton University Press, 2007), 8.

2. Jason Sokol, *There Goes My Everything: White Southerners in the Age of Civil Rights, 1945–1975* (New York: Vintage, 2007), 177.

3. Kruse, *White Flight*, 123–24.

4. Godfrey Hodgson, *America in Our Time: From World War II to Nixon, What Happened and Why* (New York: Random House, 1976), 225,

5. Kruse, *White Flight*, 259.

6. Wolcott, *Race Riots and Roller Coasters*, 221–22.

7. Andrew Kahrl, "Fear of an Open Beach: Public Rights and Private Interests in 1970s Coastal Connecticut," *Journal of American History*, September 2015, 440.

8. "Decision Awaited in Maryland Pool Cases," *Baltimore Afro-American*, July 3, 1954.

9. Wolcott, *Race Riots and Roller Coasters*, 116–17.

10. Quoted in Wolcott, "Here's the Disturbing History of Segregated Swimming Pools."

11. Quoted in Ben Keppel, *The Work of Democracy* (which itself is quoted in Robin D. G. Kelley, "Integration: What's Left?," *The Nation*, December 3, 1998, http://www.hartford-hwp.com/archives.

12. Michael Sorkin, *Variations on a Theme Park: The New American City and the End of Public Space* (New York: Hill & Wang, 1990), xv.

13. Jim Korkis, "John Hench and the Language of Vision," *Mouse Planet*, April 20, 2011, https://www.mouseplanet.com/9594/John_Hench_and_the_Language_of_Vision.

14. Eric Avila, *Popular Culture in the Age of White Flight* (Berkeley: University of California Press, 2006), 106–45.

BIBLIOGRAPHY

Abrams, Danielle. "They Gave Us a Beach: The Memory of a Black Beach on Lake Pontchartrain," *64 Parishes*, https://64parishes.org/they-gave-us-a-beach.

Adams, Judith A. *The American Amusement Park Industry: A History of Technology and Thrills*. Woodbridge, Conn.: Twayne, 1991.

Alexander, Adele Logan. *Homelands and Waterways: The American Journey of the Bond Family, 1846–1926*. New York: Pantheon, 1999.

Allen, Cleveland G. "Bishop Jones Establishes Negro Chautauqua at Waveland, Mississippi," *New York Amsterdam News*, April 7, 1926.

Avila, Eric. *Popular Culture in the Age of White Flight: Fear and Fantasy in Suburban Los Angeles*. Berkeley: University of California Press, 2004.

Benton, Andrew Morgan. "The Press and the Sword: Journalism, Racial Violence and Political Control in Postbellum, North Carolina." Master's thesis, North Carolina State University, 2016.

Berlin, Ira. *Slaves without Masters: The Free Negro in the Antebellum South*. New York: Pantheon, 1974.

Biles, Roger. *Memphis and The Great Depression*. Knoxville: University of Tennessee Press, 1986.

Billingsley, Becky. *Lost Myrtle Beach*. Charleston: History Press, 2014.

Birmingham, Stephen. *Certain People: America's Black Elite*. Boston: Little, Brown, 1977.

Blight, David W., "An American Pogrom," review of David Zucchino, *Wilmington Lie: The Murderous Coup of 1898 and the Rise of White Supremacy*, *New York Review of Books*, November 19, 2020, 25–27.

Block, Susan Taylor. *Along the Cape Fear*. Charleston, S.C.: Arcadia, 1998.

———. *Cape Fear Beaches*. Charleston, S.C.: Arcadia, 2000.

Bond, Beverly, and Janann Sherman. *Memphis in Black and White*. Charleston, S.C.: Arcadia, 2003.

Breaux, Raymond R. "Gulfside: Seventy Years of Service." *New World Outlook*, April 1993, 16–18.

Bridgforth, James Cabanisis. "The Farish District: Its Architecture and Cultural Heritage." Master's thesis, University of Georgia, 2016.

Brody, Richard. "Oscar Micheaux: The First Black Auteur." *New Yorker*, August 12, 2016, https://www.newyorker.com/magazine/2016/08/22/oscar-micheaux-the-first-black-auteur.

Brunson, James E., III. *The Early Image of Black Baseball: Race and Representation in the Popular Press, 1871–1890*. Jefferson, N.C.: McFarland, 2009.

Burke, Adrienne, and Ennis Davis. "Here Is a Plan to Revive LaVilla," *J* (Jacksonville, Fla.), June 17, 2018, https://www.jacksonville.com/story/lifestyle/magazine/2018/06/17/here-is-plan-to-revive-lavilla/11952459007.

Burns, Rebecca. *Rage in the Gate City: The Story of the 1906 Atlanta Race Riot*. Cincinnati: Emmis, 2006.

Busch, Andrew M. *City in a Garden: Environmental Transformations and Racial Justice in Twentieth-Century Austin, Texas*. Chapel Hill: University of North Carolina Press 2017.

Campanella, Catherine. *Lost Lake Pontchartrain Resorts and Attractions*. Charleston, S.C.: History Press, 2019.

Carter, Edward Randolph. *The Black Side: A Partial History of the Business, Religious and Education Side of the Negro in Atlanta*. Atlanta, 1894.

Cassanello, Robert. *To Render Invisible: Jim Crow and Public Life in New South Jacksonville*. Gainesville: University Press of Florida, 2013.

Chalmers, David, "The KKK in the Sunshine State: The 1920's." *Florida Historical Quarterly* 42, no. 3 (January 1964), 209–15.

Chandler, David Leon. *Henry Flagler: The Astonishing Life and Times of the Visionary Robber Baron Who Founded Florida*. New York: Macmillan, 1986.

Church, Annette E., and Roberta Church. *The Robert R. Churches of Memphis: A Father and Son Who Achieved in Spite of Race*. Ann Arbor, Mich.: Edwards, 1974.

Coates, James Roland, Jr. "Recreation and Sport in the African American Community of Baltimore, 1890–1920." PhD diss., University of Maryland, 1991.

Cole, Elizabeth R., and Safiya R. Omari. "Race, Class and the Dilemmas of Upward Mobility for African Americans." *Journal of Social Issues* 59, no. 4 (2003): 785–802.

Colston, Ladd G., and L. Pettis Patton. *The Critical Impact of Urban Recreation on the African American Community: A Summary of Public Opinion Survey Data from African-American Consumers Nationwide, 1992–1993*. Arlington, Va.: National Recreation and Park Association, 1994.

Corliss, Richard. "An Oscar for Micheaux." *Time*, June 6, 2002, https://content.time.com/time/arts/article/0,8599,260216-2,00.html.

Cripps, Thomas. *Slow Fade to Black: The Negro in American Film, 1900–1942*. London: Oxford University Press, 1977.

Cross, Gary S., and John K. Walton. *The Playful Crowd: Pleasure Places in the Twentieth Century*. New York: Columbia University Press, 2005.

Crowe, Charles. "Racial Massacre in Atlanta." *Journal of Negro History*, no. 54 (April 1969), 150–74.

Cullen, James. "Keeping the Peace at Lincoln Beach," *Antigravity*, September 2020, https://antigravitymagazine.com/feature/keeping-the-peace-at-lincoln-beach.

Daily, Jane. *Before Jim Crow: The Politics of Race in Postemancipation Virginia*. Chapel Hill: University of North Carolina Press, 2000.

Deanwood 1880–1950: A Model of Self-Sufficiency in Far Northeast Washington, D.C. Washington, D.C.: Deanwood History Project, 2005.

Deanwood History Commission. *Washington D.C.'s Deanwood*. Charleston, S.C.: Arcadia, 2008.

Decuir, Sharlene Sinegal. "Attacking Jim Crow: Black Activism in New Orleans, 1935–1941." PhD diss., Louisiana State University, 2009.

Denson, Charles. *Coney Island Lost and Found*. Berkeley, Calif.: Ten Speed, 2007.

De Rosset, W. L. *Wilmington up to Date*. Wilmington, N.C.: Chamber of Commerce, 1902.

Di Bari, Sherry. "Seaview Beach and Amusement Park: An African American Gem on Virginia's Chesapeake Bay." Virginia Beach Historic Preservation Commission, Shore Drive Community Coalition Presentation, September 2017.

Dickon, Chris. *Chesapeake Bay Steamers*. Charleston, S.C.: Arcadia, 2006.

Diggs, Louis. *From the Meadows to the Point: The Histories of the African American Community of Turner Station and What Was the African American Community in Sparrows Point*. Baltimore: L. Diggs, 2000.

Dittmer, John. *Black Georgia in the Progressive Era, 1900–1920*. Urbana: University of Illinois Press, 1977.

Domosh, Mona. "A 'Civilized' Commerce: Gender, Race and Empire at the 1893 Chicago Exposition." *Cultural Geographies*, no. 9 (2002): 181–201.

Dray, Philip. *Capitol Men: The Epic Story of Reconstruction through the Lives of the First Black Congressmen*. New York: Houghton, Mifflin, 2008.

Du Bois, W. E. B. "Reconstruction and Its Benefits." *American History Review*, no. 15 (July 1910): 781–99.

———. "Watching a Baseball Game at the Crescent Stars Amusement Baseball Park, New Orleans," *Crisis* 23, no. 1 (November 1921), https://modjourn.org/issue/bdr513950/.

Dunn, Marvin. *Black Miami in the Twentieth Century*. Gainesville: University Press of Florida, 1997.

Egerton, John. *Speak Now against the Day: The Generation before the Civil Rights Movement in the South*. New York: Knopf, 1994.

Ellerbee, Jason E. "African American Theaters in Georgia: Preserving An Entertainment Legacy." Master's thesis, University of Georgia, 2004.

Eskew, Glenn. *But for Birmingham: The Local and National Movements in the Civil Rights Struggle*. Chapel Hill: University of North Carolina Press, 1997.

Fairclough, Adam. *Race and Democracy: The Civil Rights Struggle in Louisiana, 1915–1972*. Athens: University of Georgia Press, 1995.

Farrell, George, and Rawl Gelinas. "The History of Chowan Beach," Chowan Beach Recreation Association, www.cb-history-preface.html.

Fields, Mamie Garvin. *Lemon Swamp and Other Places: A Carolina Memoir*. New York: Free Press, 1983.

Fields, Norma Cromwell. "Blacks in Norfolk, Virginia during the 1930's." Master's thesis, Old Dominion University, 1979.

Fisher, Timothy J. "You Must Be This to Ride: Class, Gender and Race in the American Amusement Park." Master's thesis, Washington and Lee University, 2015.

Fitzpatrick, Michael Andrew. "Shaw, Washington's Premier Black Neighborhood: An Examination of the Origins and Development of a Black Business Movement, 1880–1920." Master's thesis, University of Virginia, 1989.

Fitzpatrick, Sandra, and Maria Goodwin. *Black Washington*. New York: Hippocrene, 2001.

Fleischmann, Thomas F. "Black Miamians in the *Miami Metropolis*, 1896–1900." *Tequesta* 52 (1992): 21–38.

Fletcher, Patsy Mose. *Historically African American Leisure Destinations around Washington, D.C.* Charleston, S.C.: History Press, 2015.

Flood, Dudley, and Ben Watford. *You Can't Fall Off the Floor*. Bloomington, Ind.: Author House, 2009.

Foster, Mark. "In the Face of Jim Crow: Prosperous Blacks and Vacations 1890–1945." *Journal of Negro History* 84, no. 2 (Spring 1999): 130–49.

Frazier, E. Franklin. *Recreation and Amusement among American Negroes*. Research memorandum, Howard University, July 15, 1940. Microform, Schomburg Library, New York City.

Garrow, David J. *Bearing the Cross: Martin Luther King, Jr. and the Southern Christian Leadership Conference*. New York: Vintage, 1988.

Gates, Henry Louis, and Evelyn Brooks Higginbotham, eds. *Harlem Renaissance Lives from the African American National Biography*. New York: Oxford Press, 2009.

Gatewood, Willard. *Aristocrats of Color: 1880–1920*. Fayetteville: University of Arkansas Press, 2000.

George, Paul S. "Colored Town: Miami's Black Community, 1896–1930." *Florida Historical Quarterly* 56, no. 4 (April 1978): 432–47.

George, Paul S., and Thomas K. Petersen. "Liberty Square: 1933–1987: The Origins and Evolution of a Public Housing Project." *Tequesta* 48 (1988), 53–68.

George-Graves, Nadine. *The Royalty of Negro Vaudeville: The Whitman Sisters and the Negotiation of Race, Gender, and Class in the African American Theater, 1900–1940*. New York: Palgrave Macmillan, 2000.

———. "Spreading the Sand: Understanding the Economic and Creative Impetus for the Black Vaudeville Industry." *Continuum: The Journal of African Diaspora Drama, Theatre and Performance* 1, no. 1 (June 2014): 1–20.

Gill, James. *Lords of Misrule: Mardi Gras and the Politics of Race in New Orleans*. Jackson: University Press of Mississippi, 1997.

Gilmore, Glenda Elizabeth. *Gender and Jim Crow: Women and the Politics of White Supremacy in North Carolina, 1896–1920*. Chapel Hill: University of North Carolina Press, 1966.

Gottschild, Brenda Dixon. *Waltzing in the Dark: African American Vaudeville and Race Politics in the Swing Era*. New York: St. Martin's Press, 2000.

Graham, Lawrence Otis. *Our Kind of People: Inside America's Black Upper Class*. New York: Harper, 1999.

Grant, Nancy. *TVA and Black Americans: Planning for the Status Quo*. Philadelphia: Temple University Press, 1990.

Hale, Elizabeth. *Making Whiteness: The Culture of Segregation in the South, 1890–1940*. New York: Pantheon Books, 1998.

Henson, Elaine Blackman. *Carolina Beach*. Charleston, S.C.: Arcadia, 2007.

Hill, David. *The Vapors: A Southern Family, the New York Mob, and the Rise and Fall of Hot Springs, America's Forgotten Capital of Vice*. New York: Straus & Giroux, 2020.

Hill, Sharon. "The Empty Stairs: The Lost History of East Austin." *Intersections: New Perspectives in Texas Public History* 1, no. 1, (Spring 2012): 12–18.

Hines, Elizabeth. "Sea Breeze to Sherbet Town: An Historic African American Beach Resort Lost to Affluenza." *North Carolina Geographer* 19 (2012): 54–66.

Hodes, Martha. *White Women, Black Men: Illicit Sex in the Nineteeth-Century South*. New Haven: Yale University Press, 1997.

Hodgson, Godfrey. *American in Our Time: From World War II to Nixon–What Happened and Why*. New York: Random House, 1976.

Holly, David. *Chesapeake Steamboats: Vanished Fleets*. Centreville, Md.: Tidewater, 1994.

Hurston, Zora Neale. *Barracoon: The Story of the Last "Black Cargo."* New York: Amistad, 2018.

Ingham, John N. "African-American Business Leaders in the South 1810–1945: Business Success, Community Leadership and Racial Protest." *Business and Economic History* 22, no. 1 (Fall 1993): 262–72.

Jackson, Harvey H., III. *The Rise and Decline of the Redneck Riviera: An Insider's History of the Florida-Alabama Coast*. Athens: University of Georgia Press, 2012.

Jackson, Hope. "Stones of Memory: Narratives from a Black Beach Community." PhD diss., University of North Carolina, Greensboro, 2013.

Jackson, Kenneth T. *Crabgrass Frontier: The Suburbanization of the United States*. New York: Oxford University Press, 1985.

Janken, Kenneth Robert. *White: The Biography of Walter White, Mr. NAACP*. New York: New Press, 2003.

Jean-Laurent, Annabella. "Flashback: The 1895 Cotton States Exposition and the Negro Building." *Atlanta Magazine*, February 27, 2014, https://www.atlantamagazine.com/news-culture-articles/flashback-the-1895-cotton-states-exposition-and-the-negro-building/.

Johnson, James Weldon. *Black Manhattan*. New York: Athenium, 1972.

Johnson, Walter. *The Broken Heart of America: St. Louis and the Violent History of the United States*. New York: Basic, 2021.

Jones, Marvin T. "The Leading Edge of Edges: The Tri-Racial People of the Winton Triangle." In *Carolina Genesis: Beyond the Color Line*, edited by Scott Withrow, 187–216. Palm Coast, Fla.: Backintyme, 2010.

Jones, William H. *Recreation and Amusement among Negroes in Washington, D.C.* Washington, D.C.: Howard University Press, 1927.

Kahrl, Andrew. "Fear of an Open Beach: Public Rights and Private Interests in 1970s Coastal Connecticut." *Journal of American History* 102, no. 2 (September 2015): 433–63.

———. *The Land Was Ours: How Black Beaches Became White Wealth in the Coastal South*. Chapel Hill: University of North Carolina Press, 2012.

———. "The Making, Unmaking, and Memory of White and Black Beaches in New Orleans." *Louisiana Cultural Vistas* 23 (Spring 2012): 68–81.

———. "On the Beach: Race and Leisure in the Jim Crow South." PhD diss., Indiana University, 2008.

———. "'The Slightest Semblance of Unruliness': Steamboat Excursions, Pleasure Resorts and the Emergence of Segregation Culture on the Potomac River." *Journal of American History* 9, no. 4 (March 2008): 1108–36.

Kelley, Robin D. G. *Race Rebels: Culture, Politics and the Black Working Class*. New York: Free Press, 1996.

King, Gilbert. *Devil in the Grove: Thurgood Marshall, the Groveland Boys and the Dawn of a New America*. New York: Harper, 2012.

King, P. Nicole. *Sombreros and Motorcycles in a Newer South: The Politics of Aesthetics in South Carolina's Tourism Industry*. Jackson: University Press of Mississippi, 2012.

Kissane, Amy C. "Historic Resources of Myrtle Beach, South Carolina." National Register of Historic Places Multiple Property Documentation Form. Jaeger Company, Gainesville, Florida, October 1, 1995.

Knight, Althea, "In Retrospect: Sherman H. Dudley: He Paved the Way for T.O.B.A." *Black Perspective in Music* 15 no. 2 (August 1987): 153–81.

Kobel, Peter. *Silent Movies: The Birth of Film and the Triumph of Movie Culture*. New York: Little, Brown, 2007.

Kruse, Kevin M. *White Flight: Atlanta and the Making of Modern Conservatism*. Princeton, N.J.: Princeton University Press, 2007.

Kuhn, Cliff, Harlon Joye, and E. Bernard West. *Living Atlanta and Oral History of the City 1914–1948*. Athens: University of Georgia Press, 1990.

Lassiter, Patrice Shelton. *Generations of Black Life in Kennesaw and Marietta*. Charleston, S.C.: Arcadia, 1999.

Lauterbach, Preston. *Beale Street Dynasty: Sex, Song and the Struggle for the Soul of Memphis*. New York: Norton, 2015.

———. *The Chitlin' Circuit and the Road to Rock 'n' Roll*. New York: Norton, 2011.

———. "Sympathy for the Devil." *Oxford American*, no. 82 (Winter 2014), 123–43.

Leland, Elizabeth. *The Vanishing Coast*. Durham, N.C.: Blair, 1996.

Lewis, Catherine H. *Horry County, South Carolina, 1730–1933*. Columbia: University of South Carolina Press, 1995.

Lewis, Earl. *In Their Own Interests: Race, Class, and Power in Twentieth-Century Norfolk, Virginia*. Berkley: University of California Press, 1991.

Litwack, Leon. *Trouble in Mind: Black Southerners in the Age of Jim Crow*. New York: Vintage Books, 1998.

Lowman, Ilyshia Michelle. "Recreational Segregation: The Role of Place in Shaping Communities." Master's thesis, University of Southern Florida, 2014.

McAllister, Ray. *Wrightsville Beach: The Luminous Island*. Winston-Salem, N.C.: John Blair, 2007.

McArdle, Nancy, and Dolores Acevedo-Garcia. "Consequences of Segregation for Children's

Opportunity and Well Being." Paper presented at "A Shared Future: Fostering Communities of Inclusion in an Era of Inequality," national symposium, Harvard Joint Center for Housing Studies, April 2017.

McGrain, John. "Bay Shore Park Sparked by the Trolley System." *History Trails of Baltimore County* 41, no. 4 (Summer 2010): 1–12.

McKay, Robert. "Segregation and Public Recreation." *Virginia Law Review* 40, no. 6 (October 1954): 687–731.

McMillan, Susan Hoffer. *Myrtle Beach and the Grand Strand*. Charleston, S.C.: Arcadia, 2004.

McMillen, Neil R. *Dark Journey: Black Mississippians in the Age of Jim Crow*. Urbana: University of Illinois Press, 1989.

McQueeney, Kevin G. *Playing with Jim Crow: African American Private Parks in Early Twentieth Century New Orleans*. Master's thesis, University of New Orleans, 2015.

McQueeney, Kevin G. "More than Recreation: Black Parks and Playgrounds in Jim Crow New Orleans." *Louisiana History* 60, no. 4 (Fall 2019): 437–78.

Mason, Gilbert. *Beaches, Blood, and Ballots: A Black Doctor's Civil Rights Struggle*. Jackson: University Press of Mississippi, 2007.

Mason, Herman, Jr. *African American Entertainment in Atlanta*. Charleston, S.C.: Arcadia, 1998.

——. *Black Atlanta in the Roaring Twenties*. Charleston, S.C.: Arcadia, 1997.

Medley, Keith Weldon. "Bittersweet Memories of Lincoln Beach." *Preservation in Print* 28, no. 7 (September 1999): 18–19.

Melton, Mandy. *Anne Arundel County's Historic Beach Resorts*. Annapolis, Md.: Anne Arundel County Trust for Preservation, 2017.

Mohl, Raymond A. "Shadows in the Sunshine: Race and Ethnicity in Miami." *Tequesta* 49 (1989): 63–80.

Moore, Jacqueline. *Booker T. Washington, W. E. B. DuBois, and the Struggle for Racial Uplift*. Wilmington, Del.: Scholarly Resources, 2003.

——. *Leading the Race: The Transformation of the Black Elite in the Nation's Capital, 1880–1920*. Charlottesville: University Press of Virginia, 1999.

Muhammad, Khalil Gibran. *The Condemnation of Blackness: Race, Crime, and the Making of Modern America*. Cambridge: Harvard University Press, 2010.

Murphy, Allison L. "Fifty Years of Challenges to the Color Line: Montgomery, Alabama." Masters' thesis, Georgia State University, 2009.

Myrdal, Gunnar. *An American Dilemma: The Negro Problem and Modern Democracy*, vol. 1. New York: Harper & Row, 1944.

Nasaw, David. *Going Out: The Rise and Fall of Public Amusements*. New York: Basic, 1993.

O'Brien, William E. *Landscapes of Exclusion: State Parks and Jim Crow in the American South*. Amherst: University of Massachusetts Press, 2015.

——. "State Parks and Jim Crow in the Decade before *Brown v. Board of Education*." *Geographical Review* 102, no. 2 (April 2012): 166–79.

Onorato, Michael P., ed. *Steeplechase Park Sale and Closure 1965–1966: Diary and Papers of James J. Onorato*. Bellingham, Wash.: Pacific Rim, 1998.

Osofsky, Gilbert. *Harlem: The Making of a Ghetto New York, 1890–1930*. New York: Ivan Dee, 1996.

Packard, Jerrold. *American Nightmare: The History of Jim Crow*. New York: St. Martin's Press, 2002.

Perdue, Theda. *Race and the Atlanta Cotton States Exposition of 1895*. Athens: University of Georgia Press, 2010.

Phelts, Marsha Dean. *An American Beach for African Americans*. Gainesville: University Press of Florida, 1997.

Prather, H. Leon. *We Have Taken a City: Wilmington Racial Massacre and Coup of 1898*. Rutherford, N.J.: Fairleigh Dickinson University Press, 1984.

Repanshek, Kurt. "How the National Park Service Grappled with Segregation during the 20th Century." *National Park Traveler*, August 18, 2019, https://www.nationalparkstraveler.org/2019/08/how-national-park-service-grappled-segregation-during-20th-century.

Revel, Layton. *Early Pioneers of the Negro Leagues: Charles Mills*. [Carrollton, Tex.]: [Center for Negro League Baseball Research], 2017.

Rhodes, Jason. *Maryland's Amusement Parks*. Charleston, S.C.: Arcadia, 2005.

Rieser, Andrew C. *The Chautauqua Movement: Protestants, Progressives, and the Culture of Modern Liberalism*. New York: Columbia University Press, 2003.

Robinson, Todd E. *A City within a City: The Black Freedom Struggle in Grand Rapids, Michigan*. Philadelphia: Temple University Press, 2013.

Rogosin, Donn. *Invisible Men: Life in Baseball's Negro Leagues*. Lincoln: University of Nebraska Press, 2020.

Rohar, Donald E. "Tuxedo Junction, Where the Townsfolk Meet." *Alabama Heritage*, no. 76 (Spring 2005), https://www.alabamaheritage.com/from-the-vault/tuxedo-junction-where-the-town-folks-meet.

Rymer, Russ. *American Beach: A Saga of Race, Wealth, and Memory*. New York: Harper Collins, 1998.

Sampson, Henry T. *Blacks in Blackface: A Sourcebook for Early Black Musical Shows*. Lanham, Md.: Scarecrow Press, 1980.

Sanders, Crystal R. "Blue Water, Black Beach: The North Carolina Teachers Association and Hammocks Beach in the Age of Jim Crow." *North Carolina Historical Review* 92, no. 2 (April 2015): 145–64.

Sandler, Gilbert. *Small Town Baltimore*. Baltimore: Johns Hopkins University Press, 2002.

Savage, Beth L., ed. *African American Historical Places*. Charleston, S.C.: Preservation Press, 1994.

Schneider, David B. *Downtown Ensley and Tuxedo Junction: Introductory History*. Birmingham, Ala.: City of Birmingham, 2020.

Semuels, Alana. "Segregation Had to Be Invented." *Atlantic Monthly*, February 17, 2017, https://www.theatlantic.com/business/archive/2017/02/segregation-invented/517158/.

Shapiro, Herbert. *White Violence and Black Response: From Reconstruction to Montgomery.* Amherst: University of Massachusetts Press, 1988.

Shaw, Douglas V. "Making Leisure Pay: Street Railway Owned Amusement Parks in the U.S. 1900–1925." *Journal of Cultural Economics* 10 (December 1986): 67–79.

Smith, James G. "Before King Came: The Foundation of Civil Rights Resistance and St. Augustine, Florida 1900–1960." Master's thesis, University of North Florida, 2014.

Smith, Robyn N. "Life on the North Side: The African American Community in Sparrows Point." *Reclaiming Kin: Taking Back What Was Once Lost*, March 2018. https://www.reclaimingkin.com/wp-content/uploads/2018/03/Sparrows-Point-Article.pdf.

Sokol, Jason. *There Goes My Everything: White Southerners in the Age of Civil Rights, 1945–1975.* New York: Vintage Press, 2007.

Soren, David. *American Vaudeville: A Celebration.* Dubuque, Iowa: Kendall Hunt Publishing, 2020.

Sorkin, Michael, ed. *Variations on a Theme Park: The New American City and the End of Public Space.* New York: Hill & Wang, 1992.

Southern, Eileen. *The Music of Black America: A History.* New York: Norton, 1997.

Standley, Fred, and Louis Pratt. *Conversations with James Baldwin.* Jackson: University Press of Mississippi, 1989.

Stanonis, Anthony J. *Faith in Bikinis: Politics and Leisure in the Coastal South since the Civil War.* Athens: University of Georgia Press, 2014.

Stephenson, E. Frank. *Chowan Beach: Remembering an African American Resort.* Charleston, S.C.: History Press, 2009.

Stokes, Barbara. *Myrtle Beach: A History 1900–1980.* Columbia: University of South Carolina Press, 2007.

Suttles, Sherry A. *Atlantic Beach.* Charleston, S.C.: Arcadia, 2009.

Tagger, Barbara A. "The Atlanta Race Riot of 1906 and the Black Community." Master's thesis, Atlanta University, 1984.

Taylor, Candacy. *Overground Railroad: The Green Book and the Roots of Black Travel in America.* New York: Abrams Press, 2020.

Thompson-Miller, Ruth. "Intergenerational Trauma: Segregation Stress Syndrome and Collective PTSD." Paper delivered at the University of Chicago, Department of Sociology, Michael Davis Lecture Series, April 26, 2011.

Toll, Robert C. "Behind the Blackface." *American Heritage* 29, no. 3 (1978), https://www.americanheritage.com/behind-blackface.

———. "Blackface and the Sad History of Minstrel Shows." *American Heritage* 64, no. 1 (2019), https://www.americanheritage.com/blackface-sad-history-minstrel-shows.

Tuck, Stephen. *We Ain't What We Ought to Be: The Black Freedom Struggle from Emancipation to Obama.* Cambridge: Belknap Press of Harvard University Press, 2011.

Vaught, Kip. "Racial Stirrings in Colored Town: The UNIA in Miami during the 1920's." *Tequesta* 60 (2000): 56–76.

Vickers, Lu, and Cynthia Wilson-Graham. *Remembering Paradise Park: Tourism and Segregation at Silver Springs*. Gainesville: University Press of Florida, 2015.

Wade, Wyn Craig. *The Fiery Cross: The Ku Klux Klan in America*. New York: Oxford University Press, 1987.

Walch, Barbara. *Frank B. Butler: Lincolnville Businessman and Founder of St. Augustine, Florida's Historic Black Beach*. St Augustine: R. B. Hadley, 1992.

Wallace, Richard. "Defeat Comes to Boss Crump." *National Civic Review* 37, no. 8 (September 1948): 410–68.

Warren, Dan R. *If It Takes All Summer: Martin Luther King and the KKK and States' Rights in St. Augustine, 1964*. Tuscaloosa: University of Alabama Press, 2008.

Washington, Forrester B. "Recreational Facilities for the Negro." *Annals of the American Academy of Political and Social Sciences* 140 (November 1928): 272–82.

Washington, Les. *Generations: A Commentary on the History of African American Immigrants and Their American Descendants*. Bloomington, Ind.: iUniverse, 2002.

Waters, Roderick. "Dr. William B. Sawyer of Colored Town." *Tequesta* 57 (1997): 67–80.

Watson, Denise. "More than a 'Little Place for Coloreds': Locals Remember the Fun and Frustration of the Area's Old Segregated Beaches." *Virginian-Pilot*, July 8, 2018.

Watson, Jerome. *Turner Station: Images of America*. Charleston, S.C.: Arcadia, 2008.

Webster, Edgar. *Chums and Brothers: An Interpretation of a Social Group of Our American Citizenry Who Are, in the First and Last Analysis, Just Folks*. Boston: Badger, 1920.

Weems, Robert C. *Desegregating the Dollar: African American Consumerism in the Twentieth Century*. New York: New York University Press, 1998.

Weiss, Jessica. "A Portrait of a Community: The Life of Shaw." *Janus: The University of Maryland Undergraduate History Journal*, Fall 2004.

Wells, Ida B. *Crusade for Justice: The Autobiography of Ida B. Wells*. Edited by Alfreda M. Duster. Chicago: University of Chicago Press, 1970.

Williams, Paul K. *Greater U Street*. Charleston, S.C.: Arcadia, 2002.

Williams, Paul K., and Kathryn S. Smith. *City within a City: Greater U Street Heritage Trail*. Washington, D.C.: Historical Society of Washington D.C., D.C. Heritage Tourism Coalition, 2001.

Wilson, Mabel O. *Negro Building: Black Americans in the World's Fairs and Museums*. Berkeley: University of California Press, 2012.

Wiltse, Jeff. *Contested Waters: A Social History of Swimming Pools in America*. Chapel Hill: University of North Carolina Press, 2007.

Winick, Stephen. "Industrial Boom and Bust: The Living Heritage of the Sparrows Point Steel Mill (Baltimore, MD)." *Folklife Today* (Library of Congress, American Folklife Center & Veteran's History Project), May 4, 2017. https://blogs.loc.gov/folklife/2017/05/Industrial-boom-and-bust.

Wolcott, Victoria W. "Here's the Disturbing History of Segregated Swimming Pools and Amusement Parks." *Huffington Post*, July 21, 2019.

———. *Integrated Leisure in Segregated Cities: Amusement Parks and Racial Conflict in the Post-War North.* Presentation at the Urban History Association Annual Meeting, University of Rochester, October 2004.

———. *Race, Riots and Roller Coasters: The Struggle over Segregated Recreation in America.* Philadelphia: University of Pennsylvania Press, 2012.

Wolfe-Rocca, Ursula. "The Red Summer of 1919, Explained." *Teen Vogue*, May 31, 2020. https://www.teenvogue.com/story/the-red-summer-of-1919-explained.

Woodward, C. Vann. *The Strange Career of Jim Crow.* 3rd rev. ed. New York: Oxford University Press, 1974.

Young, Darius. *Robert R. Church Jr. and the African American Political Struggle.* Gainesville: University Press of Florida, 2019.

Zeidman, Linda. "Sparrows Point, Dundalk, Highland Town, Old West Baltimore: Home of Gold Dust and the Union Card." In *The Baltimore Book: New Visions of Local History*, edited by Elizabeth Fee, Linda Shopes, and Linda Zeidman, 175–202 Philadelphia: Temple University Press, 1991.

INDEX

Locators in italics indicate a figure.

101 Ranch Wild West Show, 206–7

accommodation and race relations, 105, 150–51
accommodations (lodging): legislation and, 4–5, 223; musician access to, 17, 79; racism and, 133–34. *See also individual hotels and resorts*
activism. *See* demonstrations, civil rights; wade-ins/swim-ins
Adams, Charles "Hoppy," 43, *45*
Adams, William L. "Little Willie," 42–44
African American Woodmen Fraternal Society ballroom (Alabama), 159–60, *161*
Africatown, Alabama, 162–63
Afro-American Insurance Company, 135–36
Afro Club (Alabama), 165–66
alcohol, 32, 33, 34, 37, 139, 143
Alexander, Will, 148
Allen, Ivan, 221
Allen, Ross, 141, 143
Amelia Island, Florida, 136
American Beach (Florida), 136–39
American Indians. *See* Native Americans
amusement parks: "good fear" and, 1–2; pools and, 195; postwar demand for, 140; segregation and, 2. *See also* fairs; theme parks; world's fairs; *individual amusement parks*
An American Dilemma: The Negro Problem and American Democracy (Myrdal), 2–3
Anastasia Island, Florida, 131–32
Annapolis, Maryland, 9–10, 42–45
Anthony Theater (Maryland), 41
Arcady resort complex (South Carolina), 78–79
Armstrong, Louis, 176, 191
Ashwill, Gary, 41

Atlanta, Georgia, 103–5, 109–15, 221
"Atlanta Compromise" speech (Booker T. Washington), 104–5
Atlantic Beach (South Carolina), 76, 79–84
Atlantic Beach Corporation, 80
Auburn Avenue. *See* Sweet Auburn (Atlanta)
Aurora, Kentucky, 217–18
Austin, Texas, 201–3
Autocrat Social and Pleasure Club (Louisiana), 174
Avant, Frank, 61–62
Avila, Eric, 224

Baker, Josephine, 191
Baldwin, James, 223
Baltimore, Maryland, 40–41, 202, 222–23
Barnes, Ernie, 5–6
Barracoon: The Story of the Last "Black Cargo" (Hurston), 164
baseball, 41, 174–75, 182, 186–87, 193–94
baseball teams: Baltimore Grays, 41; Cincinnati Clowns, 41; New Orleans Crescent Stars, 174–75; St. Louis Black Stockings, 193–94; St. Louis Giants/Stars, 194
bathhouses, 184–86
Bay Shore (Maryland), 40, 55–56
Bay Shore Amusement Park (Maryland), 40
beaches: boundaries and, 79–80; segregation and, 53–55, 64, 121–22. *See also individual beaches*
Beale Street (Memphis), 87–89
Beale Street Auditorium (Memphis), 93
Beamon, Benjamin Burdell "B. B.," 114
Beams, Walter L., 27
Bear's Cut Beach (Florida), 121–22

255

Benga, Ota, 192
Ben Moore Hotel (Alabama), 165–66
Berry, Dorothy, 103
Bethlehem Steel, 39
Bikefest (Atlantic Beach), 83–84
Bill Pickett Invitational Rodeo, 207–8
Birmingham, Alabama, 159–61
Birth of a Nation (film), 110, 130
Black America (event), 103
"Black Broadway" (D.C.), 19–20, 46
black cattle herders, 204. *See also* cowboys and cattle culture; rodeos
black cowboys. *See* cowboys and cattle culture; rodeos
blackface, 11, 12, 110
blackness, 13, 80. *See also* vaudeville
Bohemian Caverns (D.C.), 19, 20
Bolden, Charles "Buddy," 173
Bop City (North Carolina), 67–68
Boyd, Richard Henry (R. H.), 95–96
Boyd, Simon W., 219
Bridgewater, Henry, 193
Brock, Jimmy, 134
Brody, Richard, 129
Brown, George, 36–37
Brown, Margaret, 164
Brown's Grove (Maryland), 36–37
Brown v. Board of Education, 3, 5, 20, 196
Bull-Dogger, The (film), 206
bulldogging, 206
bull riding, 207
Busch, Andrew, 201
Bush, Gregory, 122
business failures and desegregation, 56, 71, 155, 166, 178, 221
Butler, Frank, 131–32, 133

Cable, George Washington, 171–72
cakewalk dances, 88
Candler Park Pool (Atlanta), 221
Carr, Fred, 42
Carr's Beach (Maryland), 42–45
Cataliotti, Robert H., 172

Cedar Haven (Maryland), 27–28
Central Jurisdiction (Methodist Episcopal Church), 147–49, 152
Chandler, Walter "Clift," 93
Chappelle, Patrick Henry, 126
Chautauqua organizations, 147–48
Cherokee Lake State Park (Kentucky), 217–18
Cherokee Nation, 107–9
Chesterfield County Fair (Virginia), 214–15
children, 1–3, 123, 176, 195, 213, 223. *See also* amusement parks
Chitlin Circuit: background of, 48–49; name of, 10; stops on, 43, 46, 70, 115, 139, 166, 202–3
chitlins (food), 48–49
Chowan Beach (North Carolina), 69–71
Church, Robert, Jr. "Bob," 92–93
Church, Robert R., 87–90, 91
churches, 143, 147–48, 152, 200
Church's Park and Auditorium (Memphis), 87–88, 91, 93
"City Beautiful" programs, 3
Civilian Conservation Corp (CCC), 216, 217
Civil Rights Act of 1875, 4, 185
Civil Rights Act of 1964, 56, 77, 133–34, 144, 155, 166. *See also* civil rights leaders; demonstrations, civil rights; wade-ins/swim-ins
civil rights leaders, 115, 121, 165, 219. *See also* Civil Rights Act of 1964; demonstrations, civil rights; King, Martin Luther, Jr.; wade-ins/swim-ins
class and intraracial tensions, 26–27, 34, 63–64, 131, 140, 221–22
Clotilda (ship), 163–64
Club, the (Virginia), 54–55
Club Bali (D.C.), 20
Cobb Island Chautauqua (Maryland), 29–30
Coconut Grove (Florida), 120
Cohen, Walter L. "Cap," 174
Collingwood Beach (Maryland), 30
Collins, Benjamin, 78
Colored Carnival Association, 162
Colored Fair (North Carolina), 211
Colored Town. *See* Overtown, Florida

Columbia, South Carolina, 211–13
Commission on Interracial Cooperation (CIC), 148
Coney Island, 33, xi–xiii
Confederate Battle Flag, 84
Congo Square (New Orleans), 171, 173
Connors, Sarah. *See* Madame Babe (Sarah Connors)
Cooke, Sam, 124
Cooper, Dudley, 54–55, 56
Cotton States and International Exposition (Atlanta), 103–5
country clubs, 79, 106–7, 110–12, 136
County Line/Upshaw, Texas, 200
cowboys and cattle culture, 204–8, 213
Craver, Sunny, 11
Crescent Stars Stadium (New Orleans), 174–75
Cripps, Thomas, 61, 126–27
Crump, Edward H., 92–93
Crystal Caverns (D.C.), 19, 20
Cullen, James, 177
Culver, Nina, 108, 109
Cummings, E. L., 17
Cunningham, Carrie, 115

Dahomey enslaved group (Alabama), 163
Dallas State Fair, 213–14
dancing, 88, 114, 160, 171–72, 200
Daniels, Josephus, 59–60
Daniels, Pete, 110
Davidson, William "Shorty," 140–42
David T. Howard Junior High School, 106
Davis, Edward Clinton, 166
Dawes Commission, 108–9
Dawson v. Mayor and City Council of Baltimore, 222–23
day laborers, 75, 78, 119
Deanwood (D.C.), 9–10
Deep Morgan (St. Louis), 191–93
demonstrations, civil rights, 133–34, 165, 195, 219. *See also* wade-ins/swim-ins
desegregation: black business failures and, 56, 71, 155, 166, 178, 221; entertainment and, 221–23; integration vs., 144, 218, 223; social consequences of, 195, 221–23; white flight and, 221–22. *See also* wade-ins/swim-ins; white flight
Diggs, Eugene, 53
Dightman, Myrtis, 207, 208
Dillard, William, 16–17
Dirt Bowl Basketball League Tournament, 99–100
discrimination: Bikeweek and, 83; desegregation and, 222; District of Columbia and, 23; legality of, 4, 134, 203; racial subordination and, 1; taxation and, 28. *See also* desegregation; racial violence; segregation
dislocation, 124
Disneyland, 224
domestic servants, 62
Dormon, James, 13
Dorsey, Dana Albert, 120–21
Douglass, Charles, 23–24, 25, 41, 75
Douglass, Haley, 24–26
Douglass Beach (Maryland), 30
Driver, Michael, 166
Dudley, Sherman, 15–18
Dudley's Circuit, 16
Dunn, Marvin, 124
Dyson, George, 79, 80

Eagle Harbor (Maryland), 27–28
East Texas, 199–203
Edgewater Beach Park (Maryland), 39, 40
Edwards, Kathleen, 54
Egerton, John, 148
E. Madison Hall (ship), 34
emancipation, 131, 199. *See also* freedmen's settlements
Ensley, Alabama, 159
Ensley, Enoch, 159
entrepreneurship, 30, 63, 153, 155, 178. *See also* business failures and desegregation
"equalization strategy," 218
excursion businesses: George Brown, 36–37; Joseph Thomas, 40–41; J. W. Patterson, 29–30; Lewis Jefferson, 30–35

Fairground Park Pool (St. Louis), 195–96
fairgrounds, 181–83
fairs, 211–15. *See also* world's fairs
Fannin Road (Mississippi), 155
Farinella, Marc, 64
Farish Street (Mississippi), 153–55
Faubourg Tremé District (New Orleans), 172, 174
Fauria, Edwin "Beansie," 174
Felton, Rebecca, 59
film. *See* movies
fires and property damage: amusement parks and, 37–38; Atlanta, 110, 113; Jacksonville, 136; racially motivated, 25, 93–94; steamboats and, 29, 33; suspicious, 34, 63–64, 144
Fisher's Island (Florida), 121
Fitzgerald, Charlie, 81–82
"Five Civilized Tribes," 107–8
Five Points Riot (Atlanta), 109–10
Flagler, Henry, 119, 125
Florida Coast Railway Company, 119–20, 125
Flying Ace, The (film), 127–29
Folly Beach (South Carolina), 76–77
"Foots, the" (show), 126
Fort Smallwood Park (Baltimore), 222
Foster, Bill, 163
Fourth Ward (Atlanta), 113
Frank, Leo, 110, 129
Franklin, Aretha, 19, 115
Franklintown, Florida, 136
Frederick Douglass Park (Kentucky), 99–100
freedmen's settlements, 199–200, 204. *See also* segregation
Freeman, Ellis, 65–66
Freeman, Rowland, 65–66
Freeman's Beach (North Carolina), 65–67
Fuller Mounds Project, 217

gambling, 32–33, 43, 56, 129, 186, 191
Gates, Henry Louis, Jr., 130, 200
Gold Bug, The (operetta), 13
Grand Strand (South Carolina), 79, 80
Grant, Nancy, 216
Greater U Street (D.C.), 19–20, 46

Great Migration, 214
Greenwood Park (Nashville), 95–96
Griset, Richard, 214–15
Gulf Beach (Florida), 219
Gulf Coast, 147
Gulfside Assembly (Mississippi), 147, 148–52

Hale, E. W., 217
Halevy, Julian, 224
Hall of Negro Life (Texas Centennial), 214
Hamilton, Bertram, 111
Hamilton, Thomas, 81. *See also* Ku Klux Klan
Handy, W. C., 11, 191
Hansberry, Lorraine, 223
Harlem Renaissance, 14
Harris, Arthur, 13
Havis, Ferdinand, 181, 182
Hawkins, Erskine, 160
Hayling, Robert B., 133
Hell's Kitchen, 13
Hench, John, 224
Hicks, Malcolm Ray "Chicken," 68
Highland Beach (Maryland), 23–26
"Hill, The." *See* Manhattan Beach (Florida)
His Honor the Barber (performance), 16
Hodgson, Godfrey, 222
Holmes, J. O., 34–35
Holmes, Johnny, 202–3
homeowners' associations, 26, 201–2. *See also* redlining
Horne, Lena, 202
Hot Springs, Arkansas, 184–87
Hot Springs National Park (Arkansas), 184–87
housing: conditions, 123; legislation, 203; soldiers and, 80, 110; worker, 31, 39, 125, 159. *See also* urban renewal
Howard, David, 106
Howard-Cunningham, Valaria, 208
hurricane damage, 55, 64, 68, 71, 77, 123, 139, 152
Hurston, Zora Neal, 163–64

Ickes, Harold, 217
immigrants, 3–4, 39–40, 222

In Dahomey (performance), 13
Independent Steamboat and Barge Company, 34–35
Indian Removal Act, 107
Indian Territory, 107–8
inequality. *See* discrimination; racial violence; segregation
Ingalls, Albert G., 185
integration, 144, 155, 214–15, 218, 221–23. *See also* desegregation
Interstate System, 124, 144

Jackson, Mississippi, 153–55
Jacksonville, Florida, 125–27, 136, 218–19
Jacksonville Expressway, 125
Jakes Colony, Texas, 204–5
Jefferson, Lewis, 30–35
Jim Crow (stage character), 11
Jim Crow statutes, 4, 14, 60, 109. *See also* segregation
jive dancing, 160
Johnson, James Weldon, 14, 41, 88
Johnson, Noble, 127
Johnson, Rosemond, Jr., 219
Johnson Beach (Florida), 218–19
Jones, Maceo, 214
Jones, Robert E., 147–51
Jones, Walter "Wiley," 181–83
"Jones Line" (Arkansas), 181
Joplin, Scott, 191
"juke joints," 200

Kahrl, Andrew, 26, 34, 64, 77, 150
Kelley, Benjamin F., 184–85
Kelley, Robin D. G., 5
Kendricks, Eddie, 160
Kennedy, Robert, 132–33
Kennesaw, Georgia, 106–11
King, Cornelius, 106–12
King, Martin Luther, Jr., 1, 133–34, 165, 199
King, P. Nicole, 80, 84
King's Dominion (Virginia), 56, 71

King's Wigwam Country Club (Georgia), 106–7, 110–12
Klein, Martin, 16–17
Koble, Peter, 130
Kruse, Kevin, 221
Kuhn, Cliff, 114
Ku Klux Klan, 81–82, 110–11, 130, 133, 207

Laicos Club (Alabama), 166–68
Langley, Walter, 36–37
Lauterbach, Preston, 48, 49, 88, 90
LaVilla, Florida, 125–26, 135
Lewis, Abraham Lincoln "A. L.," 135–36
Lewis, Cudjo, 163–64
Lewis, Earl, 5
Lewis, James, 137, 139
Lewis, Jefferson, 150
Lewis, John W., 19
Lexington, Kentucky, 99–100
Liberty City, Florida, 124
Lichtman, Abe, 10, 19
Life and Adventures of Nat Love, Better Known in Cattle Country as Deadwood Dick, by Himself, The (Love), 205–6
Lincoln Beach Park (New Orleans), 177–78
Lincoln Theater (D.C.), 19–20
Lincolnville (Florida), 131, 133, 134
Little Broadway (Florida), 120
Live at the Harlem Square Club (Sam Cooke), 124
Lofton, Tom, 66
Lofton, Victoria, 66
Long, Earl K., 177
Love, Nat, 205–6
lynching, 59, 90–91, 109–10, 129–30. *See also* racial violence
Lyons, William, 192

MacRae, Hugh, 61, 62
Madame Babe (Sarah Connors), 193
Mahogany Hall (New Orleans), 172, 173
Majestic Café (Alabama), 165–66
Mama Lou (Letitia Lu Lu Agatha Fontaine), 193

Manhattan Beach (Florida), 125, 218
Manly, Alex, 59–60
Mardi Gras (Mobile), 162, 164
Marine, Wallace, 174, 175
Marshall Hotel (D.C.), 134
Mason, Gilbert, 151
Matthews, Ralph, Jr., 25, 26
McAllister, Red, 115
McMurray, Lillian, 154
Meaher, Timothy, 163
Medley, Keith Weldon, 178
Memphis, Tennessee, 87–94, 217
Methodist Episcopal Church, 147, 148–49, 152
Miami, Florida, 119–24, 127. *See also* Overtown, Florida
Miami Beach, Florida, 121, 123
Miami-Dade County, Florida, 121–22
Micheaux, Oscar, 127, 129–30
military service and segregation, 66, 110–11, 202
Miller, Dorie, 202
Miller, Glenn, 160
Mills, Charlie, 194
minstrel shows, 11–13, 126. *See also* vaudeville
Mobile, Alabama, 162–64
Mohl, Raymond, 124
Monte Carlo by the Sea (North Carolina), 67, 68
Montgomery, Alabama, 133, 165–68, 202
Moore, D. C., 165
Morgan, James, 160
Mosquito Beach (South Carolina), 75–77
Moss, Thomas, 90
Mound Bayou settlement (Mississippi), 199
Mount Vernon and Marshall Hall Steamboat Company, 30
movies, 126–30
municipal parks, 2, 91–92, 99–100. *See also* individual parks
Muscle Shoals State Park (Alabama), 216
music: American Beach and, 137, 139; Atlantic Beach and, 80, 81; Austin and, 203; Bay Shore Pavilion and, 55; Ben Moore Hotel and, 165–66; Bohemian Caverns and, 19–20; Bop City and, 67–68; Carr's Beach and, 42, 43–44; Chowan Beach and, 70; Church's Park and, 88; Farish Street and, 153–55; the Foots and, 126; Gulfside Assembly, 149; Laicos Club and, 167; Lincoln Beach Park and, 178; MLK on, 49; Mosquito Beach and, 76; New Orleans and, 171–73, 176; Overtown and, 122, 124; Paradise Park and, 143; Sea Breeze and, 66; Shell Island Resort and, 63; St. Louis and, 191, 193; Sweet Auburn district and, 114, 115; Tuxedo Junction and, 159–60; Wilmer's Park and, 46–47. *See also* Chitlin Circuit
Myrdal, Gunnar, 2–3
Myrtle Beach (South Carolina), 78–79, 81, 82, 83

NAACP (National Association for the Advancement of Colored People), 83–84, 91, 133, 196, 217–19, 222
Napier, J. C., 95–96
Nardone, Jennifer, 200
Nasaw, David, 16
Nashville, Tennessee, 95–96
Nashville Union Transportation Company, 96
National Park Service, 216–19
National Steamboat Company, 29–30
Native Americans, 69, 107–9
"Negro areas" of national and state parks, 216
Negro Building (Cotton Exposition), 104, 105
Negro Day (Cotton Exposition), 105
Negro District (East Austin), 201–2
"Negro in Detroit, The" (Washington), 2
Negro League, 186, 193–94. *See also* baseball
Negro Motorist Green-Book, The, 42, 55
Negro State Fair (Texas), 213
New Hanover Transit Company, 65
New Orleans, Louisiana, 171–78
Nichols, Bob, 76
nightclubs. *See* Chitlin Circuit; *individual clubs*
Nolan, David, 133
Norman, Richard, 127–29, 206
Notley Hall, 29–31, 32. *See also* Washington Park (Maryland)

O'Brien, William, 1–2
Ocean Forest Hotel (South Carolina), 78–79
Ocean View Amusement Park (Virginia), 54–55
Okeh Records, 153–54
Old Creole Days (Cable), 171–72
Order of Myths, The (film), 164
Orleans Levee Board, 176–77
Ormes, Alberta "Bertie Mae," 15, 18
Overtown, Florida, 119–24

Palace Hotel and Bath House (Arkansas), 185
Palmetto State Fair (South Carolina), 213
Paradise Park, Florida, 142–44
Patterson, John "J. W.," 29–30
Payner, John H., 9
People's Company, 40
People's Defense League, 177
People's Grocery Company, 90
People's Transportation Company, 29
Peppler, Jim, 167–68
Perdido Key, Florida, 218–19
Phagan, Mary, 110
Pickett, Bill, 206–7
Pillmon, Sam, 71
Pine Bluff, Arkansas, 181–83
Pine Crest Inn (North Carolina), 63
Pine Tree Hotel (South Carolina), 77
plantations. *See* Black America (event)
playgrounds, 1–3. *See also* amusement parks; municipal parks
Plessy, Homer, 4
Plessy v. Ferguson, 4–5
politics and race, 59–60, 92–93, 109. *See also* desegregation; Jim Crow statutes; segregation
Pontchartrain Beach (New Orleans), 177, 178
pools. *See* swimming pools
Potomac River, 30, 32, 35
prohibition, 34
property. *See* real estate
prostitution, 89, 126, 172, 191, 193

race films, 127–30. *See also* movies
"race problem" in the South, 104

race relations, 147–48, 150. *See also* desegregation; racial violence; segregation
racial uplift ideology, 148
racial violence: in Atlanta, 108–11; buses and, 96; civil rights support and, 133–34; desegregation and, 77; escalation of, 100; film and, 129–30; Great Migration and, 13; KKK and, 81–82; Leo Frank and, 110–11, 129–30; People's Grocery and, 90–91; "rape" and, 59–61; swim-ins and, 195–96. *See also* fires and property damage; Ku Klux Klan; lynching
racism: athletes and, 182; "Atlanta Compromise" speech and, 104–5; black veterans and, 110–11; Cotton Exposition and, 104–5; fairs and, 214; politics and, 109. *See also* Ku Klux Klan; race films; racial violence; segregation
radio, 48, 114
ragtime, 172–73, 191
railroads, 4, 108, 119–20
Ral City, Arkansas, 184–85
Raleigh, North Carolina, 211
Ray, Carl, 140–42
real estate, 61–63, 131, 132, 136, 201–2. *See also* redlining
recreation, 1–6, 96, 99, 218–19, 222–23. *See also individual amusement parks, beaches, clubs, districts, and resorts*
"Recreation Facilities for the Negro" (Washington), 2
redlining, 202, 203
Red Summer (1919), 110–11, 148
Reevin, Sam, 16–17
Reid, Debra A., 214–15
Reid, Ira, 123
Reid, J. Eli, 69–70
religious opposition to pleasure parks, 33
resorts. *See* amusement parks; beaches; summer colonies; *individual resorts*
"respectability," 32–34, 148
retreats, 106, 147–52
Rice, Thomas Dartmouth, 11
Robinson, Bill "Bojangles," 185

Rock Creek, Maryland. *See* Brown's Grove (Maryland)
rodeos, 205, 206–8, 213
"Roomful of Blues" (Nardone), 200
Roosevelt, Eleanor, 217
Roper, Russell, 76–77
Rosebud Café (St. Louis), 191
Rosewood Park (Austin), 201, 202
Royal Peacock (Atlanta), 115

Sasscer, Landsdale G., Sr., 27, 28
Scott, Tom, 213
Sea Breeze Resort (North Carolina), 65–68
Seabrook Beach (New Orleans), 176–77
Seaview Beach Resort and Amusement Park (Virginia), 53–56
secret societies, 162
segregation: American West and, 206; amusement parks and, 2; "Atlanta Compromise" speech and, 104–5; Austin and, 201–3; beaches and, 53–55, 64, 79–80, 121–22; Bethlehem Steel and, 39–40; Black entertainers and, 14, 17; children and, 1; CIC and, 148; "congregation" and, 5; connotations of, 223; Cotton Exposition and, 104–5; *Dawson v. Baltimore* and, 222–23; fairs and, 211, 213–15; Florida and, 121, 141; Hot Springs National Park and, 184–85; immigrants and, 222; Indian Territory and, 108–9; lodging and, 132–33; in Mississippi, 149–51; national parks and, 216–17; nightclubs and, 19–20; *Plessy v. Ferguson* and, 4–5; recreation despite, 5; "safety" and, 140; as "separate but equal," 3–4; Sweet Auburn district and, 114–15; swimming pools and, 195–96, 222–23; theme parks and, 223–24; transportation and, 96; veterans and, 202. *See also* desegregation; freedmen's settlements; Jim Crow statutes; racial violence
sexual violence, 59
shag (dance), 67, 81
Shakur, Assata, 68
Shelby Farms State Park (Memphis), 217

Sheldon, Lee "Stagger Lee," 192
Shell Island Resort (North Carolina), 61–65, 70
Silver, Angela da, 192
Silver Springs, Florida, 140–41, 144
slavery and slave trade, 107–8, 163–64, 171
Slow Fade to Black (Cripps), 126–27
Smart Set, 15–16
Smith, Bessie, 191
Smith, Elizabeth Carr, 42
Smith, Hoke, 108, 109
Snake Man, 67
Social Gospel, 147
Sokol, Jason, 134
Sol Legarians, 75, 76
Solvent Savings Bank, 91–92
Somerset Beach (Maryland), 31
Sorkin, Michael, 224
Southerland, Kit, 113
Southern Consolidated Theater Circuit, 16
Southern Courier (newspaper), 167–68
Southern Mercantile Company, 182
Sparrow, Florence Carr, 42
Sparrow's Beach (Maryland), 41–44
Speir, Henry Columbus "H. C.," 153–54
sports parks. *See* baseball; Crescent Stars Stadium (New Orleans); Edgewater Beach Park (Maryland); Wilmer's Park (Maryland)
spring training, 186–87. *See also* baseball
Stagger Lee, 192
Starr, Milton, 17
St. Augustine, Florida, 131–34
steamboats, 29–30, 31–35, 36–37, 65
Steeplechase Park, xi–xiii
Stephenson, Frank, 69
St. Louis, Missouri, 191–96
"St. Louis Blues, The" (song), 191
St. Louis World's Fair, 191
Storyville district (New Orleans), 172–73
Strand Theater (D.C.), 10
streetcar companies, 3
Student Nonviolent Coordinating Committee (SNCC), 151–52
Suburban Gardens (D.C.), 9–10

Sugar Shack (painting), 5–6
Sulphur Springs, Arkansas, 182
summer colonies, 26–28, 30–31
Sweet Auburn (Atlanta), 113–15
swim-ins. *See* wade-ins/swim-ins
swimming pools, 195–96, 221, 223. *See also* wade-ins/swim-ins; *individual pools*
Symbol of the Unconquered (film), 130
syphilis, 184–85, 196

taxation, 28, 77, 83, 93
Taylor, Marshall "Major," 182
Taylor, Preston, 95–96
Tennessee Valley Authority (TVA), 216, 217
Texas. *See* East Texas; West Texas
Texas Centennial, 214
Texas Homestead Act, 204
theater, 16. *See also* minstrel shows; vaudeville
Theater District (New York City), 13
theaters. *See* Chitlin Circuit; Greater U Street (D.C.); Theatrical Owners Booking Agency (T.O.B.A.); *individual clubs and theaters*
Theatrical Owners Booking Agency (T.O.B.A.), 15, 17–18, 48
theme parks, 223–24. *See also* amusement parks
Thomas, Anthony, 39, 40
Thomas, Flavia, 39, 40, 41
Thomas, Joseph, 39, 40–41
Thomas, Lawson E., 121–22
Thomsen, Rozel, 222–23
Tidewater Power Company, 61, 62
Tilyou, Edward, xi–xii
Tilyou, George C., xi–xii
Tilyou, Mary, xi–xii
T.O.B.A. *See* Theatrical Owners Booking Agency (T.O.B.A.)
T. O. Fuller State Park, 217
Top Hat Club, 114, 115
transportation, 40, 65, 96. *See also* excursion businesses
trespassing, 24–25, 134, 167, 223
Truman Point (Maryland), 27
Trump, Fred, xii–xiii

Trumpet Records, 154
Turner, Henry McNeal, 104–5, 107–9
Turner, Lincolnia, 106, 108
Turner Station (Maryland), 39–41
Turpin, Tom, 191
Tuxedo Junction (Alabama), 159–61

United Service Organization (USO), 202
Upshaw/County Line, Texas, 200
urban conditions, 3–4, 123
urban renewal, 49, 93, 160, 203

Varn, George, 75
Vason, Lu, 207–8
vaudeville, 13–18, 88, 113–14. *See also* Chitlin Circuit; minstrel shows
Venice Beach (Maryland), 24
Vereen, Eddie, 142–43
Victory Grill (Austin), 202–3
Virginia Key Beach (Florida), 121–22
voting, 59–60, 92

Waddell, Alfred Moore, 60
Wade, Wyn Craig, 110
wade-ins/swim-ins, 133–34, 151, 195. *See also* demonstrations, civil rights
Walcott, Virginia, 196
Walker, Geder, 120
Walker, George, 12–14
Ware, Richard, 25
Ware Hotel (Maryland), 25
Washington, Booker T., 104–5
Washington, D.C., 9–20, 23, 26–27, 32
Washington, Forrester Blanchard, 2
Washington Park (Maryland), 29–30, 32–33. *See also* Notley Hall
Wells, Ida B., 90–91
WERD-AM (Atlanta), 114
West Ocala, Florida, 141–44
West Texas, 204–8
westward settlement, 205–6
White, Lulu, 172–73
White Castle Club (St. Louis), 193

white flight, 221–22
white supremacy, 104, 105
Whitman Sisters, 88
"Wigwam Building" (Atlanta), 112
Wilcox, Henry, 204–5
Wilcox Ranch (Texas), 204–5
Wilder, Andrew "Apple," 76
Wilder, Laura, 76
Wiley Jones Park and Race Track (Arkansas), 181–83
Williams, Bert, 12–14
Williams, Paul, 160
Williams, Roscoe, 167
Williams, Spencer, 172
Wilmer, Arthur, 46–47
Wilmer's Park (Maryland), 46–47
Wilmington, North Carolina, 59–61, 63
Wilmington Daily Record (newspaper), 60
Wilmington Home Realty Company, 61, 64
Wilmington Insurrection/Massacre of 1898, 60–61

Wilson Negro Park (Alabama), 216
Wiltse, Jeff, 195
Winton, North Carolina. *See* Chowan Beach (North Carolina)
Winton Triangle (North Carolina), 69
Within Our Gates (film), 129–30
Wolcott, Victoria, 222
Wolfe-Rocca, Ursula, 111
Woodmen of the Union Building, 186
Woodson, Coleman, Jr., 167
Woodson, Howard, 9
Woodson, John T., 78–79
Woodward, C. Vann, 4
world's fairs, 103–4, 191
Wright, Ernest, 177
Wright, Thomas, 61–62, 63
Wrightsville Beach (North Carolina), 61, 62, 64

Zappa, Frank, 44
Zemurray, Sam, 176

www.ingramcontent.com/pod-product-compliance
Lightning Source LLC
Chambersburg PA
CBHW021342230426
43666CB00006B/373